Profiles of Jesus

Profiles of Jesus

Roy W. Hoover, ed.

Profiles of Jesus

Published in 2002 by Polebridge Press, P. O. Box 6144, Santa Rosa, California, 95406.

Library of Congress Cataloging-in-Publication Data

Profiles of Jesus / Roy W. Hoover, ed.
    p. cm.
    Includes bibliographical references.
    ISBN 0-944344-94-1
    1. Jesus Christ--Historicity. 2. Jesus Seminar. I. Hoover, Roy W.

BT303.2 .P76 2002
232.9′08--dc21

                                           2002190892

Contents

Preface

As the Fellows of the Jesus Seminar neared the end of the twelve year period during which they systematically examined all of the words and deeds attributed to Jesus in the ancient sources, together with the reported events of his life, attention turned to the question of what kind of figure was emerging from the evidence the Seminar had found to be most probably historically authentic. More than twenty Fellows presented papers at five meetings of the Seminar over a two year period (1996–1998) in which they either drew a profile of Jesus based on the evidence the Seminar had found to be historically authentic, or critiqued important recently published work on the historical Jesus by other scholars from the perspective of the Seminar's sifting of the evidence. Six critiques were published in the journal *Forum*, New Series 1,2 (Fall, 1998). Nine of the fifteen profiles written for Seminar sessions have been selected for this volume together with three other profiles by Fellows that had appeared earlier in Westar Institute's magazine, *The Fourth R*. Lane C. McGaughy's essay, "Words Before Deeds," was originally presented at a special program on the work of the Seminar held in conjunction with the national meeting of the Society of Biblical Literature in New Orleans in November, 1996, and was subsequently published in *The Fourth R* (September-December, 1996) under the title, "Why Start with the Sayings?" A revised version of the essay was published in the above-mentioned issue of Forum and is reprinted here. The essay by Robert T. Fortna, "The Gospel of John and the Historical Jesus" was originally published in *The Fourth R* (September-December, 1995) as were also the profiles by John Dominic Crossan (March, 1991), Marcus J. Borg (May-June, 1994) and James M. Robinson (September-December, 1995). The profiles of Jesus by Robert W. Funk and Roy W. Hoover are substantially revised versions of those published in *The Fourth R* (January-April, 1996, and May-August, 1996, respectively). Brandon Scott's contribution to this volume is a lightly revised form of the profile first published in *The Fourth R* (January-April, 1997), as is that of Arthur J. Dewey which also first appeared in *The Fourth R* (November-December, 1998). Hal Taussig's "Jesus in the Company of Sages," and Mahlon Smith's "Israel's Prodigal Son" were both originally published in the issue of *Forum* mentioned above and have been slightly revised for this volume. Stephen J. Patterson's essay, "Dirt, Shame, and Sin in the Expendable Company of Jesus," is excerpted from his book, *The God of Jesus: The Historical Jesus and the Search for Meaning.* (Harrisburg, PA: Trinity Press International, 1998) and is reprinted here, with minor alterations, by permission of the publisher. Kathleen E. Corley's contribution, "Gender and Class in the Teaching of Jesus," is excerpted from her book, *Women and the Historical Jesus.* (Santa Rosa, CA: Polebridge Press, 2002) and is included here with the publisher's permission. The profile by Charles W. Hedrick is published here for the first time.

Introduction

Roy W. Hoover

After nearly twelve years of work, the Jesus Seminar produced something analogous to the result of a careful, systematic archaeological excavation of an ancient site: we, along with other scholars, had recognized that several levels of tradition are present in the gospel texts (corresponding metaphorically to the levels of occupation that become exposed in the course of excavating the site of an ancient city) and we had made it our particular aim to distinguish "the Jesus level" of the evidence from the later compositional levels that were the creations of the gospel authors and of their written sources. In finding "the Jesus level" of these sources we were able to retrieve a number of "artifacts" embedded in them that are very probably, in some cases almost certainly, traceable to the Jesus of history: sayings, stories, activities typical of him, and certain events of his life. The reports of these "excavations" were published in *The Five Gospels. The Search for the Authentic Words of Jesus* (1993), and *The Acts of Jesus. The Search for the Authentic Deeds of Jesus* (1998).

Since these "artifacts" were used by gospel authors to compose their own interpretive narratives (or, by the authors of Q and Thomas to compile a body of teaching materials that reflects a community's perspective and commitments), much of these artifacts original connection with the public activity of Jesus and its social context had receded behind the interests of the gospel authors. The question then becomes whether one can reconstruct a profile of the Jesus of history on the basis of the recovered "artifacts:" is it possible to find in the authentic "Jesus level" materials, together with other information about first-century

1

Palestine and the wider Roman world, evidence sufficient to enable one to sketch a profile that would credibly resemble the Jesus of history? That is the challenge faced by each of the contributors to this volume.

The first thing that responding to this challenge requires is to decide how best to get a handle on the various "artifacts" extracted from the texts of the gospels. To be up to this task, the excavator of these gospel texts must become an accomplished sleuth. It is one thing to uncover evidence; it is another to follow its trail. Should one start with the authentic deeds of Jesus and the assured events of his life, on the grounds that events and deeds carry more weight than words? Is the key to seeing Jesus in profile the likelihood that he was in fact a healer and exorcist? Or is his crucifixion the most reliable piece of evidence we have about him, and should we think that the fact that he ended up in this way casts the brightest light on the life that came to such an end? Or is the record of his deeds and other events unclear and inconclusive unless it is viewed in connection with his teaching?

Are Jesus' words, then, the better place to begin? If so, which words? Do his parables lead us most surely to his profile, or are his aphorisms more revealing of the man? Or should we look for a theme that is visible in all of these forms of evidence and thus identify the unifying point of view of the figure whom we see speaking and acting in this evidence? Alternatively, is getting the stratigraphy of our sources right the crucial move in this game of detection? That is, if we can determine what is earliest in the gospel tradition and what elements of this earliest evidence have the most independent witnesses, will that get us closest to the historical figure of Jesus? Or will the results obtained from any of these approaches remain shrouded in the fog of uncertainty unless we use the right sort of sociological or anthropological model or comparative religions typology to bring the historical evidence into focus?

All of these options and more have been exercised by scholars in pursuit of the historical Jesus in recent years; several of them are utilized by the contributors to this volume. Part of the value of this collection of profiles, in fact, lies in the opportunity to note the different strategies the contributors employ in their attempts to derive from the recovered "artifacts" something like a credible sketch of Jesus as a historical figure, even if it does not and cannot constitute a claim to have reconstructed a view of "the whole person" or an account of his whole life—aims that are beyond the reach of a brief profile and also beyond the reach of the surviving evidence.

The yield of these profiles is what can be characterized as a collection of studied impressions of Jesus as a figure of history. They are different from the first impressions the young man known as Jesus of Nazareth would have made on the peasant farmers and fishermen, the homemakers and artisans of the small towns and villages of Galilee in the first century CE. We lack the direct access they had to what he looked like and how he sounded when he spoke, and we lack the ability to observe his behavior and what we would call his personality. We are also without that sense of their life situation and prospects that would have affected the way they perceived him. But that we lack what they had is not the only thing that should be acknowledged. We also have what they lacked: the advantage of hindsight, the comparative capacities of knowledgeable and interested observers from another country, comparable in some respects to the case of the young Frenchman, Alexis de Toqueville, who, during a nine-month visit in 1831–1832, noted things about America that had not been recognized by Americans themselves. Also available to us, but not to them, is not just one, but several texts by different authors, all written within a few decades of Jesus' life, that preserve a selected residue of his life and teaching in the context of their own assessments of his significance. Profiles based on such evidence are not first impressions of the man; they are studied impressions based on that residue of his life and teaching preserved and re-presented in early Christian texts. These ancient texts share a certain fund of common knowledge about Jesus, but none is a carbon copy of another. That is true of these profiles also: they offer some differing perspectives on Jesus, but they also are in agreement about certain matters of crucial importance in any attempt to gain an informed view of him as a figure of history.

For example, all of the authors of these profiles agree that Jesus of Nazareth did not refer to himself as the Messiah, nor did he claim to be a divine being who descended to earth from heaven in order to die as a sacrifice for the sins of the world. These are claims that some people in the early church made about Jesus, not claims he made about himself. At the heart of Jesus' teaching and actions was a vision of life under the reign of God (or, in the empire of God) in which God's generosity and goodness is regarded as the model and measure of human life; everyone is accepted as a child of God and thus liberated both from the ethnocentric confines of traditional Judaism and from the secularizing servitude and meagerness of their lives under the rule of the empire of Rome. Although the contributors to this volume have differing ways of depicting how this vision of Jesus was played out in his public activity, all agree that a vision of life under the reign of God was of great importance to him and is *a* key, if not *the* key to understanding his public career.

None of the contributors think that Jesus held an apocalyptic view of the reign (or kingdom) of God – that by direct intervention God was about to bring history to an end and bring a new, perfect order of life into being. All of the contributors agree that in Jesus' teaching the reign of God is a vision of what life in this world could be, not a vision of life in a future world that would soon be brought into being by a miraculous act of God. All of the contributors also agree with the view, lucidly presented in Robert Fortna's essay, "The Gospel of John and the Historical Jesus," that although the Gospel of John has been an important source for Christian theology and piety, it is of little use as a source of information about the historical Jesus.

Several contributors have based their profiles explicitly on what the Jesus Seminar found to be the authentic words and deeds of Jesus, i.e., the elements of the gospel texts that are almost certainly (red) or very probably (pink) traceable to the Jesus of history.[1] Some of these are based almost entirely on the authentic sayings, some on both the authentic sayings and the authentic deeds. Contributors whose profiles draw upon a sociological or anthropological model or a comparative religions typology are also in substantial agreement with the Seminar's work and make use of materials in its data base in the course of their scholarly work. All of the contributors are Fellows of the Seminar.

These important agreements notwithstanding, there are some significant differences in what these authors have relied upon to construct the profiles of Jesus they have contributed to this volume. A majority have based their profiles either primarily or entirely upon what the Seminar identified as "the authentic words of Jesus." The reason for doing so was in some cases partly circumstantial: the Seminar had not completed its work on the deeds of Jesus when these profiles were originally written. In other cases profiles are based primarily on Jesus' sayings because the authors think that identifying the meaning of Jesus' words is the key to understanding both the character and meaning of his mission. In such cases the reason for focusing on Jesus' words is methodological rather than only circumstantial, a judgment that the meaning of Jesus' deeds can become clear only in light of the point of view disclosed in his words. Lane McGaughy's contribution, "Words Before Deeds," offers an illuminating and cogent argument in support of the methodological appropriateness of beginning a search for the Jesus of history by first identifying his authentic sayings. Investigating Jesus' deeds in light of his words gives us a basis for discerning the intention of his deeds and for assessing his integrity – whether he meant what he said as evidenced by whether he "practiced what he preached." The profiles by

Robert Funk, James Robinson, Brandon Scott, Roy Hoover, Charles Hedrick and Mahlon Smith can be loosely grouped together as based primarily on Jesus' words.

Several contributors are convinced that taking Jesus' social world into account and locating him in it is crucial to drawing his profile. These authors rely not only on historical evidence but also on sociological and anthropological models, or on typologies drawn from studies of comparative religions to develop a view of Jesus' social context and his relation to it. The implicit or explicit claim of this approach is that the meaning of Jesus' words can be discerned only through the lens of his social location and intention. It follows that the social meaning of Jesus' teaching emerges as of first importance, or as what stands out, accompanied as it is by religious affirmations and legitimations. The profiles by Marcus Borg, Dominic Crossan, Kathleen Corley,[2] Stephen Patterson, and Hal Taussig can be loosely grouped together as regarding Jesus' social location and/or religious typology as crucial to drawing his profile.

While it is useful to call attention to this basic divide that is apparent in these profiles, it would be a mistake to suppose that this distinction is hard-edged or absolute in every case. All of the contributors who have based their profiles primarily on Jesus' words would agree that discerning the relation between Jesus' teaching and the social world in which it took place is an important part of the task of reconstructing his profile; and the contributors who use that social world as their principal focus also make considerable use of Jesus' words. For all of the contributors the evidence furnished by Jesus' authentic words and deeds, on the one hand, and the evidence about the social realities in which he and his hearers lived, is a reciprocal one. The differences result from what kind of evidence one is inclined or persuaded to emphasize, and the range can run from a difference of degree to a difference in kind. They never are, however, distinctions without a difference. Ultimately, it seems, one has to decide whether it makes more sense to see Jesus as the pioneer of "a social movement with religious connotations," or as the pioneer of "a religious movement with social and political commitments," as Harvard Professor Francois Bovon recently put it.[3] More simply put, ultimately one is persuaded to see Jesus as first of all a religious visionary or as first of all a social reformer, however earnestly one tries to find a balance between his religious message and its social implications, or between his social reform and its religious legitimations and meaning.

Readers may wonder, if there is so much agreement among the Fellows of the Seminar about the evidence of Jesus' words and deeds and about Jesus as not holding an apocalyptic view of his life and times, why is there so much difference among the profiles collected here? The answer to this question lies partly in the nature of the evidence and partly in the nature of a scholar's interpretive strategy and method. Reconstructing history always involves more than finding the facts, and the facts never speak for themselves; they always require that someone speak for them. Both the nature of the facts and their meaning and significance must be discerned. With regard to the facts about the historical Jesus, one needs to note that the historical evidence about Jesus' teaching and actions is not comparable to a pile of bricks. Bricks retain their form and substance wherever they are placed; historical facts do not. Their form and substance depend upon how they are understood and conveyed.[4] Even in recounting the facts it is the discriminating mind of the historian that gives them a particular voice; and by the way the historian construes them the facts come to have a particular meaning and significance. Thus the facts about Jesus' teaching and actions can be understood differently, and this can result in differing profiles of him.

Secondly, historical scholarship is always the fruit of a particular perspective and a particular interpretive strategy. Human reason, honestly employed, does give us the capacity to see beyond the boundaries of tradition and conventional wisdom; but it does not give us the capacity to step outside of our own historicity – our culture and times and our own skin – and enable us to attain a point of view that is not conditioned by it. It does not follow, however, that historical scholarship can result only in interpretive fiction that can lay no claim to knowledge. It is possible to see some things clearly from a particular perspective and, undoubtedly, some things only from a particular perspective. A perspective is an angle of vision, not a form of blindness. Scholars' perspectives derive not only from the fact that they inevitably reflect their own historicity in general, but also from their judgments about what investigative and interpretive aim and method will best succeed in bringing the profile of the historical Jesus into focus. For example, do we see the Jesus of history most clearly if we propose that he was a certain type of religious figure known from studies of cultural anthropology and/or comparative religion? Or if we identify and draw out the implications of his social location in first-century Palestine? Or if we identify the vision of human life evident in his words? Or if we propose a composite method in which we attempt to weave several strategies together (in which case the method of weaving will itself be a significant factor)? The Jesus we see through lens as different as these will leave us with different impressions, even if we can see some similarities among them. Thus the perspectives of scholars often differ and the profiles of an historical figure seen from such differing perspectives will in some respects, inevitably differ. Even so, differing perspectives can be both insightful and complementary, as a number of the profiles in this volume show. They may be, but need not be, contradictory or conflicting. In other words, there can be elements of historical validity in more than one perspectival view of the historical Jesus.

Why both the earlier critical work of the Jesus Seminar to identify the historically authentic words and deeds of Jesus and the endeavors of the contributors to this volume to use that historical evidence to draw profiles of Jesus as a figure of history are important, is suggested by two eminent writers, one ancient, the other modern. The ancient writer is the Second Century BCE historian Polybius, who remarked that "just as a living creature, if deprived of its eyesight, is rendered completely helpless, so if history is deprived of the truth, we are left with nothing but an idle, unprofitable tale."[5] The modern author is sociologist Peter Berger, who suggested that "the power of religion depends, in the last resort, upon the credibility of the banners it puts in the hands of men as they stand before death, or more accurately, as they walk, inevitably, toward it."[6] Insofar as the authors of these profiles succeed in perceiving the truth about Jesus as a figure of history, they will offer to their readers views of a noteworthy young man of first-century Palestine rather than the icon of myth and creed; and in so far as the truth about the Jesus of history is relevant to the credibility of Christian faith, these profiles will have their uses for faith as well as for history.

Jesus
A Voice Print

Robert W. Funk

Jesus was a wandering teacher of wisdom. His voice emanates from
a compendium of parables, aphorisms, and dialogues the Jesus Seminar
has isolated from the mass of tradition that accrued to his name. In those
sayings, and correlative acts, we can occasionally catch sight of Jesus'
vision, a vision of something he called God's domain. Visions come in
bits and pieces, in random stunning insights, never in continuous, artic-
ulated wholes. Yet from these fragments of insight we can begin to piece
together some sense of the whole. Together those fragments provide us
with glimpses of the historical figure. Since his vision was neither more
nor less than a glimpse, the best we can hope for is a glimpse of his
glimpse.

The Aphorism
Jesus was a master of the short, pithy witticism known as an aphorism. We need to distinguish an aphorism from a proverb.

An aphorism is a proverb-like saying that subverts conventional
wisdom. "An apple a day keeps the doctor away" is a proverb. It expresses
conventional wisdom; it affirms what everybody already knows. "Let the
dead bury the dead" is one of Jesus' most difficult aphorisms. An aphorism subverts or contradicts conventional, proverbial wisdom. "Let the
dead bury the dead" attacks the fundamental obligation to care appropriately for the dead, and it does so by suggesting that many living are
in fact metaphorically dead.

Oscar Wilde was a well-known aphorist. One of his best: "We wouldn't be so concerned about what people thought of us, if we realized how seldom they do."

Flannery O'Connor was asked over and over again if she thinks the universities stifle writers. Her response, "Perhaps, but they don't stifle enough of them."

Halford Luccock, who taught homiletics at Yale University for many years, was once asked, "How many points should a sermon have?" To the question he replied, "At least one."

The Parable

The parable is a fantasy – a fantasy about God's domain, an order of reality that feeds on but subtlety transforms the everyday world. It is about an order of reality that lies beyond, but just barely beyond, the everyday, the humdrum, the habituated. In that case, the parable is also an invitation to cross over, to leave the old behind and embrace the new. The ability to cross over will depend, of course, on both the tenacity with which one holds to the inherited scheme of things, and on one's willingness to cut the ties to comfortable tradition. The parable is pitted against the power of the proven. Making the transition under such circumstances does not come easily.

The options Jesus offers his audience consistently run counter to their normal way of looking at life. Both his parables and aphorisms regularly frustrate the expectations of his hearers. Jesus develops a consistent rhetorical strategy that matches the content of his message. First, he depicts and then distorts the everyday world he and his Galilean neighbors inherit and inhabit. We shall refer to that world as the received world. Second, his parables and witticisms transform and transcend that world. He adopts and then distorts the received world in order to hint at a new horizon. The result is a fleeting glimpse of what lies beyond the boundaries of the everyday; his language and deeds constitute a knothole in the cosmic fence.

Before we attempt to summarize the content of his vision, we should explore this strategy. It will telegraph valuable hints about the content of his vision.

1. His language is concrete and specific. Jesus always talked about God's domain in everyday, mundane terms – dinner parties, travelers being mugged, truant sons, the hungry and tearful, toll collectors and prostitutes, a cache of coins. He never used abstract language. He made no theological statements. He would not have said, "All human beings

have sinned and fallen short of the glory of God." He would not have confessed, "I believe in God the Father Almighty." It never occurred to him to assert that "God is love." Jesus did not have a doctrine of God; he had only experience of God.

2. Typifications. Jesus makes use of typifications to which everyone in his audience could have given immediate assent. Travelers get mugged on the Jericho road. A manager embezzles from his employer. A woman loses a coin on the dirt floor. A judge is corrupt. A friend knocks on the door at midnight and asks for bread. A truant son asks for his inheritance and then blows it on wine, women, and song in a foreign land. People nod their heads in agreement with these generalizations.

3. Unlike other teachers, he does not cite and interpret scripture. He does not debate fine points in the law. He makes no theological statements. He would not have said, "God is the ground of being" or even such a simple thing as "God is love." He does not make philosophical generalizations. He would not have said, "I think, therefore I am," or "Homo sapiens is the only animal that has language."

4. He does not make personal confessions nor are his stories and witticisms self-referential. He would not have said, "I believe in God the Father Almighty." It is inconceivable that he said, "I am the way, the truth, and the life; no one comes to the Father except through me." On the contrary, his discourse is focused exclusively on the banalities of the everyday world.

5. Although his language was drawn from the mundane world around him, he did not have ordinary reality in mind. His language is indirect; it is highly figurative or metaphorical. We know the parable of the leaven is not about baking bread. The dinner party has nothing to do with social etiquette or with seating patterns at a banquet. The mustard seed and the sower are not about gardening. The shrewd manager is not advice about business practices. His admonition to lend to those who can't pay us back is not about banking practice. While he invariably speaks in mundane terms, about what appears to be trivial or trite matters, his listeners know he has some other, much more significant subject in mind.

6. They know that for several reasons. They know because his exaggerations, his caricatures, resist literal interpretation. Three people are invited to a dinner party; they refuse at the last moment to come; hundreds from the street are then herded into the hall. The discrepancy is fantastic. A slave has a debt of ten million dollars cancelled, but he is unable to forgive a debt of ten dollars. The contrast is ludicrous.

7. Moreover, he frustrates ordinary expectations by reversing what

we anticipate will be the case. When he proclaims, "Congratulations, you hungry! You'll have a feast," he is countermanding expectations. In the parable of the vineyard laborers, those who work only one hour are paid the same wage as those who labored the entire day. We do not think that is fair.

In the parable of the prodigal, the truant son is welcomed home like royalty, when we think he should have been reprimanded and chastised.

8. He makes free use of parody. The parable of the empty jar in the Gospel of Thomas is a parody of the jar of meal miraculously replenished by Elijah for the widow of Zarepath. The Mustard Seed pokes fun at the image of the mighty cedar of Lebanon employed by Ezekiel as a symbol for the mighty kingdom of David.

9. Parody is a form of humor, to be sure. But Jesus indulges in other forms of humor. In the parable of the lost coin, the woman spends the value of the coin she has just recovered in celebrating her good fortune. The shepherd recovers the lost sheep and promptly announces a celebration, which probably involved the slaughter of a sheep. When sued for your coat, Jesus advises his followers, to give up your shirt to go with it. That would of course leave them naked. Jesus' listeners must have laughed at these travesties on sober speech.

10. He often combines the literal and the figurative in order to create tension. "Give to everyone who begs from you" is an example. His listeners knew they should practice acts of charity, but how could they respond positively to every request without financial ruin?

11. Jesus was plied with questions, to which he never gave a direct answer. "Should we pay taxes," he was asked. "Pay the emperor what is due the emperor and pay God what is due God" was his ambiguous but not evasive response.

12. Jesus may be described as a comic savant. He was perhaps the first standup Jewish comic. A comic savant is a sage who embeds wisdom in humor, a humorist who shuns practical advice. "If someone sues you for your coat, give him the shirt off your back to go with it." That is not practical advice: to follow it is to go naked. Comic wisdom refuses to be explicit.

Yet in the stories he tells, the sage constructs a new fiction that becomes the basis for his or her own action and the action of others. The contours of that fiction are ambiguous in order to frustrate moralizing proclivities; they are also open to multiple and deeper interpretations as a way of keeping them open to reinterpretation in ever new contexts. Our task is to follow their lead and figure out how what meaning to give them in our own circumstances.

13. This way of speaking about the kingdom of God is necessary because God's domain is not immediately observable. Jesus employs tropes or figures of speech drawn from the sensible world to speak obliquely or indirectly, and therefore metaphorically, about another realm. His followers remember him warning them repeatedly, "Those here with two good ears had better listen." What he was trying to convey was subtle and covert. He was undermining the immense solidity of the received world with a vision of an alternative reality. His words communicate in a non-ordinary sense. The knowledge he communicates is pre-conceptual; it is knowledge of reality unsegmented, of an undifferentiated nexus, of a seamless universe of meaning. In his parables and aphorisms is embedded a world coming into being.

What Jesus Had to Say

James M. Robinson

We need to face up to an undomesticated Jesus, what one might call a real idealist, a committed radical, in any case a profound person who proposed a solution to the human dilemma.

What Jesus had to say centered around the ideal of God's rule ("the kingdom of God"), the main theological category Jesus created. Calling the ideal God's rule puts it in an antithetical relation both to other political and social systems, and to individual self-interest – "looking out for number one." Jesus points out that the ravens and wild flowers prosper without working to secure their needs. God cares about every sparrow sold a dime a dozen. God will not give a stone when asked for bread, or a snake when asked for fish, but can be counted on to give what one really needs. Indeed people should trust God to know what they need even before they ask. This utopian vision was the core of what Jesus had to say. It was both good news – reassurance that good would happen to undo one's plight in actual experience – and the call upon people to do that good in actual practice.

The human dilemma is in large part that we are each other's fate. We are the tool of evil that ruins the other person, as we look out for number one, having long abandoned any youthful idealism we might once have cherished. But if I would cease and desist from pushing you down to keep myself up, and you for your part would do the same, then the vicious circle would be broken. Society would become mutually supportive, rather than self-destructive. Count on God to look out for you, to provide people that will care for you, and listen to him when he calls

15

on you to provide for them. This radical trust in and responsiveness to God is what makes society function as God's society. This is, for Jesus, what faith and discipleship were all about. Nothing else has a right to claim any functional relationship to him.

Put in language derived from his sayings: I am hungry because you hoard food. You are cold because I hoard clothing. So we are all to get rid of our backpacks and wallets! Such "security" is to be replaced by "God's rule," which means both what we trust God to do (to tell the other person to share food with me), and what we hear God telling us to do (to share clothing with the other person). One does not carry money while passing by the poor, or a backpack full of extra clothes and food while ignoring the cold and hungry lying in the gutter. This is why the beggars, the hungry, the depressed, are fortunate: God, that is to say, those who hearken to God, those in whom God rules, will care for them. They are called upon to trust that God's rule is there for them ("Theirs is the kingdom of God"). One need not even carry a club for self-protection, but rather should return good for evil even with regard to one's enemies. One turns the other cheek. God is the kind of person who provides sunshine and rain even to those who oppose him. So God's children are those who care even for their enemies. In the original form of the Lord's Prayer, what followed directly upon and defined "Thy kingdom come" was: "Give us this day our daily bread." People should ask for no more than a day's ration of food, trusting God to provide for today, and then trusting for tomorrow.

God's rule ("the kingdom of God") was interpreted by Matthew's community to mean: "Thy will be done on earth as it is in heaven." This addition to the Lord's Prayer is, technically speaking, not a call for action, but, like "Thy kingdom come" which it interprets, an appeal to God. When one prays, one trusts in God to answer. But God answers by motivating people – to turn the other cheek; to give the shirt off one's back; to lend, expecting nothing in return. The person who prays to God for help is the same person whom God motivates to help: "Forgive us our debts as we forgive our debtors!"

Part of God ruling is helping the infirm with whatever medicine was available. One went from door to door, and if admitted for bed and breakfast (the answer to the prayer for a day's bread), one placed God's blessing on the house, in practice by healing the sick within as best one could ("Heal the sick and say: The kingdom of God has drawn near").

Just as the sharing of food and clothing, the canceling of debts, the non-retaliation against enemies, were not seen as human virtues, but rather as God acting through those who trust him, just so healings were not attributed to a witch- doctor's or a magician's individual technique or skill, but to God making use not only of Jesus, but of others as well. Clearly all these were things that one could not oneself do, from renunciation of self-interest to healing disease. They took place because God was doing it, God was ruling in this unusual human society – this was in fact the "coming" of "the kingdom of God"! Jesus was a faith healer in the sense that he trusted God to thrust his finger into the human dilemma (the "coming" of "God's rule"), to overcome the plight of the infirm.

But not everything had been done: Not all people lived such trust in God, not all the helpless were helped, nor all the disabled healed. Of course one trusted God to follow through to completion ("eschatology"). But Jesus' message was not intended to replace grim reality with a "pie in the sky by-and-by" utopian ideal, but rather to focus attention on trusting God for today's ration of life, and on hearing God's call to give life now to one's neighbor.

All this is as far from today's Christian coalition and even mainline Christianity as it was from the Judaism practiced in Jesus' day. The hardest saying of Jesus is: "Why do you call me Lord Lord, but do not do what I say?" One laments the absence of a "high christology," any claim by Jesus in his sayings to be divine. But what could be higher than the belief that doing Jesus' word is what acquits in the day of judgment? Christological creeds may be no more than pious dodges to avoid this unavoidable condition of discipleship. Actually do what he said to do!

People do not do what he said, not simply because of the shift in cultural conditions, but ultimately because people do not trust God as Jesus did (in spite of claims to Christian faith). This, not the Jesus Seminar's shocking negations, is what should be unsettling about finding out what Jesus had to say.

All this of course sounds incredibly naive. Once Jesus launched himself into this lifestyle, practicing what he preached, he did not last long. A reality check is called for!

Yet the bottom line is not necessarily so cynical: In concentration camps, cells of a few who can really trust each other – due to a shared ethnic, religious, or political commitment – and who are hence willing to give an extra portion of their meager food and other necessities of life to the feeblest, have turned out to have a higher chance of survival than do individuals looking out only for themselves. Selfishness may ultimately turn out to be a luxury we can ill afford. There is a paradoxical saying to the effect that when one saves one's life one loses it, but when one loses one's life one saves it. To be sure, the point here is not longevity but integrity. What Jesus had to say is thus all the more worthy of serious consideration.

The Reappearance
of Parables

Bernard Brandon Scott

How should I go about putting together a profile of Jesus? I could construct a "life" of Jesus. There is much to speak for such a suggestion because a story of Jesus' life would make it easier to make sense of it, to see how it fits together. However, one of the assured results of 150 years of the quest for the historical Jesus is that we do not have enough evidence to know how to construct such an outline. The only outline we have is the one created by the author of the Gospel according to Mark.

I have chosen a different path. I have taken the material, both sayings and deeds, that has the highest claim to be from Jesus, based on the voting of the Jesus Seminar,[1] and have asked, How does this material cohere? How does it fit together? Does it represent a consistent picture? After developing three theses which I think represent this coherent view of Jesus' sayings and deeds, I then will ask, What does this tell us about Jesus?

Disappearance of parables

There is general consensus among scholars that the quest of the historical Jesus has entered a new stage since the mid 1980s.[2] A characteristic of recent books, a trend that cuts across all of them, is the disappearance of parables. At one level this is understandable because recent scholars have sought to shift the quest from Jesus' sayings to his deeds, since the previous generation of scholars had stressed the sayings and teachings of Jesus. This shift makes the disappearance of parables inevitable.

19

The motives of individual authors vary. E.P. Sanders in his *Jesus and Judaism*[3] distrusts language because it needs interpretation and there is no way to secure that interpretation. So he turned his attention to a deed – Jesus' act in the temple – that provided the sure foundation, or so he thought.[4]

John P. Meier dismisses parable interpretation in his *A Marginal Jew* because he neither approves of the methodology nor the current direction of parable studies.[5] He attempts to figure out what the parables mean by predefining what the kingdom of God means. The kingdom of God determines the meaning of the parable rather than the parable defining the kingdom of God. Because of this procedure, one can for all practical purposes dismiss the parables. Dale Allison takes a similar tack in his defense of millenarian understanding of Jesus.[6] For both Meier and Allison it would appear that Jesus made a mistake in employing parables, since they are too pliable to make his point clearly.

John Dominic Crossan, who had established his early reputation as a parable scholar, makes minimal use of parables in his *The Historical Jesus*.[7] Since he selects material only from the earliest stages of the Jesus tradition that are multiply attested by independent witnesses, few parables get through his sieve.

Marcus Borg in his *Meeting Jesus for the First Time* employs the insights from the parable studies of Robert Funk and Crossan in seeing the world turned upside down, but parables themselves are peripheral to his understanding of Jesus as a charismatic figure.[8]

At the other end of the spectrum, N.T. Wright makes use of parables, but he reverts to a pre-Jülicher position and accepts allegory as the way to read the parables. "In the parable of the wicked tenants, Israel is the vineyard, her rulers the vineyard-keepers; the prophets are the messengers, Jesus is the son; Israel's god, the creator, is himself the owner and father."[9] Needless to say, such a march backwards is hardly the way forward.

Parables once again

I have chosen to base my profile on the parables for two reasons. (1) Proverbs, aphoristic sayings and parables dominate the database of Jesus sayings and (2) the parables of Jesus are a distinctive literary form within that group of sayings. Despite various assertions to the contrary, there is no evidence of parable tellers contemporary with Jesus. The rabbinic parable develops after the destruction of the temple in 70 C.E. and follows a very different stereotyped use. Even more, many forms in the

Jesus database that are not parables often have a "parabolic" twist. For example, the Other Cheek or Coat and Shirt turn out to be burlesques of codified law, rather than the exact codification of case law. If when someone asked for my shirt I also gave them my coat, I would soon be naked. That is, these sayings along with the parables exhibit what I and others have called the distinctive voice of Jesus.[10]

To use the parables as the base of my analysis, I have borrowed a model from surveying. To lay out a map, a surveyor establishes points and then coordinates those points. I have developed three different coordinates. Each coordinate is specified by a parable that provides the initial insight that allows me to sketch the general contour of that coordinate. I will expand the insight by relating various other sayings and deeds to form a coherent field for each coordinate. With each coordinate we are, in a sense, plotting an aspect of Jesus' map. By triangulating the three points, the whole map of what Jesus is about should come into view. How these three fit together gives us the whole field. I have not engaged in a detailed analysis of each saying in this profile but rely upon the work done in my *Hear Then the Parable*.

Coordinate 1: The Leaven

In the voting of the Jesus Seminar, the parable of the Leaven attracted the highest ranking of any parable. I take that to be significant for two reasons. The parable has not figured strongly in anybody's reconstruction of the historical Jesus and receives little attention in the history of scholarship. Also it indicates that the radical interpretation of this parable initiated by Robert Funk in *Jesus as Precursor* has won the day.[11] Here if anywhere the distinctive voice of Jesus can be heard.

Insight: God becomes unclean

The parable serves as vehicle for "the kingdom of God." How to translate the phrase *basileia tou theou* has provoked much discussion. Some prefer "the ruling activity of God," while others have suggested "God's imperial rule." The problem with "kingdom" is that the word in English is too vague, too ethereal. The more exact term is "empire" because empires were the dominant political reality of the ancient world. So I prefer to translate this phrase "the Empire of God." Empire suggests a stronger, more imperial tone and has the virtue of implying its opposite. The opposite of the Empire of God is the Roman Empire. If the term has negative overtones in English, that is all right, because Empires had bad reputations in the ancient world as well.

God is unclean

Able-bodied and sick
POxy 1224 5:2, Matt 9:12, Mark 2:17, Luke 5:31

Assassin
Thom 98:1–3

Congratulations: hungry
Luke 6:21, Matt 5:6, Thom 69:2

Congratulations: poor
Luke 6:20, Thom 54, Matt 5:3

Congratulations: sad
Luke 6:21, Matt 5:4

Corrupt judge
Luke 18:2–5

Eye of a needle
Matt 19:24, Luke 18:25, Mark 10:25

Foxes have dens
Luke 9:58, Matt 8:20, Thom 86:1–2

Leaven
Luke 13:20–21, Matt 13:33, Thom 96:1–2

Mustard seed
Thom 20:2–4, Mark 4:30–32, Luke 13:18–19, Matt 13:31–32

No respect at home
Thom 31:1, Luke 4:24, John 4:44, Matt 13:57, Mark 6:4

Scholars' privileges
Luke 20:46, Mark 12:38–39, Matt 23:5–7, Luke 11:43

Shrewd manager
Luke 16:1–8

Sly as a snake
Matt 10:16, Thom 39:3

Toll collector and Pharisee
Luke 18:10–14

Treasure
Matt 13:44, Thom 109:1–3

Two friends at midnight
Luke 11:5–8

What goes in
Mark 7:14–15, Thom 14:5, Matt 15:10–11

The parable of the Leaven arranges a series of words into a pattern that the hearer must decode. We can view the parable at two different levels. At the level of a sentence it appears to picture an everyday scene in which a woman mixes some leaven in dough to make bread. But even at the sentence level oddities appear. The woman hides the leaven. She does not mix the leaven, as one might expect. Likewise, the Greek word used here is not the neutral Greek word for hiding, but a word with strong negative overtones. She conceals the leaven in the dough. Even more, the amount of dough is extraordinary. Three measures is about fifty pounds of flour, not the normal amount for a baking session. It produces a humorous image of the woman baking such a large amount, surely for a party. So while at the level of a simple sentence the parable appears to be everyday, closer examination suggests that things are not quite normal.

The second level at which to understand the parable is as a metaphor or comparison for the Empire of God. At this level it produces a cacophony. Leaven is a symbol for moral evil, the unclean; unleaven is the proper symbol for the divine. According to Exodus, at Passover, "For seven days no leaven shall be found in your houses; for if any one eats what is leavened, that person shall be cut off from the congregation of Israel" (12:19). Twice Paul quotes the aphorism, "A little leaven leavens the whole lump," to warn that a little evil will corrupt everything (Gal 5:9; 1 Cor 5:7). It parallels the American aphorism, "One rotten apple spoils the whole barrel." And Jesus warns his disciples to "beware of the leaven of the Pharisees" (Mark 8:15). It is not too extreme to say that the juxtaposition of Empire of God and leaven is blasphemous. The comparison of the Empire of Rome to leaven would strike a Jewish audience as more appropriate.

Besides this initial negative symbol, the parable piles on other problematic symbols: a woman hides or conceals the leaven until all is leavened. "Until it is all leavened" brings the process of corruption to completion. The only symbolically positive term in the parable is "three measures," which is most probably a reference to the messianic banquet. When Abraham receives the three angelic messengers at the Oaks of Mamre, Sarah makes three cakes from thee measures of flour (Gen 18:6). The reference in the parable to three measures is where the parable at the sentence level bursts out of the everyday, because the amount is way beyond ordinary. It points to the extraordinary, something like the prophecy of Isaac's birth, a divine banquet.

This one sentence parable redefines the divine in parable. The divine is identified with the unclean, the impure. The involvement of the divine with the unclean does not result in the unclean becoming clean. The parable does not end with "until it was all unleavened." Thus the divine becomes unclean, or to restate this insight even more provocatively, God becomes unclean. On this fundamental insight I will build a profile of Jesus.

Convergence: Snakes and doves

If this is literally what the parable means, then it is nonsensical. God by definition cannot be unclean. For this reason the tradition has resisted the normal meaning of leaven and instead has sought to understand the parable in a non-threatening, actually reassuring way — from a little beginning comes a great end. But the logic of parable is different from the logic of abstract discourse. To state in abstract discourse that God is unclean makes no sense at all because the essence of God is to be clean. In abstract discourse it would make more sense to say that God's rule has nothing to do with ethnic notions of purity. But in parabolic discourse it makes sense. In metaphor the daring connection of God and unclean, of Empire of God and Leaven, produces a new insight, a new disclosure. The disjunction between the two terms that produces meaning is what Wheelwright has called a diaphoric[12] metaphor. By holding the unholdable together meaning is produced. The parable has to be heard as a poem, not as an abstract logical proposition about God. Thus to say that God is unclean is my way of trying to express in abstract discourse the diaphoric quality of the oral poetic metaphor of Jesus' parable.

So radical is the proposition that God is unclean, so counter-intuitive to normal religious thinking, indeed so offensive, that in order to demonstrate its correctness I must show how it makes sense of items in the Jesus tradition, how it can serve as a unifying insight into how Jesus re-imagined the world.

In this section I want to show how this initial insight converges with other items from the database. This allows further expansion of the insight as well as producing what I hope is a convincing pattern within the database. This pattern or arrangement should begin to make the isolated sayings and deeds form a field on the map of Jesus' vision.

The insight that God becomes unclean goes a long way toward explaining the frequent references to Jesus' association with the outcast, lepers, and sinners and the special place of women in his activity. These people find themselves accepted as they are without the need to become clean or honorable. The Congratulations also belong to this coordinate, for they congratulate people who are not obviously to be congratulated. The poor are congratulated because they are poor and to them belongs the Empire of God, not because they will be rich. This overturns the assumption that poverty and disease are God's punishment for sins that underlies the books of the Hebrew Bible from Deuteronomy to 2 Kings.

What Goes In is an explicit applying of this insight to food laws. The argument that it is not what goes into the mouth that defiles a person, but what comes out, upsets the ability of the food laws to define what is clean and holy. Jesus appears to have carried out this aphorism literally in his eating habits by not washing his hands and eating with unclean people. The function of food laws is to codify the divine so one can know where the divine is. But if foods can no longer represent and replicate the divine by marking the line between clean and unclean, then people can no longer be divided into clean and unclean.

This same rejection of the line between the clean and unclean finds expression in several parables. In the Mustard Seed the planting of mustard seed, a weed-like plant, pollutes the garden, makes it unclean. Various revisions of the parable have obscured this aspect, though it is clearly in the Q (Lukan) version. Likewise, Crossan has shown in his analysis of the Treasure that the treasure, a gift, becomes a seduction for the man, who in his joy at finding the treasure, rushes out to do an immoral thing.[13] He buries the treasure and goes and buys the field, thus signaling that the treasure is not his. He steals it from its rightful owner. This parable is a counterpoint to the Leaven. What is good, a treasure, seduces the man into doing evil. Belonging to this same coordinate is the Eye of a Needle. The rich man is like treasure, one who, according to Deuteronomy, should be congratulated, but it will be more difficult for him to enter the Empire of God than for a camel to pass through the eye of a needle.

Likewise the warning against the Privileges of Scholars, "who like to parade around in long robes" belongs here. Scholars know what is clean and unclean and who can thus represent the divine. But they should not be imitated, for the basis on which their scholarship rests has been undermined. The complex of sayings dealing with the Able-bodied and Sick clearly indicates that God is on the side of the sick. It is they who need a physician. God identifies not with the honorable and righteous, but the shamed and sinners.

Finally, into this coordinate I would place those parables that exhibit characters who do not quite seem to conform to the standard of behavior thought appropriate to the Empire of God. For example, the violence of the Assassin who tests his power by thrusting his sword through a wall shocks the hearer. Like the dishonesty of the man who finds Treasure, the wheeling and dealing of the Shrewd Manager has confounded various interpreters since before the parable was incorporated into the gospel tradition. When dismissed from his job as steward, he goes to those who owe debts to his master and drastically reduces their debts. The master of the parable is no more honorable for he has been profiting from interest[14] charged by the manger.

The shamelessness of the man who delays in welcoming his guest in Two Friends at Midnight and the Corrupt Judge who fears neither God nor people in dealing with the widow's request both exhibit behavior that confounds an audience. The very amorality of the parables has proven so problematic for most interpreters that the tradition has tried to explain it away. In the end, it is the Toll Collector standing at the back of the temple begging for mercy who goes home acquitted, and not the Pharisee who openly gives God thanks. The temple no longer sets the rules. And the toll collector is unrepentant; he is still a toll collector.

"No prophet is welcome on his home turf" because there the rules are known. So one is homeless: unlike the Foxes Who Have Dens, the son of Adam has no place to lay his head. Jesus' probable conflict with his family and village belongs to this coordinate.

What is one to do in a situation where leaven represents the Empire of God, when what goes into a person does not defile, where toll collectors go home acquitted, the poor are congratulated and home has disappeared? "You must be as sly as a snake and as simple as a dove."

Coordinate 2: The Empty Jar

In contrast with the Leaven, the parable of the Empty Jar barely made the list of authentic sayings of Jesus compiled by the Jesus Seminar. There are a number of reasons for this. The parable occurs only in Thomas, and there is little history of scholarship concerning this parable. While these two reasons alone make me hesitant to build a significant aspect of my profile on this parable, I still think it unambiguously makes an important point.

Insight: God is present in absence

At the most elementary discourse level the parable is about loss. The woman starts out with a jar full of grain but arrives home empty-handed. "The handle of the jar broke . . . She didn't know it . . . she put the jar down and discovered that it was empty." The Empire is identified with loss, with accident, with emptiness. It is also possible that the story of Elijah's miracle for the widow of Zarephath as told in 1 Kgs 17:8-16 lies in the background furnishing a contrast story to the parable. During a famine a widow feeds Elijah. When he first approaches her she says, "I have nothing baked, only a handful of meal in a jar, and a little oil in a jar." Elijah commands her to bake, but to bring him the first cake. "For thus says the Lord the God of Israel, 'The jar of meal shall not be spent . . . until the day that the Lord sends rain upon the earth." She does as Elijah commands, and the prophet, she, and her child have meal throughout the famine. The parable of the Empty Jar presents a contrast to the story of the widow with a full jar. There is no prophet to come to her aid, no end-time miracle to set things aright.

Even if I am not correct about the Elijah counter-reference, the basic narrative is clear. There is no divine intervention: she goes home empty-handed. This leads me to my second foundational insight: the Empire of God is identified not with divine intervention but divine emptiness. Recasting the insight will help to bring it into focus. God is not found in the apocalyptic miracle – one must look elsewhere.

This parable fills out aspects of the profile intimated in the Leaven. Like the leaven it identifies the Empire of God with the marginalized, the female, the unclean; and in the end all is leavened, the jar is empty.

Convergence: Spread out but not seen

The saying that most obviously belongs to this coordinate is the Coming of God's Imperial Rule. This saying explicitly rejects the ability of people to point to or observe the Empire of God. "On the contrary, God's imperial rule is right there in your presence." Both the Thomas and Lukan versions of the saying agree on these two basic points – you cannot point to it, yet it is here. This presence of the Empire of God, not observable but in your presence, spread out upon the earth but not seen,

---

Present in absence

Anxieties: birds
Luke 12:24, Matt 6:26

Anxieties: don't fret
*Thom 36:1, Luke 12:22–23,
Matt 6:25*

Anxieties: clothing
Matt 6:28

Anxieties: lilies
*Luke 12:27–28, Matt 6:28–30,
Thom 36:2*

Anxieties: one hour
Luke 12:25, Matt 6:27

Congratulations: poor
Luke 6:20, Thom 54, Matt 5:3

Corrupt judge
Luke 18:2–5

Empty jar
Thom 97:1–4

Finger of God
Luke 11:19–20, Matt 12:27–28

God's imperial rule
Thom 113:2–4, Luke 17:20–21

Lost sheep
Luke 15:4–6, Matt 18:12–13

Mustard seed
*Thom 20:2–4, Mark 4:30–32,
Luke 13:18–19, Matt 13:31–32*

Rich farmer
Thom 63:1–8, Luke 12:18–20

Satan divided
Luke 11:17–18, Matt 12:25–26

Seed and harvest
Mark 4:26–29

Sower
*Mark 4:3–8, Matt 13:3–8, Thom
9:1–5, Luke 8:5–8*

Unforgiving slave
Matt 18:23–34

indicates the paradox that the Empire of God is present in absence. There is divine action in the Empire of God, but it cannot be observed.

The first Congratulations helps us understand this coordinate of sayings. The saying says "Congratulations, you poor! God's domain belongs to you." They are in the Empire of God and are still poor. It does not say, "Blessed are you poor, for you shall be middle class." The activity of God will not be manifest in a change from poor to rich, rather it is manifest in the paradox that to the poor belongs the Empire of God. To say that God is present in absence is the same as saying that to the poor belongs the Empire of God.

In the Mustard Seed the plant does not become the great cedar of Lebanon, the more appropriate metaphor for an Empire. The mustard plant is more like a weed. In the Seed and Harvest, the harvest belongs to a farmer who does not quite know what is going on. He does not observe the activity of God because he is asleep. But the last line of the parable quotes a passage in Joel about the end-time, apocalyptic war. "Prepare war, . . . Beat your plowshares into swords and your pruning forks into spears; . . . Put in the sickle, for the harvest is ripe" (Joel 3:9–13). When the farmer puts in his sickle the occasion is not the ultimate end-time war between nations, but simply the actions of farmer who is bringing the harvest in. Even though the parable of the Sower moves towards the expectation of a dramatic harvest as a climax to its stages of failure, the harvest is quite ordinary. It is not a harvest in which one grape makes five and twenty measures of wine, as in the rabbinic speculations on the great harvest.

If images of apocalyptic expectation are rejected, the observer will need to be very sharp-eyed. Instead of watching over the ninety-nine, the shepherd may abandon the whole flock for the one that wandered away (Lost Sheep). Not a very good bargain. And the judge who does not fear God may be the one to vindicate the widow (Corrupt Judge). To push even more, it may be dangerous to ask for God's intervention. In the parable of the Unforgiving Slave, after the king forgives the slave a huge, astronomical debt, his fellow slaves observe his lack of forgiveness of another slave, who by comparison owes a very small amount. These fellow slaves go and tell the king about the slave's lack of forgiveness, at which point the king takes back his forgiveness of the debt and turns the man over to the torturers. This king is a real Hellenistic tyrant. The fellow slaves by turning in the first slave have done the same thing to him that he had done to the slave who owed him a debt. And these fellow slaves turned him over in the name of a greater justice. The king-tyrant has made the situation even worse. Now they are dealing with a real autocrat. They have no criteria for his behavior. He may forgive everything or take it all back. This is hardly a model for God's Empire.

What is one to do in such a situation? One has to be very observant and see what is actually there. "Grapes are not harvested from thorn trees, nor are figs gathered from thistles" (from the complex On Anxieties: Don't Fret). The whole complex of sayings that deal with anxiety fits in here (On Anxieties: Don't Fret, Lilies, Birds, Clothing, One Hour). One should not worry about clothes or eating or anything else.

The parable of the Rich Farmer tells the other side of this story. Having a bounteous harvest, he tears down his barns and builds new ones. Yet that night he dies. His anxiety did him no good. Furthermore, even though God intervened, no one will ever know it. Both the parables of the Empty Jar and the Rich Farmer move from bounty (full jar, great harvest) to loss (empty jar, death).

Several recent studies of Jesus have put the healing and exorcisms of Jesus at the heart of their reconstruction. Even though it is difficult to trace individual stories of healing and exorcism back to the earliest levels of the Jesus tradition, there can be no doubt that Jesus was a healer and exorcist. How does that activity of Jesus fit into this coordinate that I am developing? Does it not seem to contradict it?[15]

The most explicit saying in which Jesus refers to his exorcisms equates what he does with the finger of God. "If by God's finger I drive out demons, then for you God's imperial rule has arrived." The phrase "finger of God" is used in the story of Moses' contest with the magicians of Pharaoh's court. When Aaron strikes the dust, a great swarm of gnats appears. The magicians, unable to duplicate the feat, tell Pharaoh, "This is the finger of God" (Exod 8:15). The use of that phrase means that Jesus' exorcisms bear the same relationship to Moses' wonderworking as the Mustard Plant does to the great cedar Lebanon. Both make ironical claims that burlesque expectations.

In a similar vein, the saying about Satan's house being divided against itself (Satan Divided) indicates that there were those who saw Jesus' activity as that of Satan himself. Thus the activity of God in Jesus' own exorcisms is not obviously God's activity. Perhaps this is the context in which one should view Jesus' claim to have seen Satan Falling from Heaven like lightning. Jesus views his healings and exorcisms as divine activities, but they are not the miraculous deeds of Moses – nor does his wonder working fill up the empty jar. It still demands insight on the part of the audience. He begins by saying, "If by the finger of God," indicating that the viewer must judge what kind of activity this is. And some will judge it to be the activity of Satan.

Coordinate 3: From Jerusalem to Jericho

The Samaritan, or as I prefer to call it, From Jerusalem to Jericho, received a very high vote of confidence from the Jesus Seminar even though only a single version has survived in the gospel of Luke. This parable is one of the most popular in the tradition and one of the most frequent topics in religious art.

Insight: Cooperation, not competition

To understand this narrative parable we must take up the point of view of a Jewish audience, and thus firmly set aside the gentile perspective in which the Samaritan is a good fellow, as Luke and the tradition have insisted. From the perspective of a first century Palestinian audience, the Samaritan is the expected opponent or villain, the moral equivalent of Leaven, and and assigning the hero's role to him – instead of the priest or Levite or even the expected Israelite – is the same as finding the jar empty.

Even more this parable envisions interpersonal relations on a basis other than those of an agonistic contest. In a Mediterranean culture relations of all types were agonistic, viewed as contest, because all goods are viewed as limited and fixed and so one must always be in a contest, an agon, to get a share of the limited supply. To accept this parable as anything but a fantasy, a hearer must accept the Samaritan as helper-hero instead of expected opponent-villain and oneself as victim in the ditch. An audience is not even offered the opportunity of an agonistic contest in the narrative. The man in the ditch is passive and the Samaritan simply has compassion, effectively ending the story in mid-narrative. The Samaritan cannot even be the man's patron because their social spaces are so different. This leads to my third fundamental insight: a parable re-imagines human relationships apart from the agonistic contest. Cooperation, not competition, is the basis for human social structure in the Empire of God.

Convergence: The great leveling

Jesus' meals are probably the immediate context in which this coordinate found its most concrete expression. Eating together, sharing food in a society constantly threatened by hunger and famine, concretely demonstrated what cooperation meant. This is the context in which I would seek to understand the second and third Congratulations dealing with hunger and weeping. The archetype is Congratulations You Poor. In that beatitude there is no future in which the poor become rich. That

Cooperation not contest

Bury the dead
Matt 8:22, Luke 9:59–60

Children in God's domain
Mark 10:14, Matt 19:14, Luke 18:16

Coat and shirt
Matt 5:40, Luke 6:29

Congratulations: sad
Luke 6:21, Matt 5:4

Dinner party
Thom 64:1–11, Luke 14:16–23

Emperor and God
Thom 100:2, Mark 12:17, Luke 20:25, Matt 22:21

Congratulations: hungry
Luke 6:21, Matt 5:6, Thom 69:2

Give to beggars
Matt 5:42, Luke 6:30

God as father
Luke 11:2, Matt 6:9, Matt 6:9

Hating one's family
Luke 14:26

Leased vineyard
Thom 65:1–7

Left and right hands
Matt 6:3, Thom 62:2

Lend without return
Thom 95:1–2, Matt 5:42

Love your enemies
Luke 6:27, Matt 5:44, Luke 6:32, 35

Other cheek
Matt 5:39, Luke 6:29

Prodigal sons
Luke 15:11–32

Rich farmer
Thom 63:1–6, Luke 12:16–20

Samaritan
Luke 10:30–35

Saving one's life
Luke 17:33

Second mile
Matt 5:41

True relatives
Matt 12:40–50, Thom 99:2, Luke 8:21

Two masters
Luke 16:13, Matt 6:24, Thom 47:2, Luke 16:13, Matt 6:24

Vineyard laborers
Matt 20:1–15

beatitude should guide our understanding of the other two. "You will have a feast" and "You will laugh" do not refer to the apocalyptic future, but to the practice of cooperation within the meal events. There all will share what they have. So profound is this cooperation, so deep does it reach into the established structures of first-century reality, that the Samaritan can be envisioned as the hero-helper, and one can be commanded to "Love your Enemies."

The other side of this occurs in the Rich Farmer. He exposes himself as an epicurean. "Then I'll say to myself, 'You have plenty put away for years to come. Take it easy, eat, drink, enjoy yourself.'" He co-opts a fantastic harvest for himself. But that night he dies and so his harvest, like Joseph's in Egypt, will be available for the village. God does intervene in this parable, but to the villagers who helped the rich man build new barns, his death will be a natural one, and they will mourn for this generous man who has provided for them. They will not see the hand of God in his death, though without his death, they would have starved. He intended to keep the whole harvest for himself.

The saying about Children in God's Domain indicates who people the Empire of God. Children are an appropriate image because they cannot play the adult roles that are being rejected as inappropriate for life in the Empire. The recasting of the family is fundamental to this redefinition of community. True Relatives are no longer one's natural family, but "Those here who do what my Father wants are my brothers and my mother." The other side of this redefinition of family is the very Hating of One's Family. There is even the abandonment of a fundamental familial duty to bury the dead. "Leave it to the dead to bury their own dead."

This re-envisioned family contains a re-imagining of God as Father. The Seminar voted overwhelming that Jesus used "Abba" to refer to God as father. Regardless of how Abba is to be understood, clearly the tenor of "father" as a metaphor for God is very different than "Our Father in heaven." The latter is part of the patriarchal, patron-client world; the former is an effort to redefine family.

The parable of the Prodigal Sons exhibits in great detail a narrative of this re-imagined family. The father in the parable at times plays a foolish and shameless role and at other times a "female" role. From the very beginning of the narrative he exhibits little in the way of male honor. The admonition of Sirach about the distribution of inheritance is clear. "While you are still alive and have breath in you, do not let any one take your place. It is better that your children should ask from you than that you should look to the hands of your sons. . . At the time when you end the days of your life, in the hour of death, distribute your inheritance" (Sir 33:21–23). The father of this parable surrenders his property, a foolish act, putting himself and his family at risk. He runs and kisses his younger son instead of maintaining his male dignity. He addresses the elder son as "baby." This shameful aspect of the father has been thoroughly hidden in the history of scholarship.

Moreover, the father does not choose between his sons. He accepts both regardless of what they do. The acceptance of one is not purchased by means of the rejection of the other, as is typical in such stories of elder and younger sons in the Hebrew Bible and other cultures.[16]

Finally, there is a third act implied but unspoken in the narrative. The story ends with a younger son feasting on the fatted calf with all the signs of acceptance – shoes on his feet, a signet ring on his finger, and the father's best robe as his garment, thinking he has struck a clever bargain with the father. Meanwhile outside waits an angry elder son who still has all the property. What happens when the father dies? If the sons continue on their same trajectories, the younger pushing the boundaries, the elder feeling himself the abused family slave, they will kill each other. Or they can emulate the father. He is all forgiveness. There is nothing the sons can do that he will not forgive, regardless of the cost to him. He is willing to surrender all his male honor to preserve his sons in family. Or as another saying has it, "Whoever tries to hang on to life will forfeit it, but whoever forfeits it will preserve it" (Saving One's Life).

While exactly what is at stake in the Leased Vineyard is not very clear, it surely represents an agonistic contest run amuck. The owner who relies on the respect due him as a patron and social superior misjudges the intent of those who have leased his vineyard. These also calculate that they can get away with their acts of violence. The parable exhibits how bankrupt is a world based on agonistic contest. It is a world of unending violence.

In the Vineyard Laborers those hired first complain that by paying the last hired the same amount they have received, the master has made them equal. The laborers complaint is that the master has destroyed the order of the world. The entire Roman Empire was organized as patron-client system. The ultimate patron was the emperor, and the system worked its way downward, with his clients in turn becoming patrons for yet other clients. And their fleas have fleas too. Such a system ensures a hierarchically arranged social order in which no one is equal and every social engagement is a contest to determine one's place in the hierarchy. The Empire of God brings everyone to the same level. This parable is retold from the rich man's point of view in the Dinner Party. In order to throw his party, he must invite the homeless and forfeit the company of those rich like himself. So radical is this break between these two ways of organizing social relations that one cannot have Two Masters, something demanded by the patron-client organization of society. Calculating which master to please is a hazard of everyday life. The organization of the emperor's world is diametrically opposed to that of God's. "Give to the emperor what belongs to the emperor, give God what belongs to God."

This re-imaging of social relations finds one of its clearest expressions in those sayings burlesquing case law: Other cheek, Coat and Shirt, Second Mile, Give to Beggars, Lend without return. Case law attempts to work out in advance and in detail all the situations or cases implied by a law. These sayings of Jesus burlesque case law through a similar form and strategy. If someone asks for your shirt, give them also your coat. In such a case one would soon be naked. If you turn the other cheek, you would soon be black and blue, beaten about the face. And finally if you gave every time someone begged, you soon would be broke. These examples of case law all subvert the very effort of case law to specify what is moral. "When you give charity, don't let your left hand know what your right hand is doing."

Outcomes

The world implied in these three coordinates re-imagines a community's social experience. The Empire of God as Leaven does not warrant a license to do whatever one wants. Rather the unclean are accepted as welcomed by God as they are without the necessity of becoming clean. Likewise when the Empire of God is an empty jar, then the community must accept responsibility for its life and not fall back on the narcotic of a divine intervention to set things aright. When the Samaritan is the hero-helper, then social cooperation is defined outside the bounds of the traditional agonistic relations of a patron-client relationship. These three aspects go a long way towards redefining basic human relationships as conceived within a Mediterranean peasant culture.

The Empire of God is at the core of Jesus' re-imagining. It is the presiding symbol, whether or not it is always or ever the referent of the parables. Also the understanding of the Empire of God must be derived from Jesus' language-activity, rather than from an historical survey of Jewish literature. Such a survey produces little fruit because of the very infrequent appearance of the phrase. As a symbol, Empire of God stands for the experience that results from the language-activity of Jesus. The Coming of God's Imperial Rule clearly indicates that it is a non-empirical reality. "You won't be able to observe the coming of God's imperial rule. People are not going to be able to say, 'Look, here it is!' or 'Over there.'"

Jesus surely uses Empire in an ironical sense since the Empire of God fails to measure up when compared to the empires of David or Caesar. This irony and non-comparison is clearly represented in the Emperor and God: "Give the emperor what belongs to the emperor, give God what belongs to God." To define it negatively, the Empire of God is not like the Empire of David or Caesar. As a symbol, the Empire of God is like the American flag. It stands for a whole series of complex values that cannot be expressed clearly — that is why one needs to employ a symbol to represent it. But to go even further, I think the Empire of God functions to create through the imagination a sphere in which those who are a part of this community of envisioning can experience healing, the hospitality of the unclean, the presence of God in God's nonempirical activity.

Death of Jesus

The reason(s) for the death of Jesus probably remain beyond our grasp. Empires can and do act in authoritarian ways that escape the cool rationality of law or reason. Pilate did not really need a solid case to kill Jesus. Yet one can see in Jesus' language-activity the seeds of a conflict that could easily escalate to a confrontation and to death. And the parable of the Leaven and what it implies are sufficient blasphemy to put Jesus into conflict with the religious authorities. For them the symbol of God's activity is the unleavened, the clean. The leavened bread must be swept out to make a place pure and holy, set apart. And even though Jesus explicitly separates God's empire and Caesar's, the success of Jesus' social experiment in peasant community under the symbol of the Empire of God would pose a threat to Rome's rule. Rome's rule is built on the premise that the local population is divided and distrustful of each other. A peasantry that accepts each other, that no longer sees itself in agonistic conflict with each other, always defending their given and limited positions, even reaching out to Samaritan enemies, poses a real threat to Rome's rule by thwarting its attempts to divide and conquer.

Jesus as rebel: a social science model

One of the most perplexing problems in the quest for the historical Jesus is why Jesus opted for such a radical program. Frequently this problem is avoided and one falls back on the inevitability of history. What happened had to happen. But, of course, that is not true; it is the fallacy of the inevitable. Like most peasants in his situation, Jesus could have sat back and done nothing. At other times I suspect that an assumed Christology warrants the model. Unthinkingly we fall back on faith commitments as though those explain why Jesus chose so revolutionary an agenda.

What complicates any attempt to solve the problem is the very lack of data. We know almost nothing about Jesus' interior life, his psychological or social development. Nor do we possess even a chronological narrative in which to arrange a "life of Jesus."

Social science methods have provided a way forward. Crossan, for example, presents in his *The Historical Jesus: The Life of a Mediterranean*

Jewish Peasant a model of brokerage in the Roman Empire that produced a system on the verge of breakdown. But what Crossan has explained is why the Roman Empire was such an unstable society and why the Jews revolted in 68 C.E. What no social model can explain is why an individual decides to revolt. Social sciences deal with social groups, not individuals.

Frank Sulloway in *Born to Rebel, Birth Order, Family Dynamics, and Creative Lives*[17] has produced an impressive and controversial study seeking to explain why people rebel. While the reasons are complex, as his title indicates, the model with the most predictive power is birth order combined with various aspects of family dynamics. For Sulloway, the most important aspect in the model is birth order. Latterborn are more likely to be rebels because of the internal evolutionary dynamics of family life. Children have to find a niche in the family structure in order to prove their value to their parents. Parents invest most heavily in the firstborn, and to be more precise, the firstborn male in traditional societies. Thus the firstborn does not have to search for a niche and automatically receives a high investment from the parents. Firstborns more naturally identify strongly with power and authority. Latterborns must find their own niche in the family, so in order to succeed they must be open to experience. Openness to experience is a term psychologists employ to indicate a crucial aspect of the creative process. "People who exhibit openness are described as imaginative, flexible, creative, independent, and liberal."[18] Birth order, gender, and temperament interact to produce personality characteristics. These are, in Sulloway's argument, more determinant of the creative individual than social class. If social class were the dominant factor we would expect siblings to be very similar. Yet "siblings raised together are almost as different in their personalities as people from different families."[19] Thus family structure produces the difference.

In developing his thesis, Sulloway argues from the centrality of birth order, but other factors in a family's dynamics make the model more predictive. By itself, the birth order will not correctly predict openness to experience any more accurately than flipping a coin. But when combined with other factors, for example, conflict with a parent, then the predictive power rises substantially.

A major problem with employing Sulloway's model to understand Jesus is that we know almost nothing about Jesus' birth order. Thus we confront Samuel Sandmel's law: minimal evidence leads to maximal theories. Still I think the model can still be helpful. It can be used negatively to call into question certain assumptions. Meier envisions Jesus as the firstborn, raised in an intact family, with Joseph teaching his son Jesus his trade and schooling him in Hebrew and the traditions of Judaism. If this were in fact the case, then, according to Sulloway's evidence, the chance that Jesus would lead a radical revolution would be less than two percent. So perhaps that traditional assumption about Jesus' birth order and family situation can be set aside.

At the risk of sliding down the slippery road of speculation not built on facts, there are aspects in the tradition that can be of use. The tradition of Jesus as the firstborn very probably results not from family remembrance but from faith speculating about the significance of Jesus. James may well be the elder brother of Jesus and what little we know of him would support this theory. His assumption of power and the maintenance of family authority in Jerusalem result from the adaptive strategies of a firstborn.

Sulloway notes that the death of a parent or a missing parent has a strong effect on siblings. The firstborn becomes more conservative, the latterborn more open to experience, more likely to rebel. The existence of Joseph has long been problematic, since he appears only in the later stages of the tradition, having no mention in Mark or Q, and having no role in the sayings of Jesus. This absence of Joseph during the life of Jesus led later Christians to speculate that he was old man when he married Mary and had died by the time Jesus was active. Joseph is surely a later fiction of the gospel writers. So we have no good evidence for Jesus' father. Jane Schaberg has argued that the birth of Jesus was illegitimate.[20] Whatever the facts about Jesus' father, his absence from the family would have had a strong impact on the siblings. Finally the tradition contains evidence of conflict between Jesus and his own family. Clearly they were not part of his original group of followers. These three factors – latterborn birth rank, absence of a father, and conflict with the family – would in Sulloway's model put Jesus in the group most inclined to support a radical response.

Sulloway's model is powerful and I find it helpful. As the response to his book develops we will get a clearer idea of both its problems and its strengths. But it offers a way to begin to sort out some of issues and clarify what we can and cannot explain. The interface between the historical, social scientific, and family dynamics models is very important. The historical-social model provides evidence about the specific cognitive and ideological structures that make up a culture. Family dynamics helps us understand how an individual responds to that structure – why some support the structure while others revolt.

Parabler as poet

Jesus' revolt takes a very special form. He revolts in parable. I see no evidence that Jesus was leading a political revolution or that he had a social program in mind. He clearly affected the lives of people, but he was not a social organizer or activist. Although the idea is now out of fashion, Jesus the oral storyteller seems to me closer to a poet. The activist will always be dissatisfied with the poetic vision, but change comes about because a creative individual has had that vision.

At times it seems to me that it is easier to know what Jesus is against than what he is for. To borrow a term from computer science, Jesus' vision is against the default world, especially insofar as the default world is oppressive and destructive of the life of those he calls the poor. He is opposed to the purity code and the imperial order as models for God. He is not simply a contrarian, but often it is easier to make clear what one stands against than exactly what one stands for.

Seamus Heaney has recently addressed this issue in his *The Redress of Poetry*. I take the liberty of quoting a passage that is to the point.

> And in the activity of poetry too, there is a tendency to place a counter-reality in the scales – a reality which may be only imagined but which nevertheless has weight because it is imagined within the gravitational pull of the actual and can therefore hold its own and balance out against the historical situation. This redressing effect of poetry comes from its being a glimpsed alternative, a revelation of potential that is denied or constantly threatened by circumstances. And sometimes, of course, it happens that such a revelation, once enshrined in the poem, remains as a standard for the poet, so that he or she must then submit to the strain of bearing witness in his or her own life to the place of consciousness established in the poem.[21]

In his explanation of how poetry functions, Heaney brings out a number of points that are critical to understanding how Jesus' parables and aphorisms operated. Jesus' vision is not an alternative to the default world in the sense that it is a replacement. It is a counterweight, a counter-reality, in Heaney's terms. Thus, it is always dialogically related to that default world. The default world will almost always win in the long run, because it is the default. That is why Jesus' own language betrayed him in the end.

Jesus' parables are "a glimpsed alternative, a revelation of potential that is denied or constantly threatened by circumstance," or in my terms, constantly threatened by the default world. A glimpsed alternative is not a worked out program. It is always temporary, glimpsed. It is a possibility, not a reality.

Once enshrined in parable, it remains a standard for the poet, or in this case Jesus. Thus it is not the empire of God that drives Jesus, but the glimpse enshrined in the parable that is likened to the empire of God. It is an alternative reality only as a counter-balance to the real reality, whether the Roman Empire or the Temple state. As Heaney remarks, the poet "must then submit to the strain of bearing witness in his or her own life to the place of consciousness established in the poem." In Jesus' parables his consciousness is established and his life bears witness to that consciousness. Thus the parables provide the coordinates for understanding Jesus' deeds.

A problem with this view of Jesus is that it runs counter to the assumption that he is the founder of a new religion. This demands something new and complete, not something in counter-balance, not just a glimpse. Such a view of Jesus appears too ephemeral for what came afterwards: Christianity and the church triumphant. With my view, Jesus remains firmly attached to Judaism and is engaged in an argument within Judaism. He is part of a continuing debate. To put it too boldly, he is against the Deuteronomist and sides with Job and Qohelet.

Several scholars have strongly objected to a view of Jesus that puts his language and parables at the center. Sanders has objected that "that it is difficult make his [Jesus'] teaching offensive enough to lead to execution."[22] Meir is even more acid in his remarks.

> A tweedy poetaster who spent his time spinning out parables and Japanese koans, a literary aesthete who toyed with 1st century deconstructionism, or a bland Jesus who simply told people to look at the lilies of the field – such a Jesus would threaten no one, just as the university professors who create him threaten no one.[23]

Perhaps Meier's remark reflects his own impotency in a capitalist society rather than an objective assessment of words in the ancient world. Socrates, next to Jesus one of the most famous martyrs of the ancient world, died because of his provocative language; and the fate of Salman Rushdie in our own day demonstrates the power of words in a traditional society. Poets still have power.

To return to Heaney's argument, poetry is a redress because it envisions "a reality which may be only imagined but which nevertheless has weight because it is imagined within the gravitational pull of the actual

and can therefore hold its own and balance out against the historical situation." The redress of the parable is hope and hope has power – not
because it is a concrete program, a worked out plan or blueprint, but
because it creates the counter-reality to the default moral world. It says
things do not have to be this way.

Václav Havel was imprisoned for his poems and plays, led the vel-
vet revolution, and became the first President of Czechoslovakia and then
the Czech Republic. What Havel has to say about hope explains how
parables and the empire of God functioned as a revolutionary symbol for
Jesus and his followers. Hope, he says, is

> a state of mind, not a state of the world. . . and it's not
> essentially dependent on some particular observation of the
> world or estimate of the situation . . . it transcends the
> world that is immediately experienced, and is anchored
> somewhere beyond its horizons . . . It is not the convic-
> tion that something will turn out well, but the certainty that
> something makes sense, regardless of how it turns out.[24]

It is no accident that those who espouse an apocalyptic Jesus avoid
the parables. You cannot get from the parables to an apocalyptic Jesus,
although you can get from an apocalyptic Jesus to an apocalyptic interpretation of the parables. But such an interpretation is the default moral
world, because apocalyptic is the Deuteronomist's vision as the future
divine fact. From an apocalyptic Jesus one does get to the founder of
Christianity.

In his understanding of the redress of poetry, Heaney has captured
an insight into how Jesus' language offered to his audience an alternative
to the world in which they were trapped – a world burdened by purity
laws segregating the unclean from the clean and into further degrees of
purity or shame. A world where those on the bottom are imprisoned in
unchangeable structures and await a divine solution. A world in which
enemies threaten at every point. Jesus in his language offers a counter
world, a vision, an openness to experience. It is a "glimpsed alternative, a
revelation of potential that is denied or constantly threatened by circumstances." It may be only an imagined or re-imagined alternative, but it
derives its weight from its opposition to and careful observation of the
historical world. Apart from the gravitational pull of that historical world,
it is without meaning or open to whatever one wants it to mean.

Jesus revolts in parable and the parables create a counter-world, a
hoped for world that redresses the world as it is and surely makes sense,
regardless of how it turns out, even it if turns out to be his crucifixion.

The Jesus of History
A Vision of the Good Life

Roy W. Hoover

Introduction

The Jesus Seminar found that the evidence of the authentic sayings strongly indicates that Jesus did not think that the world would come to a catastrophic end in his lifetime and be succeeded by a new ·age brought into being by divine intervention, nor did he say that he had come into the world to give his life as a ransom for many, as the author of Mark's gospel put it (Mark 10:45). These findings raise two compelling questions. First, if an apocalyptic hope or an eschatological expectation was not Jesus' ordering vision, not the view that furnished coherence to his teaching and guided his course of action, what was? Second, if it was not Jesus' aim to die on the cross as a sacrifice for the sins of the world, what was he trying to do? While this essay addresses both questions, it is primarily concerned with the first.

Finding the unifying theme

I began my own attempt to find an answer to these questions by a close reading of the sayings identified by the Jesus Seminar as "the authentic words of Jesus" shortly after their publication in *The Five Gospels* in 1993. I decided to compile and read through these sayings, printed in red and pink in that volume, with two questions in mind. (1) Can one discern in these aphorisms and parables a unifying theme that held them together and implied a coherent point of view that characterized Jesus' teaching as a whole and guided his course of action? (2) If such an ordering vision, or characteristic and coherent point of view is discernible, could it suggest an answer to the question of what Jesus' aim was, what he was trying to do? That is, could one find in these authentic speech fragments themselves a feature or features that might enable one to assemble a mosaic that would resemble the profile of their author?

As I read the compilation of authentic sayings, I began to notice in them a repeated call to what I called "singlemindedness," a repeated summons to an unconditional trust in and commitment to the reign of God. That led me to hypothesize that this might be the motif that exposes Jesus' ordering vision to view: a vision of the good life, a life ordered by the ideal goodness that he referred to as "the reign of God."

I will suggest here that this ordering vision is most clearly expressed in two clusters of authentic sayings preserved by the author of Matthew's Gospel in what Matthew's readers later called "The Sermon on the Mount": 5:39–48; 6:24–30; and that everything else that Jesus taught and did can be seen as consistent with the point of view expressed there. The rationale for focusing on these two sayings clusters follows in the development of this essay.

It seems to me appropriate to think of the point of view reflected so clearly in these two clusters as a vision of Israel's religious ideal. This way of characterizing his vision places Jesus in the context of the religious and social situation in First Century CE Israel: the Essenes (specifically, the Dead Sea Scroll community at Qumran), the Pharisees, and John the Baptist, I suggest, all embraced what they regarded as Israel's religious ideal as the remedy for the wrongs that plagued religion and society in Israel in their time. Each of these groups had a particular and characteristic view of the Temple establishment in Jerusalem that was consistent with their vision of Israel's religious ideal. Jesus' teaching and activity can be seen as his own version of such a quest and carried with it his own view of Jerusalem's Temple.

The answer to the second question, I suggest, is that Jesus' aim was to persuade all who could hear him to embrace his vision and to accept the challenge to actualize this ideal, to live this vision. By actualizing this ideal among themselves and by proclaiming it as good news about the reign of God they could change the life of their whole society from the way it was to the way it ought to be. If that were done, what was wrong in his country would be righted and its people would come to know this good life in their own experience.

In his parables, aphorisms, and exchanges with others Jesus unfolded his vision. In fraternizing indiscriminately with any who showed an interest in what he had to say about God's reign—many of whom were among the ignored and rejected—and by healing sick and dysfunctional people, Jesus enacted his vision: in life under God's reign there are no outcasts and none are left hopeless or helpless. Jesus' articulate, enacted vision of the way things ought to be called the legitimacy of the way things are into question; and as he had reason to know after witnessing the fate of John the Baptist, anyone in a hierarchical, authoritarian society who presumed to illuminate things in this fashion would put himself in harm's way. To undertake such a task in the face of such imposing authority and power requires both extraordinary confidence in the truth and justice of the vision and uncommon courage.

Jacob Neusner, the prominent American scholar of Judaism, said of his ten year study of the Mishnah (a codification of rabbinic oral law completed around 200 CE) that his aim was "to find out who people were from the evidence of what they said, to weigh the fire of their vision. . . ."[1] My aim in this essay is similar: to recover the fire of Jesus' ordering vision from its residue preserved in his remembered words. Since my primary aim here is to identify the ordering vision that is at the heart of Jesus' teaching and that provided the basis and rationale for what he did in the name of God's reign, this cannot be a full profile, but only a first step toward a profile. It is, nevertheless, a crucial initial move, because if one can succeed in identifying a teacher's basic orientation and theme, then the possibility of recognizing the pattern and meaning of his teaching and activity as a whole is much improved. Put differently, if we cannot discern Jesus' ordering vision, we cannot see how the pieces of information about him should be connected. We have a collection of fragments, but no clear idea of the whole of which they were a part. We can see how a gospel author has connected them in his narrative, but how this compares with the connection that Jesus himself gave them in his speech and activity remains obscure. But if we can discern his ordering vision, we will be able see what the fragments mean as evidence about Jesus before the gospels, the Jesus of history, because we will know what they are fragments of: a coherent view and a clear aim.

In one of the last things he published, Amos N. Wilder, Hollis Professor of Divinity, Emeritus, at Harvard Divinity School, argued that Jesus' parables and aphorisms "rest on prior assumptions." The meaning of his sayings and stories cannot be rightly understood unless we can recognize the larger story presupposed by them. "Even if we are unsure about [the authenticity of] his eschatological sayings," Wilder wrote, "we need to formulate his historical-cosmic outlook as best we can to locate his orientation. We do not have a sufficient basis in his stories." The cultural and political crisis at the time led Jesus to conceive of "a radical formulation and intensified symbol for Israel's hope and calling," which is best understood, Wilder thought, in eschatological or apocalyptic terms.[2] In the course of the work of the Jesus Seminar, however, I became convinced, along with other Fellows, that the explicitly eschatological and apocalyptic elements of the New Testament Gospels were the work of Jesus' early interpreters, not elements of Jesus' own vision. The evidence that supports that conclusion includes the fact that there is no appeal to an eschatological hope in the important cluster of sayings preserved in Matthew's sermon referred to above, nor in the twenty-three parables identified as authentic by the Seminar.[3] Further, recent studies of the Q document (a collection of Jesus' sayings used by Matthew and Luke as a written source for their own work and from which the aforementioned sayings clusters were taken) have convincingly demonstrated that the earliest layers of Q consist of wisdom teachings to which eschatological or apocalyptic elements were added at a later time.[4] Because the earliest layer of Q is the earliest tradition we have about the teaching of Jesus, that finding heightens the likelihood that Jesus' own outlook was not eschatological or apocalyptic either.

What remains valid in Wilder's view, I think, is his insistence that if we are to understand Jesus' parables and sayings rightly, we must succeed in recognizing their prior assumptions: Jesus' own "cosmic outlook" and "orientation," as Wilder put it.[5] That "cosmic outlook" and "orientation," I propose, is a vision of the reign of God in which Jesus asks his hearers to trust God's goodness and power absolutely and to imitate God's indiscriminate generosity unconditionally. To do this is to live the good life—life ordered by the ideal of the good, the way life ought to be. This is the visionary way in which Jesus responded to the problematic social and religious situation of his time.

Jesus was preceded by others in his society who had embraced what they regarded as Israel's religious ideal as the measure of the way things ought to be in their country. Two such groups and one such individual formed an important part of the larger context of Jesus' life and public activity: the Essenes at Qumran, the Pharisees, and John the Baptist. His aim and vision can be seen more clearly in comparison with theirs.

The Essenes

The Dead Sea Scrolls have given us extensive new information about a form of sectarian Judaism that was contemporary with Jesus, but about which little had previously been known. The opening lines of the Rule of the Community (1QS), the community's charter, contain a declaration of the community's aim and ideal, and a statement of the standards that candidates for admission to the community must meet. These opening lines indicate that the community's aim was to live in perfect, uncompromising obedience to the law of God revealed in the Torah, their holy scriptures; and that candidates for admission were to bring "all their knowledge, powers and possessions into the Community of God, that they may purify their knowledge in the truth of God's precepts and order their powers according to His ways of perfection and [order] all their possessions according to His righteous counsel" (1QS 1:11–13).

Clearly, the aim announced in the opening lines of this important scroll is nothing less than uncompromising commitment to perfect obedience to the revealed law of God. Everything is to be committed to the truth and purposes of God. Nothing is to be withheld. There are to be no reservations and no exceptions. The covenantors at Qumran committed themselves to what one might call the practice of perfection.

The requirement that members surrender their financial assets to the community, an unprecedented demand in Israel's religious history, is most convincingly seen in connection with their commitment to this practice of perfection. The desire for wealth is identified in their writings as one of the principal origins of the sinful inclination to violate God's commands, while the renunciation of possessions is seen as evidence of the genuineness of a person's professed commitment to the purposes of God, i.e., to perfect obedience to all God's commandments.

Perhaps the most striking and suggestive indictment of wealth in the Qumran literature is its identification in the Damascus Document (CD) – a community document consisting of an admonition and laws – as one of the three nets of Belial (one of their terms for Satan) by which he has ensnared Israel: "the first [net] is fornication, the second is riches, and the third is profanation of the temple" (CD 4:15–18). Here the desire for riches is expressly identified as one of the three principal reasons for Israel's failure to live in obedience to the commandments of God. In numerous other passages also the desire for wealth is specified either as a root cause of disregard for God's law or as a prominent characteristic of unjust and profane men.

Qumran's answer to this scourge of riches-induced abandonment of the precepts of God's law was a total renunciation of all personal possessions and a commitment to total obedience to all of God's commands. Here, I suggest, is the key to understanding the motivation and meaning of the covenantors' surrender of their personal property to the community: renunciation of possessions was for the sake of making their

practice of obedience perfect. (We may note parenthetically that a saying of Jesus taken from Q by both Matthew and Luke and voted pink by
the Seminar implies a similarity of some degree, if not quite common
ground, between Jesus' views and those held at Qumran: "No one can
serve two masters; for a servant will either hate the one and love the
other, or be devoted to the one and despise the other. You cannot serve
God and wealth [at the same time]" (Matt 6:24 // Luke 16:13; cp. Thom
47:1, 2). You have to choose. Although their Law-centered, priest-led
community was very different from Jesus' vision-centered, layman-led
movement, on this point at least the Essenes at Qumran and Jesus
agreed.

The Qumran Essenes also called for a reform of Temple ritual and
the restoration of its legitimate priesthood, deposed by the Maccabees
in the mid-second century BCE. In brief, one might say that a perfectly
administered Temple at the sacred center of a people who were perfectly
obedient to the law of God was the Qumran community's redemptive
vision for the people of Israel. By embracing such a perfectionistic
vision, the Qumran community committed themselves to a life of complete obedience to the law of God, which they regarded as the model of
what Israel ought to be and that they hoped would one day, in God's
good time, characterize the life of the nation as a whole.

The Pharisees

The Pharisees were another group within Judaism who had committed themselves to a specific strategy intended to realize the religious
ideal of Israel. The originating aim of the Pharisees was to resist the secularizing influence of the hellenistic world by raising their commitment
to a strictly Jewish way of life to new heights. Their impulse was to resist
the social changes stemming from pagan culture by reforming Judaism
in a perfectionistic direction.

The most visible expression of the Pharisees' strategy was their
commitment to the practice of eating their meals at home according to
the rules required of the priests when they served the altar of the Temple
in Jerusalem. They thus made their homes like the Temple on the
assumption that by "eating like God, Israel became like God: a pure and
perfect incarnation, on earth in the Land that was holy, of the model of
heaven." [6]

Both the relevance and the effectiveness of this strategy are impressive. Priest and Temple are by definition set apart for divine service. That
meant that they could not legitimately be made subject to secular

authority, and that they must not sell out to commercial interests or accept paganizing practices. They were expected to maintain the integrity of their Jewish identity. By making this sacred separateness of Temple and priestly service the model for an authentic Jewish way of life, the Pharisees demonstrated how the people of Israel could retain control over much of their own lives, even though pagan rulers (Egyptian or Syrian in the third and second centuries BCE, the Romans after 63 BCE) had political control of their country. As Neusner observes, by making decisions about food (sexual behavior and marriage also) "in one way and not some other, they . . . could keep outsiders at a distance and those who. . . adhered to the group within bounds."[7]

But by embracing the strategy of democratizing the purity rules for consuming food required of priests when they served the Temple altar, thus making every Israelite a priest, so to speak, the Pharisees were aiming at more than the survival of the Jewish way of life. They wanted to live the dream, to make the ideal real. Embracing this dream was at the same time an effective strategy. The Temple excluded all non-Israelites from participation. By extending the kosher requirements of the Temple cult to the everyday social practice of eating meals in their homes, the Pharisees emphasized the distinctiveness of their Jewish identity and the differentiation of the Jewish way of life to an unprecedented degree. What legitimized this raising the wall of separation to a new height was its aim: a more perfect realization of Israel's religious ideal.

The evidence that supports the claim that the adoption of the priestly purity laws for food was a defining element of the Pharisees' strategy and practice is found both in the Mishnah and in the early Christian gospels. While the editing of the Mishnah was completed only around 200 CE, Jacob Neusner's critical study of the text led him to conclude that the final form of the Mishnah incorporates three layers of tradition that had their origins in three successive historical periods: traditions that reflect the interests and concerns of Jewish sages (1) before the fall of Jerusalem in 70 CE, (2) between 70 and the Bar Kokhba rebellion of 132–135 CE, and (3) materials that reflect the interests and concerns of the sages around 200 CE, when the final editing of the Mishnah was completed under Judah the Prince. The Mishnah includes materials in which "there are cogent traits and internally coherent formations of ideas. . .[that] differ in their fundamental interests and character" from those of the Mishnah in its final form, "so they are not the same as the end product." These different ideas are best explained, Neusner claims, as the products of the earlier periods of history indicated above.[8]

The materials in the Mishnah that originated before 70 are especially concerned with purity laws about preparing and consuming food. It appears, Neusner says, that these materials had their origin among persons who had decided that it was necessary to practice such purity in the home, not just in the Temple. The social location of such persons was probably a group of radical priests and lay people who, by adopting such measures, formed what could be characterized as a holiness sect.[9] A holiness sect is by definition a perfectionistic group: in the name of the religious ideal it calls for the transformation of the way things are into the way things ought to be.

The controversy story in Mark 7:1–15 agrees with the earliest stratum of the Mishnah in identifying such purity regulations as a characteristic concern of the Pharisees before 70. In this passage the meal-related purity practice of the Pharisees is described, and they ask Jesus why his disciples do not observe the traditional handwashing that would put them in a state of ritual purity when they eat their meals. Jesus replies aphoristically: "What goes into your mouth will not defile you; rather, it's what comes out of your mouth that will defile you" (Thom 14:4, a more crisply worded parallel to Mark 7:15). This remark can be taken as characteristic of Jesus' view that whereas the Pharisees regarded attention to purity concerns as essential for realizing what they regarded as Israel's religious ideal, such concerns were irrelevant in his understanding of that ideal.

In the "instructions for the road" found in Q, Jesus advises his disciples to eat whatever is set before them when they are invited into a home (Luke 10:8; Thom 14:4). The scrupulous Pharisee, presumably, would eat what was set before him only if it was kosher. So when they followed Jesus' advice, the disciples would have been rejecting the centerpiece of pharisaic idealism and piety as irrelevant to the aim of realizing Israel's religious ideal.

The controversy story in Mark 7 and the instructions for the road taken from Q thus document the collision of two competing models of idealistic religious vision. For the Pharisees, observing purity laws, especially at meals, was of crucial importance in maintaining Jewish identity and tradition. For Jesus, such a concern was irrelevant for his vision of life under the rule of God. The traditional wisdom of the Pharisees was about how things are "supposed to be." The visionary wisdom of Jesus was about how things ought to be. An observer at the time might have noticed that both the Pharisees and the provocative young wisdom teacher from Nazareth were religiously serious, but such an observer could not have missed the difference between their points of view and practice.

Josephus, the first century Jewish historian, characterizes the Pharisees as the group within the Judaism of that time who were the most exacting in their interpretation of holy scripture and observance of ancestral tradition. Their reputation for expertise as interpreters of Jewish religious law is reflected in one saying in the gospels also that may go back to Jesus in some form: Pharisees and scholars have the keys of knowledge in their possession, but have used them to close the door to knowledge rather than to open it (Thom 39:1, 2; Matt 23:13, Luke 12:52). Paul's brief reference to his life as a Pharisee also appears to be consistent with Josephus' report of the Pharisees' reputation as exacting interpreters of scripture and strict observers of their religious law: "I was a practicing Pharisee and faithfully observed the Jewish religious law. . . . My practice of the righteousness called for in the law was flawless" (Phil 3:5, 6 my paraphrase). In other words, Paul was perfect so far as his observance of religious law was concerned.

Temple purity, then, furnished the Pharisees with their model of the religious ideal, and holy scripture, exactingly interpreted, gave the model its authority. This was a formidable combination. History has attested its durability even though the Temple itself was destroyed by the Romans in 70 CE. As Jacob Neusner has noted, the model embraced by the Pharisees extended through most of Israelite history and continues even to the present day. [10]

John the Baptist and the Therapeutai

Josephus says that the Sadducees, the Pharisees, and the Essenes were the three groups that constituted the principal forms of Judaism in first century Palestine. Two of these hoped to reform the Judaism of their time by commitment to what they regarded as Israel's religious ideal. There were others. John the Baptist's deliberate location at the Jordan River seems to imply a symbolic appeal to the ideal of Israel's origins, when from the banks of the Jordan they first took possession of the Promised Land, according to the biblical story. That he offered baptism as a cleansing from sin in that location seems to imply that he regarded the Temple establishment in Jerusalem as religiously bankrupt, incapable of mediating the spiritual cleansing and moral renewal the nation urgently needed. In his preaching, John forecast the recovery and fulfillment of Israel's religious ideal neither in a reform of the Temple nor in the imitation of its purity food laws, but in an imminent apocalypse. The axe is already aimed at the root of the trees, he said (Matt 3:10, Luke 3:9). John, then, called his hearers to return to the religious genuineness and purity of their origins as the only way they could prepare for the new age that was about to come into being through the direct intervention of God.

Philo of Alexandria tells us about another group of religious idealists known as the Therapeutai, an order of ascetic Jews in Egypt who sought to actualize Israel's religious ideal by separating themselves from the unclean world and by devoting themselves "to prayer and the praise of God. . . and the study of holy writings." [11]

The figure and groups mentioned in the foregoing do not constitute a complete inventory of reform-minded or revolutionary figures and groups known to have been active in first century Palestine or Egypt; but those mentioned were contemporary with Jesus and active during the same time he was, and their aims were grounded in and motivated by a particular understanding of Israel's religious ideal which can be compared with his. They also make it clear that commitment to some version of Israel's religious ideal was not uncommon in the Judaism of Jesus' day. It was part of the larger religious and cultural environment in which he grew up. While it may be unlikely that the young man from Nazareth had ever heard of the Therapeutai in Egypt, it is very likely that he knew about the Essenes at Qumran and the Pharisees in his region and beyond. He certainly knew about John the Baptist when he walked away from Nazareth and journeyed down to the Jordan River to hear John and to be baptized by him. But if Jesus was initially drawn to John's preaching and baptism, it was not for long.

Jesus' ordering vision

I suggest that Jesus had his own vision of Israel's religious ideal and it was his vision of that ideal that gave his teaching and his course of action their aim and coherence. Not the imminent last judgment and end of the world, but the attraction of the ideal is what motivated and empowered him. He called it the reign of God.

Jesus' ordering vision comes most clearly into view, I think, in these two blocks of sayings in Matthew's sermon on the mount:

> Don't react violently against the one who is evil: when someone slaps you on the right cheek, turn the other as well. When someone wants to sue you for your shirt, let that person have your coat along with it. Further, when anyone conscripts you for one mile, go an extra mile. Give to the one who begs from you; and don't turn away the one who tries to borrow from you.

Love your enemies and pray for your persecutors. You'll then become children of your Father in the heavens. <God> causes the sun to rise on both the bad and the good, and sends rain on both the just and the unjust. Tell me, if you love those who love you, why should you be commended for that? Even the toll collectors do as much, don't they? So be "perfect," just as your heavenly Father is "perfect." (Matt 5:39–42, 44–48. Parallels: Luke 6:27–36; Thom 95:1–2.)

No one can be a slave to two masters. No doubt that slave will either hate one and love the other, or be devoted to one and disdain the other. You can't be enslaved to both God and a bank account! That's why I tell you: Don't fret about your life – what you're going to eat and drink – or about your body – what you're going to wear. There is more to living than food and clothing, isn't there? Take a look at the birds of the sky: they don't plant or harvest, or gather into barns. Yet your heavenly Father feeds them. You're worth more than they, aren't you? Can any of you add one hour to life by fretting about it? Why worry about clothes? Notice how the wild lilies grow; they don't slave and they never spin. Yet let me tell you, even Solomon at the height of his glory was never decked out like one of them. If God dresses up the grass in the field, which is here today and tomorrow is thrown into an oven, won't <God care for> you even more, you who trust God for so little? (Matt 6:24–30. Parallels: Luke 12:22–31; Thom 36:1–2.)

In the commentary on these passages in *The Five Gospels* Robert Funk notes that the three aphorisms in Matt 5:39–41 form "an exceedingly tight series" and that they seem never to have circulated as individual sayings. "These cleverly worded aphorisms provide essential clues to what Jesus really said. And the consensus among Fellows of the Seminar was exceptionally high."[12] About the passage in Matt 6:25–30 Funk remarks, "It is possible that we have before us here the longest connected discourse that can be directly attributed to Jesus, with the exception of some of the longer narrative parables."[13] These excerpts from Matthew's sermon, then, appear to represent things at the core of Jesus' teaching and the fact of their connectedness serves not just to make a point, but to express a point of view. They convey to us, I suggest, a sense of Jesus' ordering vision, that view of things that furnished his teaching with its coherence and guided his course of action.

Supporting evidence

Recent scholarship on the Q Gospel and on the archaeology of Galilee offers three converging lines of evidence that support the claim advanced in this essay about the importance of these sayings clusters for identifying Jesus' ordering vision. The first is James M. Robinson's report, in his introduction to *The Critical Edition of Q*, that there is now a substantial consensus among leading Q scholars in the United States and abroad that several clusters of "sapiential speech" [i.e., instruction and exhortation that represents itself as wisdom] existed at an early stage in the development of the Q document, and that the two passages on which this profile focuses belong to this early stage.[14] These clusters, then, are widely thought to be among the earliest gospel tradition preserved in our sources.

The second is John Kloppenborg Verbin's answer to the question of what constitutes the theological center of Q. (James Robinson has characterized Kloppenborg Verbin's recently published *Excavating Q* as "without a doubt the most thorough, wide-ranging, and convincing analysis of Q" [ever published].)[15] "The center of Q's theology," Kloppenborg Verbin says, "is not Christology [that is, claims about Jesus' status, such as Messiah, Lord, Son of God] but the reign of God. . . . The kingdom sayings of Q1 [the early layers of the Q document] are connected with exhortations to a countercultural lifestyle that includes love of enemies, nonretaliation, debt forgiveness, and a willingness to expose oneself to danger, all undergirded by appeals to the superabundant care of a provident God."[16] Most of the elements in this summary of what is at the center of Q's theology are highly visible in, indeed appear to be based upon, the sayings clusters on which this profile of Jesus focuses. So these clusters should be seen not only as very early tradition, but as at the center of that very early traditions religious wisdom and vision.

Third, on the basis of an extensive archaeological survey of Galilee and close attention to the social location that is reflected in the text of Q, Jonathan L. Reed concludes that "the Q community can be placed with reasonable certainty in Galilee, in a social setting among the larger villages such as Capernaum, but with first-hand awareness even of the urban centers of Sepphoris and Tiberius."[17] In summarizing the results of his study, Reed is even more specific about its significance for anyone interested in the historical Jesus:

> By locating the Sayings Gospel Q in Galilee, a significant
> continuity between the contexts of Jesus and the early Jesus

traditions was established. Thus, the socio-economic and religious context for Jesus' teaching and for the essential message preserved in the early Gospel layers is the same, a point that helps bridge the gap between Jesus and the Jesus traditions.[18]

Reed's survey of recent archaeological discovery in Galilee and its implications for and relation to early Gospel tradition is too rich and detailed to be effectively summarized here; but taken together with the statements of Robinson and Kloppenborg Verbin noted above, the import of his findings for research on the historical Jesus seems clear: the two clusters of early Gospel tradition which this profile of Jesus focuses upon may well be evidence about Jesus' teaching that comes as close to bridging the distance between the authentic Jesus traditions in the Gospels and the historical figure about whom they were written as we can hope to come. They are as early as any gospel tradition we know of, they are at the heart of the theology of the earliest layer of our earliest Gospel, Q, and they reflect a social setting like that of Capernaum and/or other similar nearby villages which was also the social location of Jesus' public activity. In other words, these passages probably take us as close as does anything preserved in our sources to "hearing" the voice of the Jesus of history. To use the vernacular, this is as good as it gets. At the very least, in combination these assessments constitute a substantial warrant for pursuing the hypothesis that shapes this profile of Jesus. In these sayings clusters Jesus urges his hearers to have a total trust in the generosity and care of the Father in heaven and to be singleminded in their commitment to do God's will by imitating the divine generosity. To do this is to live under God's reign.

The unifying theme as the gospel Jesus preached

These sayings do not intend to provide their hearers with explicit instructions for dealing with specific situations, but to convey a vision of what it means to live one's life under God's reign, in the confidence that once the hearers have caught the vision, they will be able to recognize on their own what a particular situation may call for. Such a vision is more powerful than an instruction manual. This vision of life under God's reign invites the hearer to abandon the ordinary, ingrained habits of dealing with life on the basis of self-defense and self-interest. According to this vision of life, self-defense is not necessary and self-interest falls short of life's true goal. Hearers are invited to see things in a new way, to imagine and act out a way of life that trusts God's care absolutely and imitates God's generosity unconditionally.

The admonitions to turn the other cheek, go the second mile, offer one's undershirt as well when one's shirt is demanded have been seen by interpreters who are on the lookout for what is socially relevant as the responses to oppression of a clever, cheeky resistance. But this seductively modern reading of these sayings has two problems: (1) it literalizes language that should probably be read as symbolic hyperbole, and (2) it obscures their intent to suggest how to realize the ideal of life under God's reign by endowing them with the nimbus of cleverer-than-thou resistance tactics. The idea of the reign of God becomes a ploy to emulate rather than an ideal to realize. That is a modern social-activist attempt to improve on Jesus' imprudent, perfectionistic remarks by turning them into tactics useful for "non-violent resistance." Jesus was not teaching his hearers how to outwit their rulers with clever in-your-face insolence, but how to act like the children of their uncalculatingly generous heavenly Father.

The saying, "Give to [anyone] who begs from you; and don't turn away [anyone] who tries to borrow from you" (Matt 5:42) asks the hearer to set aside self-interest. To withhold what one might give is to regard one's own needs and interests more highly than the needs and interests of those who lack what one has. Conventional wisdom might regard that as a matter of legitimate and prudent self-interest, to ignore which is to risk becoming destitute oneself. But in Jesus' field of vision, that is looking out for oneself rather than trusting in the Father's care, and does not follow the example of the Father's indiscriminate generosity. It would fall short of demonstrating that one is the child of such a Father, and would indicate, therefore, that one was falling short of living under the reign of God.

The admonition to love your enemies is truly extraordinary. It not only contravenes what Matthew represents as the conventional wisdom, it also exceeds all of the enlightened and prudent advice discoverable in Ancient Near Eastern and Graeco-Roman literature that urges humane treatment of the enemy. The key to understanding this extravagance in Jesus' saying is not in defining the meaning of the term *love*, although that is helpful, nor in identifying the enemies in question, but in recognizing Jesus' saying as a way of refusing to accept the idea that it is all right to treat enemies differently from friends: the one who grasps what it means to live under God's reign will treat friends and enemies in the same way, because God does.

In the sayings that follow the admonition to love one's enemies in Matthew's text, the indiscriminate generosity of the Father in the heavens is offered as the sole basis of that admonition, and the aim of becoming his children is its only motivation. There is no appeal to the imminent end of history and the creation of a new age by divine intervention as grounds for showing one's enemies unusually generous consideration. There is no appeal to cheekiness as the preferred weapon of the weak either. Rather, in causing the sun to rise on both the bad and the good and in sending rain on both just and unjust God is shown to be unvaringly magnanimous. This behavior of the heavenly Father is called *perfect* in Matt 5:48 and is recommended as the model for all who want to become God's children. Matthew's phrasing in v. 48 more closely corresponds to what the historical Jesus probably said than does Luke's version of the saying: "Be compassionate in the way your Father is compassionate" (Luke 6:36). Luke's rendition softens the saying by turning an impossible demand into a possible virtue (and one appealing to modern sensibilities); Matthew's rendition lets the hard saying stand: "Be 'perfect,' just as your heavenly Father is 'perfect.' "

Both the Greek term *teleios* and its English equivalent *perfect* usually refer to a form of excellence that cannot be improved upon, a complete or flawless skill or quality. But in the Greek translation of the Hebrew Bible known as the Septuagint (LXX), the term *teleios* is always used to translate Hebrew terms that mean "unblemished," "undivided," "complete," "whole," – meanings conveyed by *teleios* in some Greek usage, but not its predominant meaning in Greek literature. Matthew's use of the term *teleios* = *perfect* in this saying undoubtedly reflects the meaning it always has in the Septuagint and which fits the context here exactly. Jesus' admonition, as Matthew transmits it, means, "Make your imitation of the heavenly Father whole-hearted, singleminded, the only thing you think about and aim for, your one ambition" – because, as Jesus also said, " you cannot serve both God and your own self-interest" (Matt 6:24). The admonition is unconditional. Jesus does not ask his hearers to be as considerate toward their enemies as the circumstances permit. The circumstances are irrelevant. Only the model of God's generosity and goodness is relevant. In Jesus' ordering vision it is never right to do wrong; it is always right to imitate and trust in God's goodness.

This reading of Jesus' admonition to love one's enemies is consistent with the other representations of Jesus' teaching in this section of Matthew's sermon (5:21–48), both in forms close to Jesus' own speech and as reflected in Matthew's reformulations: there is to be no anger, no divorce, no lying, no retaliation, as well as no distinction in the treatment of friend and enemy (in effect, no hate). In other words, to live under God's reign means to do God's will "on earth as it is in heaven" (Matt 6:10b). The Seminar regarded the wording of that petition of the Lord's Prayer as Matthew's; yet, I suggest, that piece of Matthew's rhetoric reflects the spirit of Jesus' ordering vision.

The love called for here is not affection, for which the Greek verb *phileo* would have been used, but unconditional good will, in Greek *agapao*, the verb used throughout the New Testament to characterize God's love for humankind. In fact, the distinction between the love of human friendship and the love of God is the point made in the rhetorical questions by which the import of Jesus' saying is drawn out in Matt 5:46,47 (cited above). The love of human friendship is reciprocal; it is based on acceptance and affection that is returned. The love of God is unilateral; it is grounded in God's unlimited goodness, not in the mutuality of the likeminded. The love of friendship typically links people who have something in common. The love of God is a generosity that transcends all differences between people and peoples.

Since in his teaching Jesus is articulating his vision of Israel's religious ideal, not offering solutions for particular problems, the enemies he urges his hearers to love are unspecified. If asked which enemies he had in mind, he might well have responded, "All of them."

In all of these sayings we are confronted with an unyielding call for the singlemindedness that Matthew called "being perfect." The same rigorism meets us in the demand for a total trust in the divine benevolence we find in Matt 6:24–30, the second cluster of sayings on which this profile is based. The elementary everydayness of the "cares" that are to be abandoned as antithetical to complete confidence and reliance upon God's care for us is quite stunning: even ordinary concerns about how one can be assured of food and clothing are said to be inconsistent with a total trust in the benevolence of the heavenly Father. "The prudent conscience will have an immediately unfavorable reaction to these words," Reinhold Niebuhr noted. "No life can be lived in such unconcern for the physical basis of life." Any attempt to "explain" such teaching by claiming that it could have seemed attainable to peasants in First Century Galilee who lived the simple life of subsistence farmers misses the point. "The fact is," Niebuhr saw clearly, "that this word contains a completely unprudential rigorism in the ethic of Jesus which appears again and again."[19] The pure idealism of Jesus' religious vision that we encounter in these sayings is what poses the most significant challenge for developing a Christian ethic and should be acknowledged, not explained away.

The social implications of a religious vision

Sociologist Peter Berger notes that "the *same* human activity that produces society also produces religion, with the relation between the two products always being a dialectical one. Thus it is just as possible that, in a particular historical development, a social process is the effect of religious ideation, while in another development the reverse may be the case." [20] In the case of Jesus it is the religious vision that generates the social implications: he has much to say about how one should think about life under the rule of God and what what kind of behavior it calls for, but he does not have much to say about a social program. As Henry J. Cadbury observed decades ago, when the rich young man is told to sell everything he has and give the proceeds to the poor (Mark 10:21) nothing is said about how needy the poor are and how morally necessary it is to meet their needs.[21] The poor can always use the money, of course, but the demand Jesus makes of the young man is not what is required to implement a social program. He is not asked to share the wealth by increasing the wages he pays his hired hands and thus act in the interest of social justice. He is asked to *discard* his wealth to demonstrate his uncompromising commitment to the reign of God. As Jesus had said, "You cannot serve two masters; you cannot be devoted to God and devoted to making as much money as you can at the same time" (Matt 6:24). In some respects Jesus' view here is similar to that demanded of the members of the dissident Essene Community at Qumran, as previously noted, even if the conception and style of his mission are different. Every candidate for admission at Qumran was required to surrender all of his possessions to the community, not in order to achieve a democratic egalitarianism – the Qumran community was hierarchical, not democratic; but to assure his freedom from one of the "nets of Belial" – the lure of wealth that would ensnare him and keep him from a complete devotion to the Law of God.

In a similar vein C. G. Montefiore once observed that in calling on his hearers not to retaliate against the evildoer (Matt 5:39) "Jesus, perhaps one-sidedly, is really thinking much more of the doer than of the recipient; that is to say, *in this particular passage* [italics in the original] he is not thinking so much of the redemption of the evildoer as he is of the ideal conduct for those who have to do with the evildoer, or generally, of the ideal for man. Still less is he thinking of society as a whole and of the effect of not resisting evil upon the State."[22] More recently Hans Dieter Betz noted that both Paul in Rom 12:9–12 and 13:9–10, and Jesus in

Matt 5:39, "prescribe desistance from retaliation because it is the just action required by God, not because it is effective. Even if the evildoer continues to do evil, nonretaliation remains the just thing to practice." [23]

This is not to say that there are no social implications in Jesus' teaching. It is rather to say that he did not work these out and propose them in his teaching. It probably did not occur to Jesus to work out such implications of his vision. He clearly left more up to God than many of us would. He called on his hearers to trust God to provide what they needed, as God did for sparrows and wild flowers. It would be consistent with this advice for Jesus to believe that he could trust God with the outcome of his mission, just as the farmer trusts God with the outcome of sowing the seed for his crop. God gives the increase; so don't worry about tomorrow. God will take care of tomorrow. Jesus'aim, it appears, was to live the vision in the confidence that he could trust God with the consequences; and if that was indeed Jesus'aim, then his mission was a religious movement with social implications, not a social movement with religious implications.

The social context of a religious vision

Although Jesus himself did not work out the social implications of his religious vision, the social context in which he conceived it can perhaps help us understand why he and his followers were willing to buy into it. This is an aspect of the gospel Jesus proclaimed that surely calls for another essay as a companion to this profile, but perhaps in the space available here I can sketch the gist of the matter.

The historical evidence indicates that the Jewish people in First Century Palestine would have had good reasons for thinking that they were living at a time when their political, economic, and religious lives were all under illegitimate rule. Rome had seized political power from warring members of the Maccabean royal family in 63 BCE and remained in political control of the country not only during the whole of Jesus' lifetime, but for centuries thereafter. Political authority was thus wielded by powerful foreigners who were not hesitant to use military force to maintain their rule. For many of Jesus' contemporaries, nevertheless, nationalistic feelings survived just below the surface of daily life, both as a nostalgic view of the historically recent Maccabean past and as a hope for the future. Nationalistic feelings evoked several rebellions against Roman rule during the period of more than a century and a half, from the inauguration of the reign of Herod the Great in 37 BCE to the Bar Kochba rebellion in 132–135 CE. None succeeded. While Jesus did not launch an armed rebellion against Roman rule, his thematic "reign of

God" rhetoric was not politically innocent. It plainly involved the notion that the reign of Rome was not the order of life to which one's first allegiance should belong and it summoned hearers to forms of commitment and behavior, including economic behavior, that took their cue from something other than the priorities of Roman policy. But all too obviously, Jesus' attempt to persuade his society to embrace his vision did not succeed either. As Alfred Loisy remarked a long time ago, "Jesus proclaimed the Kingdom of God, but what happened was the church." This was the not insignificant historical effect of his life and teaching, but it was an unintended consequence, not what he had aimed for.

The coming of Roman rule not only displaced Jewish political control of their affairs, but substantially altered the economy as well. As Oxford Professor of Ancient History Fergus Millar has written, ". . . the most distinctive feature of Roman rule in a new area would be the imposition of the census and of direct taxation." [24] These practices were important instruments used by Roman authorities to centralize the organization of the economy. This restructured economy reduced the autonomy of peasant farmers and put pressure on them to increase their productivity. The level of tax revenues Roman rulers wanted could be realized only by an increase in production. Whereas before the Romans seized power a peasant farmer typically produced only as much as he thought he needed, after the Romans took control of the economy, a peasant farmer was pressed to produce a cash crop. In modern terms, it was no longer enough to break even; you had to produce a profit. This pressure to produce made "making money" an unavoidable concern of daily life and produced a troubling crop of economic winners and losers. The economic displacement of the less productive and the concentration of wealth among the more productive and channeled to Roman rulers and their collaborators was the cost of Roman "modernization."

Making productivity the principal value of the economy devalued all other economically related values, including concern for those who were pushed into poverty by the competitive and bureaucratic nature of the "new economy." The relation between the pursuit of wealth and concern for the common good became frayed and was for some completely broken. The "new economy" was organized to increase and concentrate wealth; it seems not to have occurred to the ruling classes that they should pay some heed to the economic condition of "the little people" beyond their mere subsistence. An objection to such Roman-imposed "economic facts of life" is probably reflected in Jesus' insistence that "you can't serve God and devote yourself to making money at the same time." You have to choose.

Herod the Great's architectural ambitions had made Jerusalem's temple one of the grand monuments of the early Roman imperial world. But earlier, Roman rulers had deposed the hereditary high priest and proceeded to install a series of wealthy Judeans in that office who were subservient to their wishes. This practice continued until the temple was taken over by the rebels early in the Jewish-Roman War and soon thereafter destroyed by the Roman legions. Thus the men who held the highest holy office of Jewish religion were wealthy Roman appointees and collaborators, rather than the legitimate hereditary successors, and the integrity of the institution was in that respect compromised.

The Romanization of the political and economic system and the compromised leadership of the temple conspired to produce a sense of alienation for some, and perhaps for many Judeans and Galileans during this period. The Essenes, alienated by the appointment of an illegitimate candidate to the office of high priest, had withdrawn from Judean society to their retreat at Qumran in the late Second Century BCE, soon after the Maccabean revolt, and remained there in isolated dissent until 68 ce when they were apparently overrun by the Tenth Roman Legion early in the Jewish-Roman War. Judas the Galilean led rebellions against what he regarded as the illegitimate rule of Rome after Herod the Great's death in 4 BCE and again in 6 CE when Coponius was appointed the first Roman procurator of Judea. This was the first time Rome had imposed direct rule on the province rather than governing indirectly through a person from the native population, such as Herod the Great and his descendants. This change in the nature of governance evoked a vigorous protest in Jerusalem, and provoked Judas the Galilean to organized violence. John the Baptist represents another kind of protest against the illegitimacy and injustice of the way things were in the temple and in the society and held out the hope of a return to the integrity of Israel's origins.

In the face of all of this Jesus had his own dream of a new day and a new life. Seen as a vision of what life could be in contrast to the way things were under the rule of Rome, his teaching about the rule of God offered an alternative that differed from the other forms of Judaism in his world and that was appealing to some who heard him. Much as Martin Luther King, Jr. invoked American ideals as pointing the way to a better life in a more just society in his "I have a dream" speech on the steps of the Lincoln Memorial in Washington, D.C. on August 23, 1963, so Jesus invoked the Jewish ideal of the reign of God as pointing to the way things ought to be for the Jewish people of Galilee and Judea. Seen in the historical context of America in the 1960's, King's dream of a society of equal dignity and justice was a powerful and uplifting vision of a society liberated from the racial discrimination against Black Americans that was then prevalent; and seen in the context of First Century Israel, Jesus' dream of a society devoted to and trusting in the reign of God was a powerful and uplifting vision of a society liberated from the grip of Roman imperial rule with its economic servitude. Neither of these dreams was a small thing to hope for. Both of them involved utopian elements that could not be fulfilled completely, but both also pointed people in the right direction: toward hope for a more humane and just society.

The First Century Jewish historian Josephus indicates that Judas the Galilean led an armed rebellion when the Roman authorities began to impose direct taxation on Judea in 6 CE, on the grounds that it "infringed on God's sovereign rule over Israel." [25] Judas of Galilee understood very well that what the Romans were implementing would destroy the traditional Jewish way of life, and he was not pleased. Two decades later another Galilean, Jesus of Nazareth, was not pleased either, but he responded to the changes that had been imposed on his society with an idealistic vision and a subversive wit, rather than with weapons. Jesus was a Jewish gadfly, not a Jewish Rambo.

Ethical and theological implications

While some of Jesus' hearers at the time, as well as later readers of his words, may well have dismissed his teaching as hopelessly unrealistic, what actually happened among early Christians was more interesting. They recognized that Jesus' vision of life under the reign of God was a theologically, socially, economically, and politically unfinished work. That is why so many of his followers, both early on and even yet, have moved to "complete" it, to spell out what the vision implied about what they were to believe and what they were to do. That is a large part of the reason why there was so much diversity in Christian faith and practice from the very beginning, and why there has continued to be so much debate about these matters down to the present day. Perhaps we should not regard the fact that Jesus' vision of life under the reign of God is an unfinished work as unfortunate. The unfinished character of Jesus' work, in effect, invites anyone so inclined to "complete" what Jesus began in one's own way and as one's own work. That is certainly what the Apostle Paul did and what the authors of the Gospels did also. But with this interpretive and constructive freedom comes an inevitable responsibility: every interpreter will be held accountable for the perspicacity and pertinence of his or her thought and judgment, and every builder will have to answer for the fitness and quality of what he or she constructs. The fire of critical judgment and the relentlessness of history will put all such ventures to the test.

The prospects for an unfinished profile

This initial contribution to a full profile is largely based on only a few of the sayings regarded by the Seminar as very likely going back to the historical Jesus. Even if these sayings are thought to be exceptionally important for recognizing Jesus' ordering vision, we still must ask whether or not the larger body of evidence about him supports the claims made in this brief sketch, or are consistent with those claims. Here are some indications of why I think it may:

The first two petitions of the Lord's prayer (Matt 6:9, 10) can be understood to express the view that when God's name is truly revered, God's kingdom comes. Matthew's phrasing expresses the point: this happens when God's will is done on earth as it is done in heaven.

The man who sells everything he owns to gain one exquisite pearl (Matt 13:45–46 // Thom 76:1) is a disaster as a businessman, but an exemplar of the singlemindedness that God's reign calls for. According to Jesus, the Kingdom of God is about properly valuing goodness, not about prudently valuing property.

The Samaritan who does the generous thing for the man beaten and robbed on the road to Jericho models life under God's reign, whereas the principled clerics who pass the victim by in order to assure that they would not be hindered from carrying out their religious obligations are otherwise and mistakenly ruled (Luke 10:30-35).

The "perfect" generosity that characterizes God's reign is depicted in the father's acceptance of his prodigal son and in contrast to the elder son's ungenerous calculations (Luke 15:11–32).

The shrewd manager outrageously exhibits the singlemindedness that characterizes the one who lives under the reign of God (Luke 16:1–8). His self-interested behavior is ethically questionable, but his focus is admirable.

The poor, the hungry, and the sad are fortunate in finding it easy to be singleminded about God's reign. They have less to distract them and less to lose than do those who are well off (Matt 5:3–4, 6 // Luke 6:20, 21; Thom 54, 69:2). The rich farmer, on the other hand, pathetically misses the point (Luke 12:16–21 // Thom 63:1–3). He thinks his life depends upon his store of goods; actually, it depends on God.

Those distracted by lesser cares miss the biggest party of the year, maybe of their lives (Thom 64:1–12; Matt 22:1–14, Luke 14:16–24).

Neither sickness nor demonic derangement belong in the life over which God reigns.

Jesus dined and fraternized with anyone who would give the idea of God's reign the time of day, and was mocked as a drunkard and glutton for it. But for him it was an exhibition of the care-free way things are under God's reign and therefore ought to be.

When he went to Jerusalem that spring, he came to the attention of Roman and Jewish authorities who understood as well as they needed to that such a religious message could have a subversive affect on the perceived legitimacy of established authority. That sort of thing could thus mean trouble for them, especially if it drew a crowd; and they were committed to defend their legitimacy, about which they had no doubts.

Along such lines as these the ordering vision of Jesus proposed here seems capable of serving as a crucial element of an explanatory model by means of which we can read the evidence and reconstruct a fuller account of the Jesus of history.

In this essay I have focused on the nature of Jesus'ordering vision. It is a profile based on the results of the Jesus Seminar's search for the authentic words of Jesus published in *The Five Gospels* (1993). By comparing Jesus' religious vision with that of certain other religious Jews who were his contemporaries, I have also called attention to Jesus' religious location—his place on the spectrum of religious belief and practice in his society. Beginning a search for Jesus as a figure of history by analyzing his sayings is the best way to recover Jesus' own point of view, as I argued above and as Lane McGaughy explains elsewhere in this volume. Focusing on Jesus' teaching as the point of departure for sketching his profile is also warranted by sociologist Peter Berger's observation, noted above, that while the relation between religion and society is always a dialectical one, it is just as possible for a social process to be generated by a religious ideal and ideas, as for the reverse. Berger's recognition of the dialectical relation between religion and society is more persuasive, in my view, than any theory of social determinism; and in the case of Jesus of Nazareth it seems to me more likely that the religious vision generated social implications than that a social agenda generated a religious legitimation.

Postscript

We would do well to ponder the wisdom of Reinhold Niebuhr when we consider what we are to make of the lofty demands of Jesus' ordering vision, if we hope to derive some inspiration and guidance from it. The familiar notion that we have only to ask, "What would Jesus do?"

and expect to find an answer in some Gospel text that we can simply adopt as a rule that can become the practice of our daily life is undiscerning. As Niebuhr observed,

> The ethic of Jesus does not deal at all with the immediate moral problem of every human life–the problem of arranging some kind of armistice between various contending factions and forces. It has nothing to say about the relativities of politics and economics, nor of the necessary balances of power which exist and must exist in even the most intimate social relationships. The absolutism and perfectionism of Jesus' love ethic sets itself uncompromisingly not only against the natural self-regarding impulses, but against the necessary prudent defenses of the self, required because of the egoism of others. It does not establish a connection with the horizontal points of a political or social ethic or with the diagonals which a prudential individual ethic draws between the moral ideal and the facts of a given situation. It has only a vertical dimension between the loving will of God and the will of man. . . . The ethic of Jesus may offer valuable insights to and sources of criticism for a prudential social ethic which deals with present realities; but no such social ethic can be directly derived from a pure religious ethic. [26]

It must be added that such a clear, intellectually honest recognition of the utopian elements in Jesus' teaching did not inhibit Reinhold Niebuhr from proceeding to develop impressively insightful and effective treatments of Christian theology and ethics, and it need not discourage any reader of these lines from doing so either. Any intellectually honest attempt to take up that task will nevertheless be obliged to acknowledge that the reign of God is an ideal kingdom in Jesus' ordering vision, an ideal goodness that may inform, but ultimately transcends the moral virtue attained or attainable by any individual or by any society. It was and is a goodness that transcends what is realizable in history even when it offers our life in history a sense of direction. How to respond to an inspiring, ennobling, but impossible ideal is the challenge that all of Jesus' spiritual heirs have been and are obliged to deal with. That is the legacy he has left to any who may choose to treasure it.

Jesus of Nazareth
A Profile Under Construction

Charles W. Hedrick

Premises

1. The early Christian gospels, both canonical and non-canonical, are theological interpretations of Jesus. Hence, all information they contain serves the interest of early Christian faith in some way.
2. Early Christian literature contains no verbatim sayings of Jesus. What is attributed to him was given its present form in the early Christian movement, both in the oral period and later when the traditions had been reduced to writing.
3. Thus the words attributed to Jesus in early Christian literature are the words of early Christian faith, and their description of his activities constitutes the early Christian view of how the Christ ought to have comported himself.
4. We may hope to hear an echo of the voice of the historical man, and sketch in barest outline some details of his life.
5. The criterion of dissimilarity/distinctiveness is the most reliable tool in the search for the words of the historical man.
6. The findings of the Jesus Seminar constitute an irreducible minimum of the historical data.[1]
7. It is not possible to know what Jesus thought of himself.
8. Inferences may be drawn from the historical data. An inference is a reader's interpretation of data and should not be confused with the data itself.
9. The same data will allow different inferences.

10. A reconstructed Jesus is not Jesus as he actually was, but Jesus at his most radical dimensions. The reconstruction, if it is reliably done, has eliminated much of what Jesus had in common with first-century Palestinian Judaism and earliest Christianity.
11. Thus we can hope to see the historical man only in his most radical dimensions.
12. Responsible profiles are always "under construction." By its very nature the data and our critical methodologies will not allow a final definitive view of Jesus.[2]

Sketching his personal vita

It appears probable that Jesus was born, and certainly raised, in Nazareth. The two birth narratives in Matthew and Luke, despite their many differences, agree that Jesus came from Nazareth. It was a city that apparently did not have a good reputation in the Hellenistic period (John 1:46), and was not mentioned in the Hebrew Bible. Growing up in Nazareth, in the "Galilee of the Gentiles" (Matt 4:15), may have contributed to Jesus' relaxed attitude toward Torah.

Bethlehem was mentioned in the Hebrew Bible in connection with a specific messianic prophecy, or so the early Christians believed (Micah 5:2; Matt 2:4–6; John 7:42), and hence the early Christian association of Bethlehem with Jesus (Matt 2:1; Luke 2:4–6): it better fitted their faith than did Nazareth. The association of his birth with the reign of Herod the Great (d. 4 BCE) is a historical memory. Matthew and Luke independently agree in this regard (Luke 3:1, Matt 2:1), but neither relates it to the character of Jesus. His mother was Mary, and his father was unknown. This makes sense of the rabbinic traditions about Jesus[3] and accommodates the fact that Joseph is completely missing in Mark and barely present in Luke. He had brothers and sisters (Mark 6:3 = Matt 13:55–56; Gal 1:19).

He was baptized by John the Baptist, who had preached a baptism of repentance for the forgiveness of sins (Mark 1:4–5, 9). Perhaps this is one reason Matthew (3:13–15) and Luke (3:18–21) try in different ways to distance Jesus from John, but they could not deny the association. Jesus was caught up in the Baptist's movement and became his follower. When John was arrested (Mark 1:14), Jesus began his own career of preaching and was, in turn, followed by others, as he had followed John. His association with Capernaum and Galilee is plausible, but whether his activities extended beyond the general area of the Galilee is not certain. Mark restricts his activities to the region of Galilee, while John extends his area of influence to Samaria and Judea. The Romans crucified him during the time that Pontius Pilate was Prefect of Judea (26–36 CE).

Reassembling the fragments of his public discourse

Jesus' public discourse, to judge from the fragments that have survived, primarily took the form of aphorism and story. He apparently liked to play with language and had a sense of humor. For example, he chided those who criticized others for the slightest infraction while they themselves had glaring faults, or as Jesus put it: "You criticize other people for flecks of sawdust in their eyes with a two-by-four sticking out of your own" (Matt 7:3–5 = Luke 6:4 – 42 = Thom 26:1). And, of course, his humor, like all humor, had an edge to it. We must presume that recognizing oneself as the butt of the joke would have led to self-reflection, or anger and hostility – as humor usually does. His aphorisms were not easily understood, and no doubt stumped his hearers as they tried to make sense of these oblique pithy sayings. For example, he offered the paradoxical advice: "Be as sly as snakes and as gullible as pigeons" (Matt 10:16 = Thom 39:3), which, of course, is quite impossible if one gives equal attention to each directive. Most of his aphorisms, no doubt, left his auditors scratching their heads looking for some way to orient themselves in the odd kind of "world" represented by his sayings: "Don't let your left hand know what your right hand is doing" (Matt 6:3=Thom 62:2), "Let the dead bury their own dead" (Matt 8:22 = Luke 9:60), "It's not what goes into you, but what comes out of you that defiles you" (Mark 7:14–15 = Matt 15:10–11). Each of these aphorisms, as well as others, is capable of being heard in different ways. That is the nature of the aphorism. There was no one point, but almost as many "points" as there were auditors.

His stories comprise a rather large block of his fragmentary public discourse. These stories are now little more than plot summaries, but they are far more subtle and complex than they appear on the surface. Slightly more than one third of them (10) are connected to the imperial rule of God by an introductory frame. Approximately two-thirds of them are not so introduced, but are associated by early Christians with assorted theological concerns. Since most of his stories are not associated with God's imperial rule, it should at least be suspected that the ten "kingdom" stories were linked to the imperial rule of God by the early Christians, and not by Jesus. The subject matter of these stories concerns the commonalities of life in first-century Palestinian Judaism under the early Roman Empire. One striking feature of their contents is that only one of them (the Pharisee and toll collector; known only from Luke 18:10–13) deals overtly with a religious issue. In a broad sense, of course, many of them may be construed to be religious, but the fact remains that the issues overtly addressed in the stories deal primarily with secular matters in first-century Palestinian life. Their plot complexity and social engineering lead readers to find in them diverse and competing abstract values relating to theology, morality, politics, and economics. What they show us in themselves, however, is that Jesus was a shrewd observer of life around him; at the level of their social construction one may catch a glimpse of Jesus' interests and begin to infer something of his ironic sense of values.[4]

As to content, the fragments of his public discourse give us some insight into his public career and, perhaps, by inference, some idea of his own sense of personal identity. His ideas brought him into conflict with his own tradition. For example, he had the idea that the Sabbath was intended for the benefit for human beings, rather than imposed on them as an onerous religious obligation limiting their lives (Mark 2:27). This view competed rather dramatically with that of the Pharisees, for whom strict Sabbath observance was a major plank of their teaching. He rather severely criticized the principal religious teachers of his tradition, the Pharisees (Luke 11:43, Matt 23:5–7) and the scribes (Mark 12:38 = Luke 20:46), as much for their insensitivity to the poor and other "outsiders," as for what he regarded as their self-centeredness and hypocrisy. His lax attitude about dietary practices (Mark 7:14–15=Matt 15:10–11) would also have thrown him into serious disagreement with these same leaders over Torah interpretation. He had nothing to say about sin and its forgiveness that would have pleased temple supporters. He dismissed the entire temple cult with "God will forgive you as you forgive others" (Luke 6:37). His bold statement that "God's imperial rule belonged to the poor" (Luke 6:20 = Thom 54:1) could easily have been heard as a complete rejection of the Jewish religious establishment, a position that would not have endeared him to the priestly caste and the Sadducees, and made his isolation from the leaders of his religious tradition virtually complete. He clearly sensed the isolation (Mark 6:4 = Matt 13:57 = Luke 4:24 = John 4:44 = Thom 31:1).

His interest in the welfare of the poor was matched by his censuring of the wealthy (Matt 19:23–24 = Luke 18:24–25 = Mark 10:23, 25). In fact, he seemed to regard the service of God and the accumulation of wealth as mutually exclusive (Matt 6:24 = Luke 16:13), and he prohibited the lending of money at interest even to a Gentile (Thom 95:1–2), something permitted by the rabbis. He called on the wealthy to give away their wealth (Thom 95:1–2), even if it meant that they themselves would be reduced to poverty (Thom 69:2; Matt 5:42). Such attitudes, in general, would not have been shared by the wealthy and the powerful.

His cavalier attitude toward wealth and possessions in general (Matt 8:20 = Luke 9:58 = Thom 86), and his lack of concern about providing for the basic necessities of life (Matt 6:25–30 = Luke 12:22–25, 27–28 = Thomas 36) would have made his philosophy quite unrealistic even to farmers, who also lived life on the edge, always depending on God's blessing of the fields for their livelihood. The practical-minded, as successful farmers tend to be, would no doubt have argued that some advance planning was necessary, but Jesus advocated simply asking God for whatever was needed (Matt 7:7–11) day by day (Matt 6:11; Luke 11:9–10). He apparently advocated a penniless, itinerant (Matt 8:20 = Luke 9:58) existence, and the acceptance of charitable gifts for daily sustenance from whoever offered them (Luke 10:7–8; Thom 14:4). In a sense he always depended on the kindness of strangers. Such an attitude may have been a bit naive, but it clearly reflects a strong trust in God and God's concern for the welfare of even the least significant person in the human family (Matt 10:29–31 = Luke 12:6–7). In the view of Jesus, God was a caring father (Matt 6:9) who did not discriminate among his children in the human family on the basis of their morality or obedience to Torah, but showered his material blessings in the world indiscriminately, even to the evil (Matt 5:45). One could count on God to provide whatever was needed for daily sustenance.

He appears to have placed few requirements on people. His soulmates were those who did the will of God (Matt 12:50), but he never explicitly defined what constituted the will of God. Presumably, it would have involved loving everyone, but in particular it would have included the least in the human family (Matt 10:29–31 = Luke 12:6–7) and whoever you counted as your enemy (Matt 5:44 = Luke 6:27,35). Only in this way could true love be demonstrated, since everyone could be counted on to love those who returned their love (Luke 6:32). Obedience to the will of God was a consuming passion for him and overrode every other commitment (Luke 14:26). Only in this way can life be lived freely, and with meaning (Luke 17:33); otherwise one is always bound by the empty pursuit of this world's goods and vain attempts to achieve personal security. True life consists only in trusting and being obedient to God.

He taught that one should live at peace in the world; one should not resist even the evil acts of others directed against one's own person (Matt 5:39–42; Luke 6:29). But that attitude of peace did not extend to coexistence with those demonic forces he conceived as opposing God in the world. Although God apparently controlled nature (Matt 5:45), Satan ruled in human affairs, and, as a consequence, humanity was in thrall to Satan's evil empire (Luke 11:17–22), and under the control of Satan's demonic forces (Luke 11:24-26). Jesus aimed to break Satan's control over human beings (Mark 3:27 = Matt 12:29 = Thom 35:1–2) by exorcising his demonic henchmen (Matt 12:27–28 = Luke 11:19–20). Jesus was supremely confident that Satan's power was already broken, for he had seen "Satan fall, like lightning from heaven" (Luke 10:18).

Satan's evil empire was crumbling before Jesus, who described himself as the agent and initiator of God's imperial reign (Matt 12:28 = Luke 11:20). He was not part of a vanguard of the imperial rule of God; rather God's imperial rule was already present in what Jesus was doing and saying (Luke 17:20–21 = Thom 113:2–4). Yet in some sense God's imperial rule was not yet fully realized, and Jesus prayed for its full realization in the world (Matt 6:10 = Luke 11:2). He challenged his auditors to take up the cause of God's imperial rule (Luke 9:60), and declared that passion for the cause would override even the strongest of the natural urges of some of those who embraced it (Matt 19:12). Only those who stood outside the circles of earthly power (Luke 6:20 = Thom 54:1), and were uncorrupted (Matt 19:14 = Luke 18:16) by the empty quest for security and wealth (Matt 19:23–24 = Luke 18:24–25) participated in God's imperial rule. Material prosperity and its accouterments, on the other hand, characterized Satan's evil empire (Mark 12:17 = Matt 22:21 = Luke 20:25 = Thom 100:2–3).

God's imperial rule was in the process of reversing human values, which were the means by which Satan controlled human affairs. Thus God's rule could be characterized by childlike innocence (Mark 10:14), poverty (Luke 6:20), and humility (Matt 5:3); that is to say, God's rule was not part of the structures of worldly power (Mark 10:23, 25) that dictated existing human values. Under God's imperial rule, those formerly disfranchised are empowered. Grieving is replaced by consolation (Matt 5:4); and weeping by laughter (Luke 6:21). Hunger disappears (Luke 6:21), and the injustice characterizing Satan's evil empire is replaced by the flowering of justice (Matt 5:5) under God's imperial rule (Luke 11:2 = Matt 6:10).

Characterizing his public career

Jesus' principal activity involved public (oral) address and, hence, he was called teacher and rabbi in the early gospel literature. Looking for some ancient category in which to place him, modern scholars call him a sage or wise man. He was certainly not a teacher, sage, or wise man in the modern (or even ancient) sense of the word, i.e., in the sense that he passed on the content of community wisdom. As the fragments of his public discourse make vividly clear, he was at times a sharp critic of society, morality, and religion. Indeed a major theme of his public discourse, the imperial rule of God, involved a new way of conceptualizing life that completely reversed conventional value systems. He apparently conceived of life in mythical categories: human beings were under the control of satanic power. As a healer/exorcist, he was in effect contesting, and destroying, Satan's evil empire, and facilitating God's imperial rule.

His vision, i.e., the fictive constructs under which his public discourse was integrated, can only be inferred from his words. That vision brought him into conflict with the fictive constructs of first-century Palestinian Judaism (Sadducees/temple cult, Pharisees). While there is no evidence that he criticized Roman Imperial authority, it too would have been seen by him as part of Satan's evil empire. He believed in God and found in his personal faith a sense of authority for his public acts and discourse. He believed God was working through him to reclaim complete control of human affairs. When fully realized, God's imperial rule would bring a reversal of human values and overhaul the structures of society. Quite predictably, therefore, Jesus found his natural place among the poor and irreverent on the margins of society, rather than in its main stream. The "righteous" and the religious authorities were particularly subject to his scathing wit and censure. Likely the reversal of values he announced and its implied challenge to the power structures of human society brought about his death. The fact that he was killed by an official act of the governing authority suggests that his public career was viewed, in some sense, as a serious threat to the public welfare.

Answering some specific questions

1. Was Jesus born of a virgin? No. That was one way some early Christians expressed their high view of Jesus' person and authority. Others explained it differently. Both Mark and John were able to describe Jesus without mentioning a virgin birth. John described the preexistence of Jesus (1:1–18) with no reference to virgin birth. In Mark's account of the baptism, the special character of Jesus is validated by a voice from heaven: "You are my favored Son; with you I am well pleased" (Mark 1: 11).

2. Did Jesus think he was the messiah? We will never know the answer to this question. It was clearly an early Christian infer-

ence that he was. His followers gave him that title, but he was not the only son of Israel to hold it. Other messianic figures are found in the history of Israel.

3. Did Jesus think he was the Son of God? We will never know the answer to this question. It was an early Christian inference that he was. Only four times in the New Testament is he portrayed as accepting that appellation from others (Mark 14:61–62;[3] Mark 8:29–33 = Matt 16:15–23; Luke 9:20–22; John 4:25–26). Jesus "never indisputably uses of himself the title 'Son of God.'"[5] Ascriptions of divinity to people of unusual character or accomplishments–Julius Caesar, Augustus, Apollonius, Herakles, Asclepius, etc.–was the way people in Hellenistic antiquity indicated their special character.[6]

4. Was Jesus resurrected from the dead? No, if by that expression is meant that his dead body was resuscitated. While one may infer from Mark's empty tomb story (Mark 16:1–8) and the Gospel of Peter (9:1–10:5) that Jesus was physically resuscitated like Lazarus (John 11:1–44), the earliest reflection on the nature of Jesus' body at his resurrection was that of Paul (1 Cor 15:35–57). Paul clearly distinguishes between the resuscitation of a physical body and a "spiritual body" (1 Cor 15:42, 44, 50, 52–54). According to Paul, Jesus was raised "spiritually, rather than physically."

5. Why was Jesus crucified? The answer is unclear from the gospels. Perhaps as a result of his confrontation with his own culture and public discourse about the imperial rule of God, he was seen as a political threat, and the Romans simply crucified him to prevent problems. This one question – why did Jesus have to die? – plagued earliest Christianity, and there were various attempts to answer it. For example, for Mark his death was a "ransom for many" (Mark 10:45); for John it was Jesus' moment of glorification (John 12:27–33; 13:31–36) and the casting out of the world ruler (John 12:31); for Paul, the death of Jesus was the means by which human beings were reconciled to God (Rom 5:6–11).

6. Did Jesus expect the world to conclude in a cosmic catastrophe? While certainty is not possible, it seems unlikely. The earliest fragments of Jesus' public discourse suggest that God was in control of the natural world. The problems lay in the realm of human affairs, which was controlled by Satan.

7. Did Jesus cause a disturbance at the temple in Jerusalem? Such an event is consistent with his public discourse.

Jesus as a Peasant Artisan

Arthur J. Dewey

Tao will always be nameless, an Uncarved Block although it is a thing of no account, no one in the world would make it his subject.

Tao Te Ching [1]

Flight's greatest gift is to let us look around, and when we do we discover that the world is larger than we have been told and that our wings have helped make it so.

William Langewiesche [2]

My profile of the historical Jesus works along a particular grain. Moving among the fragments of sayings the Jesus Seminar has determined likely to be authentic, I shall examine the craft of this peasant artisan. Not an exercise in taxonomy, this is an experiment to work out what Jesus was about. It appreciates the texture of his imagination. How did Jesus craft his words? What did he envision as he worked? How did his words invite his listeners into his vision? As it was for the ancient Taoist and is for the modern pilot Langewiesche, the discovery of vision is not a static meditation. Rather, it is a matter of seeking the "grain" of reality and learning to live within that vision. What we can make of those words?

The social description

Recently great strides have been made to place the historical Jesus within a peasant society. Scholars like Richard Horsley and Dominic

Crossan help us reimagine the contours of the world Jesus inhabited. Because of this work, scholarship can never return to an historical Jesus abstracted from the gritty reality of his day. At the same time, however, this descriptive effort can keep at arms length the deeper issues of the historical Jesus. Determining that Jesus was a peasant craftsman (*tekton*) is only the beginning of the profile of his artisanship.

Social descriptions work primarily from the "outside in." Jesus becomes a "given" among the fragmentary data of his peasant world. Yet social description cannot detect the creative activity of the wordsmith of God's Empire. The categories used for such an analysis are still too broad, too imprecise, to catch the possible artistry within the fragments. If the historical Jesus was an artisan, then how did he go about "crafting" his work? You can, for example, assemble all the relevant data on modern flight, utilizing all the scientific, social and economic reports. But none of this captures the vision of the pilot who sees what flight is all about. Not every pilot catches the vision of reality that is emerging with the age of flight. Nevertheless it is there, providing human beings with a new and compelling vision of reality.

The task of the craft

The work of an artisan is not a mechanical act. Working in wood or stone demands envisioning "what is there within" the material. The excellent craftsman recognizes the possibilities of the material in his hands. He "sees" what is "there" and works painstakingly toward it. The task is to see a vision and to use the grain in seeking to realize that vision.

The same is true for an artisan in words. The wordsmith attempts to sound things out through the clash and reverberation of words. Moreover, the wordsmith performs his touch and go work in the echo chamber of his listeners. The storyteller searches for the words to communicate a vision that generates, sustains, and moves the words forward.

The historical Jesus was not only a craftsman but an artisan of words. Within the available fragments of the likely authentic material are there clues to this artisanship?

Rubbing the fragments together

This profile begins with those sayings the Jesus Seminar has judged to be from the historical Jesus. The original task of the Seminar was to distinguish the voice of Jesus from later voices. Now the task before us is to see what we can make of the data that have been deter-mined as authentic. How can we assess this fragmentary material consid-ered authentic? If there is no overall narrative frame for these sayings (the gospel superstructure falls out as later redaction), how do we begin to associate the words of the historical Jesus?

Certainly one can simply list the sayings. But that is hardly a sat-isfactory solution. The evidence, admittedly in fragments, suggests a most creative, engaging speaker. It is quite appropriate to reintroduce the principle of coherence. In the first phase of the Seminar the fellows employed this critical principle. We asked whether a saying under con-sideration was consistent in some fashion with a saying or sayings already judged to be from the historical Jesus. But now we must do this on a more nuanced level. One can, for instance, begin to link the vari-ous sayings along conceptual lines. Other members of the Seminar have begun this work with some significant yield.

I would take another path in the hope that there may be some correlation with other profiles. If a convergence in understanding the sayings of Jesus results from a variety of approaches, one may have more confidence in the continued search for the historical Jesus.

This profile focuses on how the sayings and parables of Jesus were crafted. I am interested in the very texture of the sayings. Can we detect any significant similarities, particularly among sayings, which on the sur-face seem to have little in common?

Moreover, I would begin with sayings that are not immediately familiar or associated (Thomas 65 and 26 below). I would begin with a more difficult saying to see whether we can detect the craftsmanship of the speaker in the very lines. From these opening observations can we build as we move to other sayings? In other words, can we detect some imaginative structures or strategies that are embedded in the way these sayings work?

The term "consistency" should be underscored in this discussion. We are not only trying to say how sayings cohere with each other, but we are asking whether there is some inner consistency in these frag-ments. While we run the risk of proving too much or too little, we must try to see whether this is possible even in a rudimentary way. Can we detect a consistent vision or approach to life in these sayings? How do we go about doing this? Moreover, since we are in an oral culture, does not the audience also play a hand in our investigation? How does the wordsmith anticipate their engagement?

Let us then take two sayings judged authentic and yet apparently unrelated to one another. Can we detect some inner consistency, some artistic construction or strategy in them? How so? Can this help us to come to terms with the other sayings of the historical Jesus?

The Revolting Tenant Farmers (Thomas 65)

> He said, A [...] person owned a vineyard and rented it to some farmers, so they could work it and he could collect its crop from them.[2] He sent his slave so the farmers would give him the vineyard's crop.[3] They grabbed him, beat him, and almost killed him, and the slave returned and told his master.[4] His master said, "Perhaps he didn't know them."[5] He sent another slave, and the farmers beat that one as well.[6] Then the master sent his son and said, "Perhaps they'll show my son some respect."[7] Because the farmers knew that he was the heir to the vineyard, they grabbed him and killed him.[8] Anyone here with two ears had better listen!

The Seminar has already noted the tradition's allegorical overlay to this story of Jesus (Mark 12:1–8; Matt 21:33–39; Luke 20:9–15a). As it comments in *The Five Gospels*,

> If Jesus told this parable, the story ended with the crime, whereas the allegory ends with the punishment.

Beginning where the Seminar's comments leave off, a further reading of Thomas 65 suggests a number of imaginative lines. Though the original audience would have focused primarily upon the defiant farmers, the construction of the parable forces listeners actually to imagine two sides: the farmers' and the absentee landlord's. The insurgence of the farmers will receive eventual reprisal. By simply following the logic inherent in the political and social forces of the first century, listeners would realize that the farmers' hope for restoration would be frustrated. Their impetuous action would be met with the landlord's response, supplied most likely by Roman legionaries. The listeners are left to envision the limits of both sides as well as the violence that either supports the system or would address the oppression. What sounded initially quite enthralling is, upon reflection, a devastating vision. The oppressive situation is not tolerable, but simple-minded action is ultimately suicidal. Listeners would conclude wisely that neither side wins. Both absentee landlord and miserable tenants are caught in a situation that demands more than reacting according to the usual way of doing things in first century Palestine.

"Timber!" — Thom 26:1-2 (Matt 7:3-5; Luke 6:41– 42)

> Jesus said, "You see the sliver in your friend's eye, but you
> don't see the timber in your own eye.[2] When you take the
> timber out of your own eye, then you will see well enough
> to remove the sliver from your friend's eye.

In voting Thom 26:1–2 Pink the Seminar noted the saying's
hyperbole. The Seminar also saw this saying as being consistent with the
forgiving sense found in other sayings of Jesus (Luke 6:37, the Lord's
prayer). But there is more to be mined here. If this witty advice has merit,
it assumes listeners who can reflect on the contradictions in their behavior. The "Timber" saying also seems to reflect a wordsmith, who was
aware of the burden of self-contradiction. These two observations may
be the closest we can get in the case of an oral performance to identifying assumptions. The Seminar has concluded from its analysis of the
sayings of Jesus that Jesus challenged people's behavior and world views
and that his "Empire" language engaged the political situation of his
time. Is there some place in the evidence where we can detect this
method of challenge? Does Thomas 26 begin to suggest how Jesus did
this?

An experiment

As an experiment, what happens if we link the story of the "revolting tenant farmers" with the "timber" saying? Can we detect any consistency in imaginative construction or strategy in these two sayings? For
Jesus' listeners the social assumptions of the first century world would
be the "timber" that interfered with their understanding of the story of
the tenant farmers and the absentee landlord, whose actions in turn convey certain embedded social beliefs. Unless those listening to the story
recognized the limits of such perspectives, they could not even begin to
imagine another response to that violent social reality. In brief, the story
challenges the listeners to become aware of the "timber" in their own
social imagination.

This conjoined reading gives us a clue about the imaginative strategy of the historical Jesus. The story of the rebellious tenants is neither a
simple call to revolutionary action nor a cautionary moral tale. Both
characterizations overlook the craftsmanship –and the craftiness – of the
storyteller and the response of the listeners. Jesus created the story so
that his audience could work it out on their own. The story truly grasps
the listeners only insofar as they enter into its fabrication. They must

retell the story and work out the implications on their own. At that point they could well take it literally as a call to action, or recognize the impending doom of such action. But is there a further option? What if the listeners saw the limits of both perspectives? What if the gruesome consequences awaiting the tenant farmers in the story were set over against the larger picture, which is being set before their eyes? They could easily extend the story and imagine the landlord's reprisal against the insubordinate tenant farmers. The listeners' own social assumptions – a peasant's world that requires either fight or flight, opposition or submission to dominating power – would limit their view. But what if the parable was designed precisely to challenge those limits?

This is where the "timber" saying becomes helpful. Here is an indication that the historical Jesus was aware of such limitations. Indeed, all of the parables and aphorisms of Jesus play provocatively against the presumptions of the first century imagination.

The double focus of the sayings

In both the "revolting tenant farmers" story and the "timber" saying, we have a stereo effect. The story challenges the listeners to hear both sides (the farmers' side and the absentee landlord's side), and the saying works only if the listeners move from the observation of the "splinter" to that of the "timber," from an initial surge of hope to a sober sense of reality. It is precisely in the tension between the two that meaning is discerned.

We find this double focus throughout the parables and sayings of the historical Jesus. Its implications are particularly clear in the following examples.

The Vineyard Laborers (Matt 20:1–15) exploits the stereo effect. As the story starts, the "proprietor" repeatedly goes out to hire more workers; but when it's time to settle accounts, the listeners' identification shifts to the hired hands. The conclusion proves doubly unsettling: not only are the laborers who worked the entire day disgruntled, but any who sympathized with the workers' expectations are also put off. The story challenges listeners to hear both the demands of the workers and the stance of the owner; they will have problems with the outcome if they have assumed society's system of rewards. The demand "from below" confronts the patronage system of the first century. The peasant cry for a fair wage collides sharply with the controlling reality of the wealthy landowners. Moreover, the final comment by the owner goes beyond the frame of the story. Is it not an indirect challenge to the way in which the audience

"sees" the imagined situation? The final, domineering tone would rever-
berate within the peasant imagination. What would you make of this double demand for equity and prerogative?

The story "A man going down from Jerusalem" (Luke 10:30–35) further explores this double vision. Jesus' audience would have expected the
third passer-by to be one of their own, a Judean. Either a Pharisee (an
heroic figure for many Judeans at the time) or a common Israelite (playing
to peasant resentment of upper classes) would be a likely character. The
arrival of a despised Samaritan shatters their expectation and exposes the
double focus of the parable. The centuries-old antipathy of Judean versus
Samaritan is flung in the face of the Judean audience, who must be
stunned by what the Samaritan did for the victim (with whom they would
have immediately identified) and troubled by the words of the Samaritan
left ringing in their ears (v. 35b). A new and disturbing perspective of the
"other" directly confronts the listeners' social stereotypes, the "timber" of
their social identity.

The parable "A man who had two sons" (Luke 15:11–32) incorporates not only the double focus but also the attempt to go beyond each
side. Due to the simple opening line, the listener expects two focal points;
the story is not over with the return of the younger son. The bargain the
storyteller made with his audience is kept with the introduction of the second son. The matter of focus becomes more complicated as the relationship of each son to the father is explored. Despite the dysfunctional
relationships evident in the story, the intriguing figure of the father
responds with surprising tolerance to both sons, each of whom has managed to insult and misunderstand his father. The story ends abruptly
before the older son can answer, and the audience, having entered into
the perspective of each son, must now conjure up the possible response of
the older brother. Or would they become entangled with only one side of
the story? Or would they see something deeper in the father's words and
deeds? Would that change their configuring of the older son's response?
What would they make of all of this?

If we turn to other sayings of Jesus, we see that the comic dispro-
portion of "the eye of the needle" (Mark 10:25) works precisely by its double focus. First there is the humorous exaggeration of the camel and the
needle's eye, then the comparison to a wealthy person's chance to get into
God's domain. The humor generated by the initial part of the comparison
serves to explode a fundamental social assumption of elite and peasant
alike in the first century: that wealth implies favor with God. This oral cartoon was designed to dislodge the "timber" of the peasants' construction

of how the world is governed. Moreover, this comic bit fed on the social resentment the peasants felt towards those they imagined to be superior and thereby more valuable.

The aphoristic command, "Love your enemies" (Luke 6:27b; Matt 5:44b) also plays upon a double perspective. First, it disputes the conventional wisdom that enjoins primary concern for those within one's social group. Second, it admits the alienation in Palestinian society (village feuding, oppression by the rich, Roman occupation). The audience could easily identify their enemies. Third, it challenges the listeners to replace a simplistic obedience with a radical reconfiguration of their social categories. As the Seminar rightly puts it in *The Five Gospels,* "Those who love their enemies have no enemies." The challenge of the aphorism is clear: can you imagine acting differently towards those outside the circle of your people? The saying carries a concussive effect; it keeps on echoing in the resisting areas of the listeners' hearts.

Such reimagining by means of a double focus can be seen in the shrewd peasant advice in Matt 5:39–41. The general injunction "Don't react violently against one who is evil" (Matt 5:39a) can be more literally translated: Do not oppose on the same level one who intends evil (towards you). We can easily see the dual implications of this advice. The listeners are challenged not to react on the same terms as someone who intends them harm but to take this advice seriously, which requires a reframing beyond the level of reaction.

The subsequent advice – turn the other cheek (Matt 5:39b), give up your coat (Matt 5:40), and go an extra mile (Matt 5:41) – provide three concrete instances of this double focus. The listeners are challenged to imagine not only their own response but also what the oppressor would likely do. In each instance, the predictable peasant response to an oppressive situation is rejected. Neither violent opposition nor passive submission to a social superior is advocated. Instead, the peasant listener is encouraged not only to reimagine his response but also to offer his oppressor a chance for a more human reply.

In offering the other (left) cheek the peasant (Matt 5:39b) would cause his superior to strike with the palm of the right hand rather than use the back of his hand on the peasant. This would imply a loss of power and prestige. If the superior, on the other hand, were to cease striking in order to consider the peasant's strange action, there would be an opportunity for reason to creep in. Then Matt 5:40 entails a wonderful burlesque of a court case in which a poor man is sued. By removing his only other article of clothing, he is naked before the God of Israel. This would embarrass all including the "cheapskate" who has haled him into court. The final saying provides the peasant oppressed by Roman occupiers a surprising tactic. To go an extra mile would violate Roman military law and could result in the death of the legionary who had commandeered the peasant. By making the offer the peasant has gained the advantage. In each of these cases the superior status of the opposing characters is dramatically undermined.

Matt 5:45 provides a deeper perspective on this double focus:

> <God> causes the sun to rise on both the bad and the good, and sends rain on both the just and the unjust.

Such a saying flies in the face of the social conventions of the first century. Listeners would presume that God favors the good and the just. They, of course, would imagine themselves among those favored. Precisely because most listeners would include themselves among "the good and the just" a discrepancy arises. How can God be so generous, so benevolent, to "the bad and the unjust"? How can God be impartial? Again, the strategy of this saying lies in its shocking possibility, in challenging the listeners to reconsider their position before God. The usual linkage of the image of the good and the just with the image of God has been placed in jeopardy. What can you make of a statement that replaces the dualism of good versus bad, just versus unjust, with a vision of a God that transcends both social groupings?

So far we have seen that the authentic sayings and stories of the historical Jesus carry a markedly double focus, which triggers the listeners' imagination. The audience cannot take refuge in one aspect of the saying or parable, for piqued by its radical duality they are enticed to see the limits of both aspects, as well as to discern new possibilities surrounding the contrasting and colliding images.

We saw in Matt 5:45 how a background can throw the double front into relief. The disjunction between "the good" and "the bad" is recast by the image of a God who brings sun and rain to both. The social identity inherent in each is relativized and rendered problematic. Listeners who would immediately identify with "the good" and "the just" would have difficulty here.

A similar movement from foreground to background was evident in the relationship among the characters of "A man who had two sons." There the story of each son is re-focused by the response of the prodigal father, and listeners are left to fill in the older son's reply. To do so they must internalize the father's words and eschew any assertion of rights or superiority of position.

Now the notion of "background relief" opens up this exploration. Do we have any clues beyond the sayings already mentioned that allow us to see how the historical Jesus crafted his speech? Was there any particular backdrop that allowed him to imagine a double-faceted discourse?

The Empire of God as imaginative field

The Seminar has concluded that Jesus envisioned the Empire of God as somehow present and impinging. Certainly Luke 6:20a asserts a present albeit shocking reality:

Congratulations, you poor!

God's domain belongs to you.

Luke 11:20 further adduces Jesus' conviction of the presence of the Empire of God.

But if by God's finger I drive out demons, then for you God's imperial rule has arrived.

However, as Luke 17:20b–21 notes, the Empire of God is not empirically observable:

You won't be able to observe the coming of God's imperial rule.[21] People are not going to be able to say, "Look, here it is!" or "Over there!" On the contrary, God's imperial rule is right there in your presence.

Thomas 113 delivers a similar perspective:

His disciples said to him, "When will the ⟨Father's⟩ imperial rule come?"[2] It will not come by watching for it.[3] It will not be said, "Look, here!" or "Look, there!"[4] Rather, the Father's imperial rule is spread out upon the earth, and people don't see it.

The presence of the imperial rule of God serves as the background against which Jesus crafted his ordinary images. It is not an explicit phenomenon but a field in which his imagination worked on and through the images of his world. It is a region of imaginative space against which images are played and out of which unlikely options emerge. It becomes present in so far as his listeners entered into his craft of the imagination and saw those images carved along the surprising grain of the Kingdom.

This point becomes clearer when we inspect the parables that involve explicit comparisons to the Empire of God. The parable of the

Empty Jar (Thomas 97) provides a comic insight into the failure to per-
ceive what is at stake: the woman never notices the meal spilling from
her jar. The story challenges its listeners to detect that "timber" which
prevents them from seeing what is essential. In effect, the joke recoils
upon the audience.

> The [Father's] imperial rule is like a woman who was carry-
> ing a [jar] full of meal.[2] While she was walking along [a] dis-
> tant road, the handle of the jar broke and the meal spilled
> behind her [along] the road.[3] She didn't know it; she had-
> n't noticed a problem.[4] When she reached her house, she
> put the jar down and discovered that it was empty.

The parables of the mustard seed (Thom 20:2–4) and the leaven
(Luke 13:20) achieve their ends by including what is "impure," obscure,
and comic into the imaginative field of the Kingdom. Mustard plants
were considered weeds by Judean gardeners. Leaven, derogated by the
Passover tradition, always connoted impurity. Neither would seem to be
a fit ingredient for the crafting of God's Empire. And when those presumed to be expendable are ennobled (Luke 12:22–28), it is clear that
Jesus' words directly challenge the audience's grandiose maps of God's
Kingdom. The double impact of such an unlikely combination must
intend a radical reexamination of what the Kingdom is about.

Furthermore, the challenging aphorism of Matt 7:7,

> Ask – it'll be given to you; seek – you'll find; knock – it'll
> be opened for you,

is best seen within this encompassing gestalt of the Kingdom. This saying does not convey a mindless idealism. Rather, it connotes a fundamental trust of the speaker who toils, discovering through the craft of
communication the reliability of the Kingdom. Let's not overlook the
need for the artisan to have a basic confidence while shaping the vision
that he sees possible along the grain. Even the parable of the sower (Mark
4:3–8) takes on a different aspect if we can see that it reflects the labor
within the field of the Kingdom. A fundamental trust that the Kingdom
is present moves the story through and beyond mounting losses to a
yield of considerable proportions.

The myth of Empire versus an "imperial" craft

If for Jesus the Empire of God is an encompassing field in which
his labor of communication takes place, then our earlier considerations

of his parables should reflect this finding. We saw, for example, that when the double thrust of the parable of the Revolting Tenant Farmers demanded to be worked out, the inherent conflicts within the first century world of power were graphically portrayed. The parable does not attempt to resolve these differences through some mythic explanation. There is no attempt to maintain the social status quo. Seminar Fellow Brandon Scott has correctly seen that the parables of Jesus are antimyth. They do not attempt to provide a means for fictionally covering up the contradictions of society. Instead, parables shatter those mythic designs.3

But this parable does carve out images in which the social myth of the Roman world is embedded. When the listeners finally detect the limits of each side of the story, the unspoken but underlying myth of the Roman power pyramid begins to lose its grip on their imagination; the foundation of the oppressive political reality of the first century begins to disintegrate. But undermining a myth is hardly an intellectual exercise; it is a practical matter of emancipating an audience from the very thralldom of their cultural imagination. The collision of images and the storyteller's trust that the listeners' imagination can carry beyond what is spoken deliver the goods. Jesus does not work without accomplices. His listeners play an active part in this performance. Only their sustained reflection can carry them beyond blaming the immediate enemy to an inchoate sense that something far more radical is necessary. They may even detect their own complicity in this social reality.

When we consider parables with explicit comparisons to the Empire of God, we should note the increasing intensity of social critique. Speaking of "God" or "God's Empire" would immediately challenge conventional assumptions about power, the social pyramid, and the way in which the divine "associated" with humanity. Such categories are inherently mythic, for they represent the projection of the power game embedded in the social realities of the day. They slip easily into full-blown myths to explain away the contradictions of an oppressive society. At the same time they bestow a divine blessing on the status quo. Yet the parables of Jesus refuse this immediate association of the Kingdom with the usual understanding of power. The parables of the Kingdom short circuit the predictable mythic cycle. The Empire of God does not admit of immediate perception; it must be figured out.

The historical Jesus decisively takes a view "from below" and he encourages his listeners not simply to accept his words, but asks, "What do you make of this?" In figuring it out they must intuitively come to grips with the limits of their political reality. These stories and sayings do not permit the social order merely to be reiterated in power and compliance. They do not allow the view "from the top" to prevail. Instead, they challenge those at the bottom of the social pyramid to improvise another way of seeing things. In essence, the communication of Jesus' sayings demythologizes the power of the Empire.

By that strategy Jesus provokes his listeners to consider what to do with his words and challenges them to see the world anew and to live by that new vision. Each story comes true when the listeners attempt to work it out; each saying, when they embody it. And they continue the work of critical construction through further improvisation, as they pass on to others the wisdom they have detected.

The energy or the basis for working with and through such conflicting images is the presence of the Kingdom. Against this field the imagination can go to work and reconfigure a way through life. Shrewd and surprising wisdom (Matt 5:39–41) replaces a vision of submission or reactionary violence. The saying *"You must be sly as a snake and simple as a dove"* (Matt 10:16b) nicely catches this double-edged response.

Movement within the field

Let's experiment with fragments of the Jesus material to see how they are magnetized by this field of vision.

To say that the Empire of God is not immediately perceptible would imply that not everyone automatically "sees" this field. Rather, the challenge is to *"struggle to get in through the narrow door"* (Luke 13:24). Entrance into this field means becoming a "nobody" in the eyes of first century society: *Let the children come . . . God's domain is peopled with such as these* (Mark 10:14b). Even the artisan of this Empire is a nobody: *...the son of Adam has nowhere to rest his head* (Luke 9:58). The cost of entrance is nothing less than the abandonment of one's attempt to hang on, to maintain the "timber" in the eye: Whoever tries to hang on to life will forfeit it . . . (Luke 17:33).

But for those who work with the words of Jesus a breakthrough can occur. The Empire is discovered by unrelenting search – like that of a woman for her lost coin (Luke 15:8–9), surprisingly like the case of a person uncovering treasure in a field (Matt 13:44), or in single-minded abandonment like a shepherd who panics to find a lost sheep (Luke 15:4–6).

Trusting that the Empire of God is present encourages artistic breakthroughs: *Seek – you'll find* (Matt 7:7). Beyond the scripted code of first century society new possibilities emerge as the artisan works with his images. A dysfunctional family, torn apart by the rules of heredity and the shortcomings of the heirs, is recast through the prodigal gestures of a foolish father (Luke 15:11–32). A Samaritan shows up where the listeners would least expect him and embodies a shocking new model of Judean-Samaritan relations (Luke 10:30–35). Listeners are urged to figure out how *love your enemies* (Luke 6:27b) can play in a world that proscribes such imaginative trespassing. And, as we have noted above, the shrewd advice of Matt 5:39–41 encourages listeners to imagine a way to deal with the desperate conditions of peasant life.

Because of this depth of vision, the conventional contours of society can be reimagined. Concern for the purity code is recast humorously on a different level: *It's not what goes in that defiles . . . it's what comes out . . .* (Mark 7:15). Allowing for this is the vision of double aspect within the encompassing field of God: *Don't you understand that the one who made the inside is also the one who made the outside?* (Thom 89:2). A radical behavior that is no longer concerned with public confirmation or scrutiny can be sculpted: *Don't let your left hand know what your right hand is doing* (Matt 6:3); *If you love those who love you, what merit is there in that?* (Luke 6:32). Even such privileged cultural symbols as the sabbath and the emperor are revised and await the listeners' further reconstruction: *The sabbath day was created for Adam and Eve, not Adam and Eve for the sabbath day* (Mark 2:27); *Give the emperor what belongs to the emperor, give God what belongs to God* (Thom 100:2b.).

This underlying vision is neither an apartheid holding pattern, nor a separation of parties into respective spheres in order to contain the conflict. Rather the vision invades, transgresses, and goes beyond boundaries. This field of God offers a new outlook to those on both sides of a conflict. We have already seen this in the aphorism to *love your enemies* (Luke 6:27b), the surprising selflessness of the Samaritan who aids the "man going from Jerusalem" (Luke 10:30-35), the shrewd advice to oppressed peasants (Matt 5:39–41), the vision of a God who is generous to both "good and bad," "just and unjust" (Matt 5:45) and the magnanimity of "the man who had two sons" (Luke 15:11–32). All of these pieces the historical Jesus artfully crafted to engage and expand the social consciousness of his audience. But a further element to this act of communication is decisive: the words come true only when they are reconstructed by Jesus' audience, when he has successfully challenged them into working out these new designs. Active listening entails continued artistic response. Each saying invites a subtle crafting of the Kingdom.

Israel's Prodigal Son
Reflections on Reimaging Jesus

Mahlon H. Smith

Because there is *only* reconstruction.

J. D. Crossan[1]

We need a fiction that we recognize to be fictive.

R. W. Funk[2]

Project: Distinguishing fiction from fact

Historical reconstruction & the human imagination

The shift in the Jesus Seminar's focus from assembling a data base of historically reliable information about Jesus to comparing profiles of him involves a critical change in methodology. Describing a person is a synthetic exercise that is qualitatively different from amassing data. Finding facts is an act of digging: extracting items from a site that currently obscures their original function. Describing is an act of construction: combining accessible elements into a new structure, even if it is a reconstruction of the past.

Descriptions are not found; they are assembled out of what has already been discovered. Thus, they are "fictions" in the root sense of that term:

- they are items that have been shaped by someone; and
- they are visual aids produced by and for the human imagination.[3]

As Gerd Theissen has noted, it is this constructive element that makes *any* description, including those designed to be historical or religious, fictive.[4] For, as a construct of a particular human imagination, a description is always subject to deconstruction and creative reconstruction when new data are discovered or when the old are viewed from a different angle.

Nowhere is this more evident than in the case of Jesus. The central thesis of L.T. Johnson's critique of the Jesus Seminar and two centuries of NT literary criticism is that the real Jesus cannot be equated with "a historically reconstructed Jesus" since "historical reconstructions are by their nature fragile and in constant need of revision."[5] Instead, he argues:

> Corresponding to the Christian claim, there is a "real Jesus"
> *in the texts* of the New Testament as they have been transmitted to this generation. It is a Jesus inscribed literarily in
> the New Testament *compositions as compositions.*[6]

Even the Seminar's most vociferous critic here concedes that the descriptions of Jesus in the gospels are literary constructs – i.e., the products of the poetic imaginations of some ancient scribes. His argument is solely with the presumption of modern scholars to reconstruct these canonical texts, since a reconstructed Jesus, he contends, is "a product of scholarly imagination."[7] Johnson's point seems to be that, as ancient artifacts, the profiles of Jesus composed by the authors of the gospels can claim historical superiority over any later scholar's composition.

The synoptic gospels themselves, however, validate reconstruction of the image and message of Jesus recorded in inherited texts. Gospel scholars are virtually unanimous on one point: two of these gospels are literary revisions of the third. Luke explicitly introduces his work as a systematic account based on his research into previous records (1:1–4). If that is not a description of historical reconstruction by a latter-day scholar, what is? If historical reconstruction cannot clarify the real Jesus, then what are Luke and Matthew doing in the church's canon? Are their divergent revised descriptions of Jesus merely the product of their "scholarly imagination"?[8]

Every image depends upon someone's imagination. Historical research is the discipline that keeps the meanderings of the human imagination in touch with demonstrable facts by clarifying whose imagination is responsible for which image. As Theissen notes, the advantage of constructs of the historical imagination is that they are "relatively free of arbitrariness, [and] capable of being corrected by sources."[9] Any descrip-

tion of Jesus is someone's fiction. What makes one description historically superior to others is not its antiquity but the fact that it accounts
for everything known about the primary data better than the alterna-
tives.

The Jesus Seminar has spent a dozen years assessing every saying
and narrative report of Jesus in the ancient records to distinguish primary evidence that can be traced to Jesus himself from later developments in the tradition. To bring all this historical data into clearer focus,
Fellows are of course free to adjust the density of particular elements
from previous voting by suggesting reasons for a different weighting.
But the rationale for such correction must come from insight into the
capability of particular items to account for other historically probable
data rather than from the unexorcised prejudices of our own poetic
imaginations. Our quest is to find what R. W. Funk calls a "true fiction":
a profile that captures the features of the Jesus who generated these
proven facts.

Relative viewpoints & narrative tensions

Neither ancient nor modern profiles of a historical person like
Jesus should be paraded as absolute fact. A historical fact – whether
verbal or visual – is the rugged residue of a dynamic process that has
outlasted its original environment. A profile of a person is inevitably
more fragile and tentative (as Johnson rightly noted), since it depends
to a large degree on patterns evident to a particular viewer at a given
time and place. It is for just this reason that the gospels are misrepre-
sented by Johnson and others who claim they are definitive descriptions of Jesus. They are, rather, a series of drafts of a sketch by
admirers of Jesus dependent on second-hand testimony a generation
or more after his death. As such, the impressions presented by each
author are subject to clarification and correction by comparison with
those of other gospel profiles and analysis of the evidence they all
present.

Even in photos of a living subject, quite different – even contrary – impressions may be caught on different days by different
lenses. Only profiles of artificial cartoon characters, like Charlie
Brown, never change. Instead of a static picture of Jesus, the gospels
present a person who made a wide spectrum of impressions on people with whom he interacted. So, if it is a really historical Jesus we
seek to describe rather than a comic book Christ, our profiles are
bound to be fleeting glimpses, consciously tentative and candid rather
than portraits pretending to be definitive and comprehensive.

Since the Jesus Seminar methodically minimized elements imported from worldviews not distinctive of Jesus, the odd bits of surviving genuine sayings, deeds and biographical data read like a badly disintegrated manuscript in need of extensive shuffling and filling in to be restored to a coherent pattern. This is a sensitive and controversial task. The Seminar's suppression of the perspectives of gospel narrators and regrouping of their data has already led L.T. Johnson to declare the whole historical quest invalid:

> It is *not* legitimate on the basis of demonstrating the probability of such items [that "Jesus said and did"] to then connect them, arrange them in sequence, infer causality, or ascribe special significance to any combination of them. This is why the abandonment of the Gospel narratives throws open the door for any number of combinations. Once that narrative control is gone, the pieces can be (and have been) put together in multiple ways.[10]

What disturbs the author of this decree, along with many other conservative Christians, is that historical reconstruction presents new insights into the character of Jesus apart from the plot set by the post-crucifixion creed. Johnson insists, in effect, that Jesus' spiritual skeleton should not be disturbed but simply reverently viewed in the narrative caskets that Matthew, Mark, Luke and John provided. His edict cannot be enforced, however, without reducing gospel study to rote repetition. Taken literally it would put an end not only to historical reconstruction but to all preaching and exegesis as well, since the gospels would have to be read as written without comment on one passage's importance or relation to other material either inside or outside that text.

Even casual reading of the canonical gospels shows that none of these authors was bound by the "narrative controls" of previous accounts. For each has, in fact, reconfigured the basic bits of Jesus' words and deeds, inferred causality and ascribed special significance to connections not made by the others, to produce profiles of Jesus that are contradictory at key points.[11] It is the demonstrable narrative freedom of the gospel writers that created the quest of the historical Jesus in the first place. If the synoptics were controlled by a single "messianic pattern," as Johnson claims, then everything they report would simply illustrate and reinforce the same paradigm. But any unbiased reader of Mark and the other gospels – a reader, that is, who does not assume *a priori* that they all say more or less the same thing

– can see that this is patently not the case. Rather, each gospel reports sayings and deeds of Jesus that not only subvert the paradigms championed by others but which stand in dialectical tension with the author's own profile of Jesus.

H. S. Reimarus' insight, that to hear the original voice of Jesus, one has to distinguish *his* viewpoint from that of later gospel writers, is just as cogent today as it was two centuries ago:

> I find great cause to separate completely what the apostles say in their own writings from that which Jesus himself actually said and taught, for the apostles were themselves teachers and consequently present their own views; indeed they never claim that Jesus himself said and taught in his lifetime *all* the things that they have written.[12]

The fact that many passages in the gospels do not fit well within the narrative frames in which they are now preserved not only justifies their separation but mandates rearrangement in a tighter, more stable pattern that is closer to the intrinsic logic of the mind that generated them.

Hermeneutical honesty & historical guarantees

Having adopted a historical method that highlights distinctive patterns of Jesus' voice and behavior, the problem the Jesus Seminar now faces is how to clarify the logic that motivated him, without imposing an alien viewpoint. R.W. Funk has observed:

> The facts are meaningless unless held in solution in some narrative or paradigm, some configuration that makes them hang together, cohere.[13]

But what is to guarantee that a particular narrative or paradigm – your reading or mine – is true to the original text? Not the text of Mark or some other gospel writer, that is, but the fabric of a life woven in word and deed by Jesus himself. The restoration of these threads is what the historical quest is all about.

The bulk of the pieces we have to work with are patterns Jesus himself constructed over an uncertain span of time and space. But drawing the right connections is up to us. Funk compares the nodes of historical data to dots on a page.[14] These unnumbered dots represent Jesus' viewpoint; the lines connecting them represent our insights. The first is an ancient fact; the second is patently a modern fiction. If we were writing a novel, this would present no problem. We could imitate Theissen in forewarning readers: "Of course I have invented the narrative framework."[15] Yet, to concede that history is the invention of the historian is not the relevant point here, since this phase of the historical quest was designed to sort out what *probably* happened at the generative level of the Jesus tradition.

Funk's suggestion that Fellows label the elements of their profiles "data" or "insight" is an admirable adaptation of Theissen's type of hermeneutical honesty to the historical task. Most who have claimed to represent the real Jesus – whether in print or in pulpit – deliberately blur the distinction between given fact and interpretive fiction. Yet, Funk's tactic only calls attention to the problem of the hermeneutical circle. It does not circumvent it. Nor does it provide others with a reason other than personal taste for preferring a new insight over more traditional interpretations. *Some* moderns may find a modern historian's profile of Jesus more appealing than those sketched by first century authors. But the only truly historical rationale for preferring the new profile of Jesus to the old is that – in spite of its apparent novelty – it is demonstrably closer to the shadows that Jesus himself cast.

Puzzles: Reconstructing Jesus' viewpoint

The paradigm paradox: "Who do you say I am?"

Jesus has been described as a person who defies classification – a conclusion that anyone who has studied him is bound to come to sooner or later.[16] But, from either a historical or religious perspective, it is impossible to leave him at that. For, despite the claims of Christian mystics, one can neither understand nor relate to an enigma. The human mind cannot focus on the pieces of any puzzle – the Jesus tradition included – without searching for a pattern that ties them together. So the first step in drawing a historical profile of Jesus is to find a functional paradigm that makes sense out of what he probably said and did.

1. *Search*. Recognition that inherited sociological models do *not* adequately account for an essential portion of the primary Jesus database is the engine that started and continues to drive the historical quest. The reason scholars shift from one controlling paradigm to another – from the classic Hellenistic image of Jesus as a divine wonder-worker to Reimarus' politically motivated Jewish messiah to Schweitzer's apocalyptic visionary to Bornkamm's prophetic rabbi to an iconoclastic itinerant Galilean sage (Theissen, Crossan, *et al.*) – is due less to current cultural preferences than to a continuing conviction that Jesus can be correctly understood only on his own terms.

Although it is easy to demonstrate that people unwittingly project their own shadows on Jesus – or anyone else for that matter – Schweitzer's celebrated claim that "each epoch found its reflection in Jesus; each individual created Him in accordance with his own character" should be seen for what it is: a poetic exaggeration that is more rhetoric than fact.[17] Any description of anything inevitably reflects the viewpoint and values of the author rather than the subject. I describe things as I see them. But what I see is not limited to my own reflection. Rather, I describe whatever draws my attention: phenomena that both attract and repel, inspire and perplex. Schweitzer himself is evidence that distortions of Jesus' image are more often due to latent hero worship than to historical research that distinguishes Jesus' perspective from one's own.[18]

Reimarus' principle is still the first commandment of scholars dedicated to the historical quest:

> It is not to be assumed that Jesus intended or strove for anything in his teaching other than what may be taken from his own words.[19]

The past two centuries of debate have simply tightened the controls for pinpointing the patterns of speech and action that reflect Jesus' viewpoint rather than those of others. Since it is always easier to recognize someone else's fictions than one's own, our first task is to test whether the traditional paradigms are adequate for understanding Jesus *on his own terms*.

2. *Models*. The problem with the templates that have dominated the historical quest thus far – messiah, prophet, sage (and variants: "teacher" or "rabbi") – is that, while intrinsic to our sources, they are uniformly extrinsic to Jesus' own viewpoint. Although these models probably echo characterizations of Jesus by contemporaries, they represent insights by primitive admirers rather than patterns projected by Jesus himself. They are, therefore, no more historically objective than characterizations of Jesus by contemporary detractors – e.g., "a glutton and a drunk, a pal of toll collectors and sinners" (Matt. 11:19 // Luke 7:19) or "agent of Beelzebul" (Mark 3:22 etc.).[20] In fact, the positive paradigms are more plausibly accounted for as reactions to the negative, rather than the reverse. They are attempts by Jesus' supporters to fit the unconventional, even scandalous, things that Jesus said and did into social patterns defined by Jewish tradition: that is, to connect prickly points of data with familiar positive lines of interpretation.

Yet, the oldest narrative sources illustrate the failure of traditional roles to account for Jesus' pattern of behavior. Both Mark and the Johannine signs source independently prove that Jesus' earliest fans could *not* find a positive paradigm that fit him exactly. Instead of agreeing that Jesus' performance followed a single "messianic pattern" (as L.T. Johnson repeatedly alleges)[21] the gospels preserve the residue of a primitive debate over rival profiles of Jesus, anticipating the current phase of the Jesus Seminar by almost two millennia. Was Jesus the Messiah (John 1:41, Mark 8:29)? or "the Prophet who is to come" (John 6:14, Mark 6:15b)? or Elijah (Mark 6:15a, 8:28c)?[22] or even the shade of John the Baptizer (Mark 6:14, 8:28b)? Mark subjects the idolizing christology of the most prominent pillars of the apostolic church (Peter, James and John) to repeated ridicule as indicating a failure to understand Jesus (Mark 8:33, 9:6, 10:38), while the fourth gospel has Jesus caustically castigate admirers – including his own mother (John 2:4) – for expecting him to reveal himself through some significant word or gesture.

The primitive Christian solution to the problem of dissimilarity between traditional messianic expectations and the facts of Jesus' life was to modify the messiah paradigm by melding it with another traditional icon (Isaiah's suffering servant) that better fit Jesus' fate, to produce a powerful paradox: a dying savior. Scholars since Schweitzer, however, have generally abandoned the messianic model altogether due to lack of reliable evidence that Jesus deliberately posed as a messiah of any sort. It has long been conceded by most critically trained scholars that messianic consciousness was a figment, not of Jesus' own mind, but of the minds of some of his early Jewish fans.[23]

3. *Hero?* The same must now be said of the other traditional paradigms, prophet and sage, which in one guise or another have been favored in historical profiles of Jesus for the past half century.[24] The issue here is not whether one can find evidence to show that Jesus had things in common with Amos or Jeremiah or Qoheleth or Haninah ben Dosa or Diogenes of Sinope. It is, rather, whether Jesus wittingly mimicked the social roles such men defined. Sages and prophets are, after all, intellectual heroes and brokers of ultimate truth. They are readily admired by liberal, bourgeois scholars and preachers like me. Such admiration has blinded many historical questers – myself included – to the fact there is no solid evidence that Jesus aspired to the respectable social status of any kind of prophet or sage.[25]

Jesus' own sayings are evidence that he deliberately disavowed the type of admiration that prophets and sages invite. The one prophetic allusion that can reliably be traced to him is the impersonal observation that prophets in general lack respect at home (Thom 31:1, John 4:44, Mark 6:4).[26] Although the context of this saying in canonical sources implies that it was an indirect self-reference, it is important to note that the gospels are unanimous in identifying Jewish crowds rather than Jesus himself as the source of any explicit claim that he was a prophet (Mark 6:15, 8:28; John 6:14). Far from enhancing his status as a prophet, Jesus' impersonal observation about prophetic reputations actually deflates it by pointing out that he was not regarded as a prophet by those who knew him best. In form this saying is a proverb, like Jesus' less certain comment that stone buildings are not eternal (Mark 13:2). Taken at face value both statements are designed to counter unqualified awe before an imposing phenomenon with a generalized observation about the relativity and impermanence of even the most prominent person or thing.

From a purely phenomenological perspective, the style of Jesus' sayings fits the paradigm of sage better than prophet or messiah. The tentativeness of worldly grandeur is, after all, a fundamental insight of classical wisdom. So, was Jesus really a sage? We, like Josephus, may characterize him as such.[27] Yet, the mere fact that Jesus used aphorisms to express pithy observations about reality is still no guarantee that *he* would have accepted classification as a sage. For the wine Jesus poured into the skins of traditional wisdom was so volatile that it stretched the social mold of sage beyond the breaking point. Like the most radical philosophers – Socrates or the Cynics – he did not pose as a *wise* man. In fact, he warned people to *avoid* the trappings of social respect enjoyed by scholars – including the fellows and academic critics of the Jesus Seminar.[28] By thanking God for hiding from sages what was evident to infants (Luke 10:21 // Matt. 11:25), Jesus turned his wit against anyone who pretended to be wise.[29] So it would be ironic indeed if the author of this sentiment presented himself as a sage of any stripe.

4. *Social inversions.* The inverted social logic of many of the most clearly genuine Jesus sayings is the basic reason for doubting that Jesus consciously identified with the role of either prophet or sage. The Jesus who told people that God's *basileia* – the office of the divine ruler – belonged to paupers (Luke 6:20, Thomas 54) or to youngsters (Mark 10:14b, Thom 22:1) obviously had a worldview that turned traditional social structures upside down.[30] Jesus, moreover, expressly identified with those at the bottom of the social pyramid. At some point in his life he was a homeless wanderer who could ironically quip that birds and foxes had a more secure existence than he (Matt 8:20 // Luke 9:53 // Thomas 86).[31] And even as an adult, Jesus shamelessly referred to God with childish familiarity as "Papa" – *Abba,* that is (Mark 14:35; Galatians 4:6).[32] Instead of self-consciously posing as mediator of ultimate truth and paradigm of social virtue, he identified himself as a sibling of anyone who heeded the one he acknowledged as Parent (Matt 12:50, Thom 99:2).[33]

The author of these sayings did not claim ontological, social, intellectual or moral superiority over anyone. Jesus did not claim to be a hero and he steadfastly refused to pose as mediator of anything. Rather, he urged others to be confident that whatever they sought their Papa would grant (Matt 7:7–11 // Luke 11:9–13). The only dignity he ascribed to himself was the lot he shared with all other humans as offspring of Adam (and Eve): freedom to wander at will (Matt 8:20 // Luke 9:53 // Thomas 86) and to determine how to spend his time even on the sabbath (Mark 2:27–28).[34] At an early date, admirers of Jesus misinterpreted indirect remarks that implied he was a "son of God" or "son of Man" as exclusive titles which exalted him above mere mortals. Paradoxically, however, these are the paradigms that Jesus himself invoked as the lowest *common* denominators to identify himself with fellow humans. Instead of claiming a favored position for himself as "the *firstborn* among many brothers," as Paul later characterized him (Rom 8:29), Jesus insisted that in *Abba's* family the last are given priority, while those who put themselves first are sent to the end of the line (Matt 20:16, Mark 10:31).[35] Thus, *he* could claim with unqualified hyperbole what none of his supporters would have dared: that John the Baptist was the greatest person who ever had a mother (Luke 7:28a // Matt 11:11a).

Yet, Jesus knew, in a household where "Papa" is in charge, it is the *smallest* child rather than the greatest that really matters (Luke 7:28b, Matt 11:11b).[36] Instead of characterizing the cosmic Parent that rules the human household as a strict patriarch who cared for the obedient and castigated the undisciplined, he represented God as a self-consistent Provider who shed sunshine and rain on the unruly and upright alike (Matt 5:45).[37] Rather than describe his *Abba's* realm as a heavenly throne room more eternal than the loftiest redwood, Jesus whimsically likened it to minuscule bits of organic matter in the cosmic kitchen: common mustard weed (Thomas 20, Mark 4:30–32) or a fermenting scrap of sourdough (Luke 13:20–21, Matt 13:33).

Jesus himself did not shun the common or even the corrupt. He neither withdrew from the uneducated masses nor frequented the exclusive table-debates of the leading intellectuals of Jewish culture – the self-styled *hakhamim* (literally: "sages"). On the contrary, his indiscriminate socializing invited notoriety as a "pal of toll collectors and sinners" (Luke 7:34 // Matt 11:19). Instead of commending those who believed in him, he merely congratulated anyone who did not take offense at his outlandish quips and uncouth social behavior (Luke 7:23 // Matt 11:6).[38]

Only in a topsy-turvy world would Jesus' behavior be thought to fit the definition of a sage. In a status-conscious hierarchical society of either the first or twenty-first century he would more likely be regarded as a clown or a fool.[39] Like the family of Francis of Assisi twelve centuries later, Jesus' own relatives considered him insane (Mark 3:21). Most religious folk, preachers, and biblical scholars today, if they ever met him, would probably be inclined to agree. But those who embrace Jesus' paradoxical vision of God's inverted priorities would concur with an equally paradoxical Pharisee named Paul: that God's fool was saner than any human sage (1 Cor 1:25).

   5. *Jesus' fiction.* What we need then is a paradigm that does justice to Jesus' intimacy with both God and sinners, to both his sense of the human family and his sensitivity to the social scandal his own behavior provoked; a paradigm that is totally consistent with his vision of God's paradoxical concern for his most difficult child. A fiction? Certainly; yet a fiction that is as durable and distinctive as anything Jesus said or did: a paradigm that was not the figment of someone else's mind, superimposed on him either before or after his death. In order to reconstruct a historically reliable profile of Jesus, what we need is a figure from Jesus' own imagination: a fictive character based on his personal experience.

   The prodigal son is the one ancient prototype that makes perfect sense out of the surviving pieces of genuine Jesus tradition, whose author is otherwise bound to seem more of a historical oddity than the platypus: a comic Jewish Cynic. However close the latter may come to an accurate profile of Jesus, it remains a composite sketch drawn at a distance. Without eyewitness comparisons of Jesus to those deliberately shameless social gadflies whom contemporaries derided as "doggies," modern skeptics can easily challenge the historical plausibility of such a subject.[40] The prodigal, on the other hand, is almost certainly a snapshot from Jesus' own imagination, and thus a better representation of his viewpoint than any characterization of him by fan or foe.[41]

   My thesis – that Jesus is best profiled in one of the more disreputable figments of his own imagination – might be heresy in the eyes of both theological and literary dogmatists. But, for now, it is the most promising vaccine against the infectious human tendency to idolize Jesus or reinvent him in our own image. The crucial historical question is whether Jesus found the model for the anti-hero of his longest narrative parable in observation of someone else or in personal experience of *Abba's* treatment of himself.

The parable perplex: "You don't get this?"

   The past century of research into Jesus' sayings has confirmed the synoptic parables as the most reliable selection of gospel *logia* for analyzing Jesus' distinctive perspective on the world. It is ironic, therefore, that the parables have generally been overlooked as the best reflection of Jesus' personal experience.[42] B. B. Scott has compensated for the "disappearance of parables" in the most recent historical portraits of Jesus by presenting them as a revolutionary poet's window on an alternate world.[43] Without disputing that insight, I would argue that they are also a mirror in which Jesus cast his reflections on his own interaction with historical contemporaries.

1. *Metaphor.* The primary advance in parable interpretation in recent years has been the conclusion of specialists that the graphic scenes Jesus plotted are understood better as metaphor than as advice.[44] Measured by conventional standards of justice and ethics, both the images and plots of the bulk of Jesus' parables range from the strange to the subversive, especially when compared to first-century Jewish codes of social purity. Read as metaphors for God's *imperium*, however, – that is, the divine management of a less than perfect human economy– most of the parables are less problematic, at least for those who like myself prefer to think that the Force which governs the universe is inclined to equilibrium rather than to the survival of only the fittest.

But, as J. D. Crossan astutely noted in echoing Marianne Moore, as metaphor "a parable gives us 'imaginary gardens with real toads in them.'"[45] The point of metaphor is, after all, to invoke a phenomenon within the auditor's own experience that makes something abstract or obscure as painfully tangible as a hot potato. Jesus' imaginary gardens are loaded with real toads, warts and all. His parables about leaven (Matt 13:33 // Luke 13:20–21), a mustard granule (Thomas 20, Mark 4:30–32) and a Samaritan (Luke 10:30–35) were framed for Palestinian Jews with intimate experience of each. Only later *goyim* who had no first-hand acquaintance with the pejorative connotations of such phenomena in Jesus' native culture could readily accept them as theological symbols without raising an eyebrow.

2. *Anti-heroes.* Except for classical satirists, Jesus was the first narrator to focus public attention on the exploits of the anti-hero. The protagonists of several of his longer narrative parables are particularly disreputable individuals whose role in each respective plot shatters stereotypical thinking. Though preserved only by a gentile scribe (Luke), these parables reflect a completely Jewish perspective.[46] But first-century Palestinian Jews would be no more inclined to imagine the charitable behavior of Jesus' Samaritan than their twentieth-century descendants to fabricate the story of a Nazi like Oskar Schindler. Without some cogent point of reference in the real world either plot would strike a

Jewish audience as a totally incredible and politically perverse fantasy.[47]

Likewise, the incompetent manager who acts out of self-interest (Luke 16:1–8) and the wayward son who wastes his inheritance (Luke 15:11–32) were probably just as common in Jesus' culture as they are, unfortunately, in ours. But the experiences of each of Jesus' anti-heroes in escaping discipline by a higher authority, though strikingly similar, are disturbingly unexpected in a culture that demands social justice – disturbing, that is, unless one sides with the deviant.

In other words, these narrative parables are likely to have been dismissed as unworthy fantasy by Jesus' contemporaries unless they were prepared to grant the reality of the toad in each magic garden. To have functioned as a real metaphor, the behavior of the protagonist of any of these parables would have had to be as much a recognizable phenomenon on the historical horizon of both author and audience as the behavior of the sprouting mustard seed or the leavened dough. Lacking reference to some third party, these parables must have been provoked by some familiar element in the experience of Jesus, his audience or, most likely, both.

3. *Viewpoint.* We gospel scholars, as distant auditors, usually interpret the plots of the parables as quasi-didactic fictions through which a clairvoyant Jesus attempted to acquaint people with his vision of God's relation *to them.* But this simply lets the shadow of the traditional view of Jesus as mediator, teacher, sage in the back door. Non-literal instruction is instruction nonetheless. Although Jesus may not have represented himself as the ultimate broker of God's *basileia*, he would have behaved as such, *if* he formulated his parables to tell others what God meant for *their* lives. As designer of these imaginary gardens he would, in effect, be identifying his hearers as toads, calling attention to all their warts.

As reader-response analyses of the parables of the Samaritan, the unjust steward and the prodigal have often pointed out, however, Jewish auditors – ancient or modern – would be less likely to identify with the agent at the center of any of these plots than with the passive bystanders in the margins: the mugged merchant lying flat on his back in a ditch along the Jerusalem-Jericho highway, consumers who owe more to a creditor than they could ever hope to repay, the dutiful son who felt an injustice when his undisciplined sibling was honored instead. In each case the face of the disreputable figure on whose behavior the parable hinges remains blank. People in desperate straits, whose garden has lost its magic, might be ready to entertain the notion that even a toad could serve as a prince charming in disguise. But unless one materialized and acted as such, the toad in each of these parables – the helpful Samaritan, the debt-canceling manager and the celebrated prodigal — was bound to be regarded as an improbable fantasy.

Thus, the most plausible explanation of Jesus' penchant for casting disreputable figures in the leading roles of his narrative parables is that these fictions reflect to some extent his own experience and notorious behavior. In spite of modern literary critics' protests to the contrary, authors — ancient or modern — inevitably project their own experiences into the characters and scenes they imagine. Poets, after all, are as much subject to quantum physics as historians. The personal perspective of any artist invariably sets the field of vision of all he or she portrays.

4. *Transactional analysis.* As poetry, a parable, like other art, is born as a creative reaction to a set of stimuli in the artist's own experience; so it inevitably retains traces of the artist's encounter with particular phenomena. Since the phenomena depicted in parables function as metaphors, however, a modern attempt to reconstruct a parable's *originating* pretext in Jesus' experience might seem an exercise in pure speculation. For art is not bound to the artist's studio but may be rehung almost anywhere. Still, no picture can hang in a void. The hermeneutical consequence of refusal to retrace a parable's roots within Jesus' personal horizons is to let it be transplanted into an imaginary garden designed by someone else: the author of a synoptic gospel or some latter day interpreter like you or me. Funk was right to insist that as poetic speech no parable can be reduced to a single fixed point.[48] Every metaphor comes with as many handles as there are hearers. But the identification of a particular set of metaphors as parables of Jesus of Nazareth is a historical judgment that presupposes probable historical grounds for claiming they are the product of the imagination of this individual rather than some other. Like any claim of historical authenticity, those grounds require reconstruction.

Since speech is inherently transactional, reconstruction of a dialog is possible and justified when — as in the reconstruction of ancient manuscripts —the missing elements are suggested by the *vocabulary* and *logic* of the lines that have been preserved. A hypothetical pretext for one of Jesus' parables can be considered probable when it is supported by other documented evidence: biographical data or verbal challenges that Jesus' supporters are not likely to have fabricated. Moreover, the validity of the reconstructed transaction can be tested further and confirmed by its coherence with standards of social interaction advocated by Jesus himself. Three principles that are particularly relevant here are "love your enemies" (Matt 5:44 // Luke 6:27), "turn the other cheek" (Matt 5:39 // Luke 6:29) and "take the timber out of your own eye" before attempting to remove a speck from a sibling's (Thomas 26).[49] The author of these sayings was obviously dedicated to creative, non-abrasive strategies of social interaction. Since these striking injunctions are traceable to Jesus, a reconstruction of Jesus' verbal transactions that illustrates them is historically more probable than one that does not.

(5) *Ironic repartée.* Jesus' quips — about a wedding party fasting (Mark 2:19); the healthy needing a doctor (Mark 2:17); harvesting grapes from thorns (Matt 7:16 // Thom 45:1); blind leading the blind (Luke 6:39 // Thomas 34); or a camel passing through the eye of a needle (Mark 10:25) — amply demonstrate his mastery in invoking familiar phenomena to get others to recognize the absurdity of a scene. They are rapier thrusts of a sharp wit to win a point not easily parried.

The same ironic wit is evident in the plots of Jesus' parables. As verbal illustrations, parables usually originate as a response to verbal stimuli: supporters' questions or skeptics' challenges. It is a historical fact that certain socially precise Jews branded Jesus a pariah. It is also a fact that Jesus' longer narrative parables create imaginary gardens that reveal the behavior of such social toads to be benign. These stories turn slander into magic. Thus, a positive twist in a scandalous scenario is a good sign that the parable was created as Jesus' retort to an opponent's slur.

Slander is often cast in socially pejorative images. An excellent example of the type of repartée that graphic invective invites is found in the synoptic story of Jesus' encounter with a Lebanese woman (Mark 7:24–30 // Matt 15:21–28).[50] Jesus at first refuses the foreigner's request for aid by invoking a table metaphor about the inappropriateness of throwing children's food to "dogs" (Mark 7:27).[51] Instead of disputing the demeaning canine image, the woman seizes it to turn Jesus' logic against himself, by pointing out that dogs get to eat the children's scraps (Mark 7:28). Thus, in this case at least, a parabolic plot was suggested by verbal sparring. Jesus' concluding commendation of his female opponent for getting the better of him makes this sparring match a scene that is not easily dismissed as a fabrication by some fan of Jesus like Mark.

A Jesus who formulated metaphors to thrust could just as easily seize them to parry.[52] This element of creative *repartée*, which is usually ignored in parable interpretation, is what makes the narrative parables ideal nodes for reconstructing a historical profile of Jesus: not as literal descriptions of his life but as metaphors suggested by situations he actually encountered.

(a) *Creative debt management.* The parable of the manager who was fired for incompetence (Luke 16:1–8) is particularly perplexing when viewed as a pedagogical metaphor for either social ethics or divine action in general.[53] Surely, the image of a boss commending the unprofitable behavior of an employee who had just been dismissed for wasteful management is a metaphor designed to undermine any economy.

But the point of this parable becomes transparent when read dialectically, as Jesus' retort to critics of his own behavior. It is certain that Jesus was himself accused of sloppy accounting in his social relationships, for no fan would have caricatured him as "a pal of toll collectors and sinners" (Matt 11:19 // Luke 7:34; Mark 2:16).[54] Almost as certainly, Jesus assured debtors that they could avoid the ultimate bill collector simply by not collecting what was owed them (Matt 6:12; 18:23–24). This is exactly what the dismissed manager does during his last days on the job. Rather than pick up the gauntlet by protesting his innocence and slapping his accusers with libel charges, the parable's protagonist simply acknowledges his limitations and makes the most out of the options available in the time he has left. Similarly, instead of challenging his critics' charge of incompetence, Jesus simply appropriates it to validate his questionable behavior in discounting the debts of others. Thus, the parable of the shrewd manager paints a connection between these two facts– a line not invented by any modern scholar, but drawn by Jesus himself.

The parable of the disreputable manager can therefore be cited as evidence that Jesus actually lived by his precept of turning the other cheek (Matt 5:39 // Luke 6:29). Instead of striking back, Jesus disarms his opponent by exposing his own vulnerability. It is a vulnerability that the opponent cannot exploit without shaming himself, since he issued the charge of incompetence in the first place. Funk's description of the function of Jesus' parables in general is especially true in a dialectical situation like this, where the controlling metaphor was probably proposed by Jesus' opponent:

> They present a world the listener recognizes, acknowledges.
> Then he is caught up in the dilemma of the metaphor: it is
> not his world after all![55]

The opponent presumes to dictate the terms by which the real world is judged. Jesus' parable restructures that world by showing that a generous, non-judgmental lord is actually in control.

(b) *Suspect savior.* The parable of the Samaritan also fits better in a dialectical context than in a didactic one. The primary problem with the traditional interpretation of this story as a lesson in neighborliness is that only a Samaritan audience would be in position to take it this way. For Luke presupposes that the auditor is supposed to imitate the agent in the parable who showed compassion on the victim. Having just finished portraying Jesus' chief disciples as invoking a heavenly holocaust on a Samaritan village that did not offer them hospitality (Luke 9:51–56), Luke knew full well the animosity between Jews and Samaritans. So, if he designed this parable to fit his narrative context, the identity of the characters would have been inverted. For he introduces the parable as Jesus' response to a Jewish lawyer's question: "Who is my neighbor?" (Luke 10:29); and he concludes with Jesus telling him: "Go and do the same *yourself*" (10:37). Thus, the parable would conform to Luke's narrative horizons only if the fictive benefactor were a Jew and the victim of the mugging a Samaritan. Any Jews who heard another Jew portray a Samaritan in the role of benefactor would accuse the speaker of siding with the enemy.

This is, in fact, a charge that the fourth gospel claims Jesus himself faced from erstwhile Judean supporters: "Aren't we right to say that you are a Samaritan and demon-possessed" (John 8:31, 48).[56] Such a venomous description is hardly likely to have been fabricated by any later fan of Jesus, especially the author of the gospel in which Jesus calls a Samaritan woman a theological ignoramus for not recognizing that "salvation is from the Judeans" (John 4:22). While the fourth evangelist has Jesus dismiss the idea that he is motivated by a malevolent spirit, it is noteworthy that he does not deny the Samaritan label (John 8:49). This omission is hardly evidence that the author of the fourth gospel thought Jesus was literally a Samaritan or let the label stick to curry Samaritan support for Jesus. For Jesus' alleged response shows an acute awareness that the intent of this epithet was to defame him.

The ultimate shame for a first-century Palestinian Jew was to be branded a Samaritan by compatriots. Josephus reports that Jews charged with kosher or sabbath violations often found refuge in Samaria.[57] Thus, we have good historical evidence that religious Judaeans were likely to label a non-conformist Galilean a "Samaritan" – especially one from a village near the Samaritan border like Nazareth, and who claimed that nothing ingested could defile a person (Mark 7:15) and that the human being per se was "lord" of the sabbath (Mark 2:27–28).[58]

What is historically suspect about the scenario in John 8 is not the hostile epithet ascribed to some Jews, but rather Jesus' alleged provocation. If Jesus called fellow Jews offspring of "the father of lies" (John 8:44), then they were justified in characterizing him as an ethnic blood-enemy. But the voice that characterized Jews as "children of the devil" is probably that of a non-Jewish gospel writer rather than the Galilean, Yeshua of Nazareth. Indeed, it is totally incompatible with Jesus' self-critical caution to rid one's own vision of flaws before focusing on someone else's faults (Thomas 26).

Jesus' parable of the Samaritan, on the other hand, is a perfect, non-aggressive retort to a Jewish charge of heresy, which is, after all, the valence of the label "Samaritan" in a story told by a Jew to fellow Jews. The "neighbors" chosen for the main roles in this plot are parties to a longer rivalry than that of the Montagues and Capulets. But like Shakespeare's Romeo and Juliet, Jesus' story of a Samaritan in Judean territory spotlights a scene where common humanity momentarily triumphs over blood feud. Since the Jewish merchant just lies there, the point of the parable is not to tell Jews how to behave or to try to make them trust Samaritans in general, but to assure them that a particular "Samaritan," whom they regarded as a dangerous heretic, was really their friend.

Drawing a dialectical connection from Jesus' parable of the Samaritan to Judeans who characterized Jesus himself as such provides indirect evidence that Jesus treated even his harshest critics with love (Luke 6:27). If Jesus called those who characterized him as an enemy "liars," he would only have proven them right. Instead, he takes them at their word. Whether or not Jesus was an observant full-blooded Jew is irrelevant here. The fact is that some other Jews saw him as a heretic. Hence, they were not lying in characterizing him as such. To prove that their perception was wrong, Jesus accepted the Samaritan slur without blinking, but then went on to tell his Jewish accusers a story in which one such character went out of his way to save a victimized Judean. Jesus did not shun contact with destitute Jews who were ritually unclean any more than did the stranger in this parable. Thus, his story of this enemy as rescuer was probably designed to help Judeans see his own disregard for canons of purity in a more favorable light.

(c) *Problem child.* If the benefactor toads in the previous pair of parables were designed by Jesus as self-profiles drawn from his detractors' point of view, then the prodigal son is an even more transparent disguise.

- The prodigal was impatient, asking his father for an immediate share of his estate (Luke 15:13). Likewise, Jesus demanded his Papa's domain (Luke 11:2), confident that whatever he requested would be granted.[59]
- Unlike the cautious servant in another parable (Matt 25:14–30 // Luke 19:12–26), the prodigal does *not* keep his capital but, rather, exhausts it with an unconservative lifestyle (*zon asotos*)

among outsiders (Luke 15:14). Jesus himself mocked efforts to preserve life (Luke 17:33) or property (Luke 12:16–21) and perplexed conservative Jews by fraternizing with those they regarded as riffraff (Mark 2:16).[60]

• The prodigal provokes his dutiful brother to issue a contemptuous denunciation: "that son of yours devoured your living with prostitutes" (Luke 15:30). Jesus too was caricatured as a shameless libertine – "A glutton and a drunk! A pal of toll collectors and sinners!" (Luke 7:34 // Matt. 11:35) – and assured conservative critics that toll collectors and prostitutes had a prior claim on his Papa's estate (Matt 21:31).[61]

• The prodigal's homecoming prompts his father to celebrate with a feast (Luke 15:23–24). Jesus regarded the present as a time to celebrate, brashly comparing his own presence to a bridegroom (Mark 2:19) and his Father to a person who threw a dinner party for everyone (Thomas 64).[62]

• The prodigal's sober brother stayed outside the celebration for his disreputable sibling (Luke 15:28). Likewise, Jesus' brothers remained outside the circle of those who idolized him (Mark 3:31–32 // Thomas 99) – until after his death (Acts 1:14).[63]

• The prodigal's brother is portrayed as a dutiful, self-righteous son who can tell his father without fear of contradiction: "I never once disobeyed any of your orders" (Luke 15:29). Jesus' brother Ya'akov (James) was nicknamed "the Righteous" (Thom 12:2; Eusebius *Eccles. Hist.* 2.23.4–7) and was held in high repute by "those who were strict in keeping the laws" (Josephus, *Antiquities* 20.200–201).[64]

Any of these parallels alone could be regarded as figments in the mind of this modern reader that were not intended by the original tale spinner (Jesus). But their number and the fact that they have been tightly woven into the most complex and most realistic of Jesus' stories, which Luke presents as explanation of Jesus' own behavior, prevents easy dismissal as unintentional coincidences.

(d) *Allegory or autobiography?* The very length and realistic dramatic development of the plot of the prodigal puts it in a class by itself as reflecting more of the world as Jesus imagined it than any other saying. The basic plot—a father's benevolent concern for all his children, the bad seed as well as the good—makes it a perfect illustration of Jesus' uncommon aphorism envisioning the morally blind impartiality of divine providence (Matt 5:45//Luke 6:35); and the fact that the parable's characters fit the Matthean form of that Q aphorism better than the Lukan indicates that it is probably not the product of Luke's own imagination. Moreover, recognition of a healthy dose of Jesus' autobiographical input in the construction of this parable resolves problems that have long perplexed scholars regarding its structure and focus and avoids the temptation to allegorize both cast and plot.

As an author, Jesus had to get the inspiration for his characters from somewhere. Although the motif of sibling rivalry between a father's sons over the inheritance was a familiar mytheme in Jewish tradition, the characterization of the sons in this parable is *not* based on any standard Hebrew story. Instead of shrewdly cheating his older brother out of his birthright (like Jacob) or rising to power in a foreign land (like Joseph), the younger son is portrayed as a self-indulgent problem child who irresponsibly squanders his patrimony and is reduced to degraded circumstances in an alien setting. Though his return may occasion a celebration, it does *not* prompt the father to declare the younger son his heir or strip the understandably jealous elder son of his favored status. Since the interaction of characters in this parable does not conform to traditional Jewish mythemes it is better explained as a reflection of the world that the author personally experienced or at least deemed possible.

Moreover, the narrator who created this plot had to have some motivation for developing it in such detail. If the point of this parable was simply to illustrate the father's joy in the return of the prodigal, the character of the elder son and the conclusion would be superfluous. The lost sheep or lost coin (Luke 15:4–6, 8–9) make that point better. If the original intent was to shame critics of Jesus' association with sinners (Luke 15:1–2), then the father's concluding assurance that the elder son is his eternal companion and heir (Luke 15:31) is an inappropriate punch line.[65] If the author of this story were Paul, then it might be passed off as an allegory of all God's children, with the elder brother personifying Israel and the younger, the *goyim*. But the scenario and *dénouement* preclude such an application.[66] At first glance, Luke's fictional setting suggests a plausible allegorization of this parable within Jesus' world (prodigal = sinners; brother = Pharisees). Yet, the dramatic development of the brothers' roles and the father's dialog are still strangely out of sync. The prodigal returns on his own initiative. Luke, on the other hand represents sinners as responding to Jesus' initiative (Luke 5:32, 19:10). The dutiful brother is assured that he is his Father's eternal companion and heir, while Luke characterizes the Pharisees as "moneygrubbers" (Luke 16:14) whose self-righteous prayers are rejected by God (Luke

18:10–14). The difficulty in making the structure and details of this parable match Jesus' message or *Sitz im Leben*, has led some scholars to suggest it has been rewritten. Since its characters and plot are not typically Lukan constructs, however, it is more likely that the original point of the story of the prodigal has eluded interpreters to date.

Taken at face value the parable of the prodigal is a drama about the resolution of family tensions. One need look no further than Jesus' own family to find his inspiration for this plot. The story has been designed to reduce a dutiful son's resentment regarding the fuss being made over a disreputable younger brother. This parable neither favors the prodigal, nor rehabilitates his reputation nor censors his older brother. On the contrary, by conceding the latter's perception of his impetuous sibling's folly (Luke 15:30) it focuses on getting the firstborn to join the party by assuring him of his father's constant favor. So, the most likely auditor for whom Jesus crafted this story is his own brother James, who emerged as undisputed leader of the Jerusalem-based wing of the Jesus movement soon after his controversial sibling's death.[67]

An autobiographical interpretation of this parable, with the father's two sons as fictionalized versions of Jesus and James, is the simplest solution to the perplexing problem of accounting for the unique features of its composition. One does not have to resort to forced or imperfect allegorizations to recognize Jesus as model for the disreputable venturer and James the Just as prototype of his self-righteous brother.[68] One need only concede that the traditional christologically motivated characterizations of Jesus as "firstborn" and "the holy one" are not biographical facts.

The fact that this parable concludes without indicating the older son's response is evidence that it was composed before Jesus' own brothers decided to associate with those who celebrated Jesus' presence. B. B Scott notes that this most intricate plot of all of Jesus' parables has been left without a proper ending.[69] The simplest explanation of this fact is that the author composed it as an open invitation and was awaiting his big brother's reply. At a later date, during James' presidency, this invitation could have been used as an olive branch to Pharisees (like Paul) and other law-abiding Jews, as the setting in Luke suggests. In any case, the fact that this parable focuses on persuading a brother who is standing outside to come in makes it a logical sequel to the scene in which Jesus' own brothers (and mother) are described as outsiders (Mark 3:31–35 // Thomas 99).

The author of the parable of the prodigal was more concerned with restoring personal relationships than his own reputation. In characterizing himself as the disreputable son, Jesus once again concedes his critic's pejorative caricature of him.[70] In not censuring his elder brother's jealousy he demonstrates his commitment to his own principle of reconciliation: focus on your own flaws rather than those of your brother (Thomas 26). Modern fans who cling to a historically distorted reputation for Jesus, an image that was concocted by ancient partisans who never understood this witty self-effacing Jew may fail to find the historical Jesus' own profile in this uncensored fiction designed to overcome alienation between two brothers. But it provides the best model for making a coherent reconstruction of many of the other unquestionably genuine pieces of the Jesus puzzle. It remains to be determined, however, whether the line between the story of the prodigal and its creator is limited to stylized character icons or whether it involves more precise autobiographical insights into Jesus' self-image.

Plot: Correcting synoptic chronology

The Baptizer's successor: "Are You the One?"

While the character of the prodigal son bears unmistakable similarities to unvarnished glimpses of Jesus scattered through the gospels, the plot of this parable does not follow the outline of Jesus' career made familiar by the synoptics. Anyone who recognizes that Jesus had a rather shady reputation among decent first century Jews might be prepared to grant that he based the description of this disreputable son on his own public image. But the career paths of creator and creature do not appear to be at all parallel. The impetuous prodigal starts by earning a scandalous reputation but is reduced to penitence. The synoptic account of Jesus' public career, on the other hand, starts when Jesus leaves a preacher of repentance (John) to return to his homeland where he begins to act up, scandalizing his family and Pharisees by flaunting his freedom from all religious regulations. In the parable the father's celebration is occasioned by his wayward offspring's return to the relatively sober discipline of the family fold. Jesus' celebration was not with his biological family but rather with toll collectors and sinners. Since the synoptic account of Jesus' homecoming is diametrically opposite the plot of this parable, cautious scholars can be excused for not immediately conceding that the prodigal is a reliable self-portrait of Jesus.

The discrepancy between the scenarios of parable and gospels is a cogent objection to the historicity of the plot of the prodigal, however, only if the chronology of the synoptic accounts can be proved to be historically reliable. But this is hardly the case.[71] Matthew, Mark and Luke are certainly mistaken in describing a Sanhedrin trial and Jesus' execution during Pesach.[72] So, if their chronology of the climax of Jesus' career is unreliable, how can their sequence of events at its beginning be trusted? If the Passion narrative is demonstrably a christological construct,[73] can the gospel accounts of Jesus' inaugural appearance be any less so?

The introduction of Jesus career after the conclusion of John the Baptizer's has clearly been shaped by sectarian propaganda.[74] John was a highly visible and influential Jewish folk hero whose charismatic reputation almost certainly preceded and overshadowed the public career of Jesus.[75] Jesus himself granted John's superior social stature (Luke 7:28a // Matt 11:11a; Thomas 46).[76] The synoptic authors even conceded that some Jews tended to regard Jesus as a carbon copy of John (Mark 6:14, 8:28). Jesus' partisans, on the other hand, identified Jesus as John's greater successor.[77] Thus, it is hardly surprising that all the gospels (except Thomas) introduce Jesus only *after* citing the Baptizer's prediction that his successor will be far more powerful than he (Mark 1:7-8; Luke 3:16 // Matt 3:11; John 1:26-27).

Since the synoptic narrative sequence has been dictated by christological propaganda rather than reliable biographical data, it cannot be invoked to disprove an autobiographical basis of the parable of the prodigal. The Markan outline is an obvious author's fiction, with incidents arranged by motif rather than historical causality. The literary refinements of Matthew and Luke disguise but fail to alter the artificial character of the synoptic sequence. Chronological indicators provided by Mark and his editors are simply products of redactional activity.[78] None of the anecdotes that the synoptics string together to develop their portraits of Jesus contain built-in markers to indicate their original order. They are reported *after* the stories of Jesus' baptism and John's arrest simply to illustrate the theological thesis that Jesus was John's greater successor who initiated a baptism with a holy spirit. But that very thesis poses problems that undermine the credibility of the synoptic "narrative controls."[79]

The Markan conundrum: "What are folks saying about me?"

The chronology of Jesus' relation to John the Baptist in the synoptic narratives is intertwined with the question of Jesus' public reputation. Mark opens his gospel of Jesus the Messiah (1:1) by implicitly equating the Baptizer with Elijah (1:2-6). Jesus' initial appearance is fleeting. A brief post-baptismal vision, in which the narrator tells the reader that Jesus saw the holy spirit alight on him, (1:10) drives Jesus offstage into the wilderness from which John emerged (1:12). John's arrest provides the cue for Mark to recall Jesus to center stage (1:14). The Elijah motif is introduced again when Jesus' own "reputation had become well known" (6:14). The Markan narrator reports that "some" anonymous fans of Jesus "spread the rumor that he was Elijah" or some other prophet (6:15). Herod Antipas, however, is alleged to have identified Jesus as John *redivivus* (6:16), which leads Mark to present a lurid flash-back detailing the circumstances of John's execution (6:17–28). Only when the headless Baptizer is entombed (6:29) does Jesus start to act as John's successor, since the Jewish mob is now compared to a shepherd-less flock (6:34). Yet, in Mark's report, no one – neither the Jewish peo-ple nor Jesus' own disciples – apparently gets any significance from Jesus' repeated feeding of thousands in the wilderness (6:35–44, 8:1–9) or in gathering symbolic sums (twelve and seven baskets) of remnants (8:16–21). Still, when asked about Jesus' public reputation (8:27), the disciples report the same string of paradigms (John, Elijah, prophet) that the narrator introduced two chapters earlier (8:28 // 6:15–16). Matthew makes only minor adjustments in this scenario, while Luke edits out some of Mark's more politically loaded segments.

The odd thing about this sequence is that Mark reports nothing to account for Jesus' alleged public reputation. On the contrary, the peri-copes Mark inserts between his reports of John's arrest (1:14) and execu-tion (6:16) sharply distinguish Jesus from the ascetic herald of repentance who practiced the most rigid standards of personal purity. John preached repentance as precondition of forgiveness of sins (1:4).[80] As Mark tells it, Jesus was accused of blasphemy for presuming to forgive sins (2:6–7) and shocked purity-minded Pharisees by dining with sinners (2:16) with-out once suggesting that any "sinner" need repent of anything.[81] John is portrayed as an extreme ascetic (1:6) whose disciples observed ritual fasts (2:18).[82] Mark spotlights Jesus as dinner guest of secular types (2:15–16) who cites his mere presence to justify his disciples' deviance from reli-gious abstinence (2:18–19). John was unquestionably "an upright and holy man" (6:20), whom the gospels claim characterized his successor as agent of an even more thorough-going spiritual purgation (1:8). Though Jesus was introduced by Mark as a charismatic exorcist (1:23), his public reputation was anything but pure.[83] Mark has a single foul spirit declare Jesus holy, only to be silenced (1:24–25). Everything else that Mark reports about the inaugural phase of Jesus' public career portrays him as a social deviant who repeatedly initiated contact with those whom Jews normally regarded as impure, leading Judean scholars to regard Jesus as an agent of the chief demon (3:22).[84]

The problem with Mark's scenario is not its discontinuity between the profiles of Jesus and John; Q preserved sayings that paint the respective behavior and messages of these figures in even bolder contrasting colors (Luke 7:31–35, 16:16).[85] Rather, it is Mark's timing that is historically dubious. If Jesus began to deviate from the orthopraxis of John and other Torah-minded Jews after John's arrest, he would have been rightly labeled a renegade and no Jew would ever have confused Jesus with John, much less regard him as John's greater successor. Only if Jesus' shady reputation was earned prior to his association with the Baptizer could his supporters hope to convince other Jews that Jesus was a credible candidate to fill the leadership void created by John's execution. The simplest explanation of the gospels' campaign to present Jesus as John's greater successor is that John had many supporters who, from the moment that he was arrested, had serious doubts that Jesus was fit to fill or even tie his sandals.

The chief historical flaw in the "narrative controls" of Mark and the other synoptics is that the logical sequence of profiles in Q (first John, then Jesus) has been historicized by introducing all accounts of Jesus' activity only after John's has ceased. The practice of describing Jesus' behavior after John's can be traced to the logion about children in the marketplace, which concludes with this rhetorical contrast (Matt 11:18–19 // Luke 7:33–34):

> Just remember, John appeared on the scene neither eating [bread] nor drinking [wine]; and you say: "He is demented!" The son of Adam appeared on the scene eating and drinking; and you say: "There's a glutton and a drunk, a crony of toll collectors and sinners!"

Mark apparently based the outline of his first two chapters on this rhetorical pattern and Matthew and Luke simply followed suit. Thus, in the synoptic gospels chriae commemorating Jesus' scandalous behavior are set after his baptism without ever accounting for his baptism in the first place.

It is virtually certain that Jesus was baptized by John.[86] Since John's baptism was linked to his call for repentance, then Jesus most probably submitted to baptism as a sign that he was penitent. If Jesus did penance, then his previous behavior was admittedly deviant from the social norms of Judaic religious tradition. In that case, the paths of Jesus and the prodigal are perfectly parallel. Thus, the plot of this parabolic fiction reflects Jesus' own life journey better than the narrative structure of any gospel.

Matrix for a message: "Where's he getting this?"

Beyond its ability to act as a corrective of romantic idealization of
Jesus and literalistic reading of the synoptic narratives, the parable of the
prodigal has one distinct advantage over other paradigms for reconstructing a historical profile of Jesus: it portrays a very human person
rather than an abstract type. The prodigal son is the only character in
the synoptic narratives (including Jesus) who undergoes existentially
plausible psychological development. A brash youth prematurely sets
out to establish his own fortune. Free from family discipline, his opti-
mism turns him into a bon vivant. Still fiercely independent when hard
times come, he struggles to survive without parental support until he
compares his present lot to those back home. Stripped of his arrogance
and self-assurance, he returns with no pretense of being better than anyone else, only to be overwhelmed by the generous reception of a parent
of whom he felt unworthy to be heir. Finally, he is really free to celebrate, not his own achievements but the amazing tolerance of a provider
who cares for both the rebellious and the pious. At last he sees that
his father's house is an open house that has room even for his hostile
sibling.

This sketch of the prodigal's experience that calls him to his senses
is the matrix that makes historical sense out of the most distinctive features of Jesus' own message. Using this parable's protagonist to account
for parallels in Jesus' own outlook and behavior is historically sound,
since both are products of the same mind. Jesus' insight into the psychology of the prodigal offers a window into his own mental processes.
It explains not only his scandalous reputation but his self-effacing humility and amazing tolerance of scathing criticism. It makes sense out of
both his identification with homeless paupers and his optimistic confidence that God feeds those who lack a barn or bank account. It paints a
backdrop that makes his injunction to love enemies intelligible. And,
above all, it provides a clue for solving the greatest of historical puzzles:
that this wayward prodigal son of Israel was ultimately promoted by
decent law-abiding Jews like James and Saul of Tarsus to the status of
model son and heir to their common Father's heritage.

Rescripting scripture: applying Jesus' narrative control

As a product of Jesus' imagination, the plot of the parable of the
prodigal son provides a more reliable template for reconstructing Jesus'
own early career than any gospel narrative. Of course, the details of the
fictive narrative are not literal autobiography, and therefore defy histori-
cization. But this parable offers a glimpse of experiences Jesus had prior

to the redemption of his social reputation after his baptism. Charges that Jesus caroused with irreligious types ("toll collectors and sinners") were probably the baggage that he brought with him in his own "home-coming" to John. He neither attempted to deny these charges nor claimed moral stature comparable to that of the Baptizer. Thus, the parabolic celebration for the return of the wayward son provides a more accurate insight into the existential impact of Jesus' baptismal experience than the synoptic accounts of his post-baptismal vision. Far from being an egocentric revelation that he was God's uniquely favored son, for Jesus the experience of his own unconditional reacceptance into his paternal heritage was more likely the catalyst that convinced him that the God of Israel was not a harsh judge who held sinners accountable but a benign provider who invited all offspring to join the party.

The advantage of this historical scenario over a literalistic reading of the synoptic narratives is that it is able to account for evidence that, despite a public reputation, social message, and theological vision which were almost diametrically opposed to John's, it was Jesus rather than the Baptizer who became the center of a Jewish baptizing movement that expanded to include even gentile sinners. If one adopts Mark's narrative controls in reconstructing a profile of Jesus, it is difficult to explain how any Jew could ever have identified Jesus as a prophet, much less the Messiah. If one follows Matthew's narrative controls, it is hard to see why religious Jews would have scorned Jesus as a social deviant. While Luke's narrative addresses both problems, his profile of Jesus' social tolerance does not account for claims that Jesus was heir to John. Though the plot of the parable of the prodigal son does not provide a template for integrating all the historical facts in the Jesus puzzle, it presents a more cogent paradigm than the gospel representation of Jesus as God's holy one for drafting a profile of a son of Israel who spawned a movement focused on getting all God's children, the dutiful and the prodigal alike, to celebrate together.

EXCURSUS 1

> I thank you, Father,
> Lord of heaven and earth,
> because you have hidden these things from the wise and
> the learned,
> and revealed them to infants!
> Yes indeed, Father,
> because this is the way you want it.
> — Luke 10:21 // Matt 11:25 (SV modified)

This saying was weighted gray by the Jesus Seminar because it received a divided vote (.36). As an echo of Ps 8:2 traceable only to Q, it cannot automatically be assumed to be a formulation of Jesus. But it was the fact that Q prefaced it to a quasi-Johannine christological formula exalting Jesus as sole revealer of God (Luke 10:22, Matt 11:27–28) that led the majority of fellows to consider it the creation of an early Christian scribe.

There are three good reasons for reconsideration, however:

1. *Discontinuity*. The logic of the first saying (Luke 10:21 // Matt 11:25) is contradicted by the second (Luke 10:22 // Matt 11:27–28) and is, therefore, the product of a different mindset. While the creedal formula identifies "the son" (singular) as sole broker for any knowledge of "the Father," the prior thanksgiving affirms a radically immediate knowledge of God by "babies" (plural) in general. Infants are impervious to verbal instruction by anybody. (The Greek word *népios* carried connotations of a newborn and was even used to refer to fetuses). The subversive consequences of this thanksgiving for catechetical instruction probably led some Christian scribe to append the creedal affirmation to prevent the originally independent thanksgiving from being interpreted as an affirmation of innate human knowledge of God apart from Jesus.

2. *Coherence*. The thanksgiving by itself is a perfect corollary of Jesus' genuine declaration (Mark 10:14) that God's kingdom belongs to "little children" *(paidia)*. The ironic social logic of both sayings overturns the world's hierarchical pyramid that equates wisdom and authority with seniority. The mind that formulated one saying could easily have drafted the other.

3. *Embarrassment and environment*. No follower who revered Jesus as the ultimate revealer of wisdom would have created a categorical debunking of sages in general. (Compare this saying with Paul's less paradoxical contrast of worldly and divine wisdom in 1 Cor 1–2.) Since the

author of Q presented Jesus as divine Wisdom's offspring and spokesman (Luke 7:35, Luke 11:49–51), this thanksgiving is probably not a scribal fabrication. The only voice in Christian tradition that could have composed such a gleefully positive devaluation of wisdom is that Jewish wit who regularly celebrated the Creator's subversive irony of social history: Yeshua bar Yosef of Nazareth. Therefore, Luke 10:21//Matt 11:25 should be rated at least pink.

EXCURSUS 2

Abba, Father

Much has been written in recent years to challenge J. Jeremias' thesis that the Aramaic word *Abba* was Jesus' distinctive way of addressing God, indicating his unique sense of childlike intimacy with the Deity. Yet Jeremias' observations have not yet been disproved. Though scholars have produced many examples of Jews addressing God as "(Our or my) Father (in heaven)," it remains a fact that no example of a Jew using the Aramaic form Abba as a direct address to God has yet been found apart from primitive Jesus tradition.

G. Vermes (*Jesus the Jew*, p. 211) identified a rabbinic anecdote about the *hasid* Abba Hanan as an exception (*b Ta'anith 23b*). It is not. In this story school-children (i.e., pre-teens) address this plea to *Hanan*: "*Abba, Abba*, give us rain!" Hanan then turns and addresses God with proper deference as "Lord of the universe!" and asks him to ignore the impertinence of children who fail to make the distinction between "the Abba who gives rain and the Abba who does not."

This story proves the rule that adult Jews were not accustomed to addressing God as Abba. In Palestinian Judaism Abba was sometimes used by *children* in addressing their *teacher* to show both respect and a family loyalty, much as Christians later adopted Papa as a designation of their bishop. In the case of Hanan, children deliver a petition that only the Almighty could grant, to their teacher. The teacher then forwards the misdirected petition to the Person with the authority to grant it by changing the address ("Lord of the universe"). Hanan's indirect reference to God as Abba in this context is a pun prompted by childish impertinence and, therefore, is not historical proof that either he or Jewish children in first century Palestine were accustomed to addressing God as Abba. On the contrary, this anecdote was recorded by non-Palestinian rabbinic scribes only hundreds of years after Hanan's death. Whether it is a historically reliable report or not, the fact that it was considered remarkable enough to be recorded at all, can be taken as evidence that it was regarded as a unique deviation from Judaic custom.

In first-century Greek Christian sources, the Aramaic term Abba was used as a term of direct address to God. But this term is exclusively ascribed to Jesus (Mark 14:36) or to the voice of the spirit that Paul claims God sent into "whoever is baptized into Christ" (Gal 3:27): "the spirit of his son" (Gal 4:6), which is clear evidence that "we are children of God" and "co-heirs with Christ" (Rom 8:16–17). So, while some of the conclusions drawn from Jeremias' claim that Jesus' address of God as Abba was unprecedented may have to be modified in the light of subsequent scholarship, the gist of his insight is still historically valid: Abba was Jesus' characteristic designation of God that the first generations of his followers imitated precisely because they found it socially innovative and spiritually liberating.

The Search for the
Historical Jesus
Why Start with the Sayings?

Lane C. McGaughy

The first decade of the work of the Jesus Seminar was divided into two phases: for the first five years the members of the Seminar critically evaluated the inventory of roughly 1500 sayings attributed to Jesus in Christian sources from the first three centuries of the common era. The results of this work were published in 1993 as *The Five Gospels: The Search for the Authentic Words of Jesus*. During the next five years the Seminar assessed the deeds attributed to Jesus in the surviving early Christian Gospels, and the results of this work were published under the title *The Acts of Jesus*. Any reconstruction of the historical Jesus, of course, must include both his deeds and his words, and indicate how the two are related. But since all investigations must begin somewhere, why did the Jesus Seminar begin with the sayings of Jesus rather than with his actions? And what difference if any does this make for the resulting reconstruction of the historical Jesus?

The immediate reason for reflecting on these questions is to respond to one of the criticisms aimed at the Jesus Seminar. Ben Witherington of Asbury Theological Seminary says that by beginning with the sayings of Jesus, the Seminar has produced a "talking head,"[1] a disembodied voice whose message is unclear because it has been removed from the historical, social and literary contexts within which it should and could be interpreted. In like manner Birger Pearson in the journal *Religion* claims that reconstructions of the historical Jesus should rather begin with his deeds, since "actions speak louder than words."[2] Apart from such criticisms of the Jesus Seminar's work, reflection on whether one should begin with deeds or words is important because it calls our attention to methodological issues in historical Jesus research.

From the New Quest to the Jesus Seminar

When Robert W. Funk convened the first meeting of the Jesus Seminar in 1985,[3] he invited respondents to prepare a new history of the traditions about Jesus in early Christianity, one which in effect, would update and expand Rudolf Bultmann's *History of the Synoptic Tradition*, first published in 1921, in light of textual discoveries like the Dead Sea scrolls (1947) and Nag Hammadi codices (1945) and recent methodological advances in the social sciences and literary criticism. The quick answer as to why the Jesus Seminar started with the sayings is that Bultmann did. The outline of his *History of the Synoptic Tradition* provided the ten-year agenda of the Jesus Seminar:

1. The Tradition of the Sayings of Jesus
2. The Tradition of the Narrative Material.

As the preeminent New Testament scholar of the twentieth century, Bultmann formulated the questions which have been addressed by all critical scholars ever since. He began the *History of the Synoptic Tradition* with an investigation of the sayings material because he was concerned with the relationship between the message of the historical Jesus and the preaching of the early church: Can one demonstrate a continuity between what Jesus proclaimed through his parables and aphorisms and what others proclaimed about Jesus? Were Paul and the other early missionaries saying the same thing as Jesus, though in different words and new places, or was the message of the historical Jesus distinct from that of his early interpreters? Bultmann's question formed the agenda for the so-called New Quest of the last generation since the failure of the nineteenth century Old Quest to discover the historical Jesus had removed the historical foundation of Christian preaching. Even though we do not have historical sources to construct a full biography of Jesus, and even though the sources we do have are written from the theological viewpoint of post-Easter faith, the New Questers attempted to recover at least the message of Jesus in order to determine whether the intention of Jesus' words and the intention of early Christian preaching are coherent. Thus, Bultmann and the New Questers started with the sayings of Jesus rather than the deeds because their aim was to compare messages, not actions.

The agenda of the Jesus Seminar thus evolved from the New Quest and its attempt to reconstruct the teaching of the historical Jesus. In distinction from the so-called Third Quest which is attempting to locate Jesus within the religious and social world of first-century Judaism, the work of the Jesus Seminar is best seen as a renewal and extension of the New Quest (though some members of the Jesus Seminar may see their own work as part of the Third Quest). In chapter four of his recent book *Honest to Jesus*, Robert Funk refers to the work of the Jesus Seminar not as part of the Third Quest, but as the Renewed Quest for Jesus.[4]

The scholarly route from Rudolf Bultmann's *History of the Synoptic Tradition* to *The Five Gospels* of the Jesus Seminar thus can be traced through studies like Gunther Bornkamm's *Jesus of Nazareth* (1956), which contains about twenty-five pages on Jesus' biography and about one hundred sixty-five on his message, and Norman Perrin's *Rediscovering the Teaching of Jesus* (1967), as well as such monographs on the parables of Jesus as Robert Funk's *Language, Hermeneutic, and Word of God* (1966) and *Jesus as Precursor* (1975); John Dominic Crossan's *In Parables* (1973); and Bernard Brandon Scott's *Jesus, Symbol Maker for the Kingdom* (1981) and *Hear Then the Parable* (1989).

Before the Jesus Seminar, the forum for this renewed quest had been the Parables Seminar of the 1970s and the journal *Semeia*, which Robert Funk launched in 1974 – both projects of the Society of Biblical Literature, the professional association for biblical scholars. Those who had participated in the Parables Seminar and related scholarly circles from 1965 to 1985 formed the core of those whom Funk invited in 1985 to constitute a national seminar on the Jesus tradition. The work of the Jesus Seminar thus derives from the New Quest for the historical Jesus, mediated in part by the Society of Biblical Literature and representing many of the important voices in twentieth-century New Testament scholarship.

Methodological questions about words and deeds

If one agrees with most scholars that there was at least a generation between the historical Jesus and the composition of the Gospels, then the New Questers were faced with serious methodological questions. How could the authentic sayings of Jesus be recovered if they were all assimilated to the message of the early church during the period of oral transmission? Could the Jesus tradition and Christian interpretation be separated, or had the two blended so completely that the authentic sayings can never be recovered? Gunther Bornkamm expressed this skepticism in the 1950s:

> We possess no single word of Jesus and no single story of
> Jesus, no matter how incontestably genuine they may be,

which do not contain at the same time the confession of
the believing congregation or at least are embedded
therein. This makes the search after the bare facts of history
difficult and to a large extent futile.[5]

Many still share Bornkamm's methodological skepticism; in fact
several members of the Jesus Seminar consistently voted black during the
first phase as a way of expressing their judgment that all the sayings were
transformed in the process of oral transmission. For them, the gospels
contain no word-for-word quotations of what Jesus actually said. Thus,
before the New Quest could begin to reconstruct Jesus' message, criteria
had to be formulated for separating tradition from interpretation.

On the assumption that the sayings of Jesus were repeated and
interpreted time after time, thus forming layers of tradition, Norman
Perrin argued in *Rediscovering the Teaching of Jesus* that the tradition-history of each saying must be written in order to discover its "most primitive form."[6] He used three main criteria in his study to determine the
tradition-history of Jesus' sayings:

1. the criterion of dissimilarity, on the grounds that a
   saying which differs in its emphasis both from Jesus'
   back ground and from the foreground of the church was
   preserved because it was authentic
2. the criterion of coherence which judges materials to be
   authentic if they are consistent with those judged
   authentic in terms of the first criterion
3. the criterion of multiple attestation which takes materials to be authentic if they stem from most or all the
   pre-Synoptic sources[7]

The methodological questions implicit in Funk's invitation in
1985 for scholars to rewrite the history of the Synoptic tradition have
been constantly debated and refined during the semiannual meetings of
the Jesus Seminar. This attention to method started with a paper presented by Seminar Fellow Eugene Boring at the second meeting (Fall
1985) and subsequently published in the journal *Forum*.[8] Boring
extended Perrin's criteria from three to ten and arranged them in order
of priority, beginning with multiple attestation.

Also in *Forum*, John Dominic Crossan proposed a chronological
sequence for dating the various sources which he has elaborated in his
later works on the historical Jesus.[9] As a result of this methodological
debate, a gradual shift occurred during the first phase of the Seminar
from stressing the criterion of dissimilarity to emphasizing the priority
of multiple attestation. (This partly explains why some singly attested

sayings like several of the Lucan parables were voted red and pink during the early sessions.)[10] As a result of this self-conscious attention to methodology, *The Five Gospels* begins with a lengthy analysis of rules of written and oral evidence and observations about how the Seminar determined the authentic sayings of Jesus.[11]

The continuing debate about methodology among the Fellows also led to the recognition that since Perrin's criteria were formulated with the sayings material in view, they would need to be refined for the second phase of the Seminar. In fact, the search for the authentic deeds of Jesus is more difficult than the search for the authentic sayings because the best one can hope to recover with respect to deeds are the earliest reports of bystanders about what they thought they saw, whereas the authentic sayings indicate what Jesus himself thought or intended about his mission. To quote a memorable aphorism coined by Julian Hills of Marquette University, "Sayings are repeated, deeds are reported." Therefore, beginning with an analysis of the sayings is necessary if one's aim is to recover Jesus' own perspective, rather than the perspective of those who reported his actions.

Having reconstructed the intention of Jesus' message by recovering the authentic sayings, the Seminar instituted phase two by asking whether the reported deeds of Jesus were consistent with his words. As is well known, every traditional proverb can be countered with another that advocates just the opposite. And so, though Birger Pearson cites the proverb "actions speak louder than words" to support his view that one should begin with the deeds of Jesus,[12] the Jesus Seminar investigated Jesus' deeds only after his sayings in order to determine whether Jesus "practiced what he preached." Were his actions consistent with his message? Such a procedure, far from producing merely "a talking head," would yield a benchmark for judging early Christian claims that Jesus was someone special who deserves to be imitated. By this criterion integrity would be the highest virtue. If it turned out that Jesus' actions were always consistent with his message, then he would indeed be a remarkable human being, since finitude implies that our actions do not always match our words, that most of us don't often practice what we preach. Like Socrates, Jesus was a victim of his own integrity. He could act in no other way than that revealed through his teachings, regardless of the consequences for himself.

To sum up to this point, though the Jesus Seminar may have started with the sayings because many of its members participated in the attempt to recover Jesus the teacher and parabler during the 1960s, 1970s, and 1980s, the deeper reason is a methodological one: deeds by themselves are like archaeological artifacts without a text; their meaning becomes clear only in light of the intent of the actor as revealed through his or her words.

The nature of Jesus' deeds

These remarks about the priority of sayings in reconstructing the historical Jesus raise other questions about the so-called deeds in the gospels. Apart from the fact that they are secondary reports, are the deeds in the gospels narrated in such a way that their historical specificity can be tested? The father of ancient Greek historiography, Herodotus, defined *erga* ("achievements," "deeds") as the construction of monuments or military victories which bring immortal fame because they leave visible traces behind.[13] For him, history was the listing of such monumental deeds, and biography was likewise, focused on the visible achievements of political and military heroes.[14] Following the adaptation of the biographical genre by Aristoxenus and other students of Aristotle to accommodate notable teachers like Socrates,[15] deeds became subordinate to words and redefined as miracles in order to correspond to Herodotus' view that *erga* bring fame because they are visible and leave traces behind.

The term bios ("life," from which we get the term biography) appears for the first time in the hellenistic period to mark this shift from biographies of military heroes to the lives of remarkable teachers. In *Heroes and Gods*, Moses Hadas and Morton Smith have constructed a genealogy for the genre which moves from history to biography to aretalogy, their term for the life of a spiritual hero which has become stereotypical in its form and functions as a model for moral instruction.[16] As we know from Plutarch's *Parallel Lives*, the focus was not on the unique deeds of each hero, but on the conventional moral patterns which the paired biographies illustrated. The fact that in hellenistic biographies deeds of holy figures had become highly stylized is illustrated by the way Philostratus (a philosopher of the early third century CE) summarizes the achievements of the first-century mystic Apollonius of Tyana not as historical events, but as a typical day in the life of the hero (I.16).[17] This is reminiscent of Mark's use of the iterative imperfect (a use of the past tense of the verb to indicate typical rather than specific actions) to introduce the accounts of Jesus' miracles: "In the evening, at sundown, they would bring all the sick and demon possessed to him" (1:32).

Rudolf Bultmann has shown that all the healing miracles attributed to Jesus in the Gospels are narrated in exactly the same pattern:

1. description of the illness
2. cure, including Jesus' technique
3. demonstration of cure or audience response

Since the same stylized pattern is used to recount the miracles of the disciples in Acts and in non-canonical works, it seems clear that we are dealing with a set oral form which has become a literary convention, rather than with reports of specific deeds which can be verified historically.[18] Thus, the second phase of the Jesus Seminar reached conclusions that may at first seem to be contradictory with respect to the historicity of Jesus' miracles, but which in fact honestly reflect the methodological difficulty in verifying the stylized reports of Jesus' deeds. While most of the actual miracles were colored black because they cannot be traced back to a specific historical action of Jesus, the criterion of multiple attestation prompted the Seminar to vote red on the general statement that Jesus was a miracle worker and exorcist.[19] Given the generic way in which the deeds were reported in ancient sources like the Gospels, this is probably the best historical criticism can do.

The healing of the centurion's boy (Matt 8:5–13; Luke 7:1–10; John 4:46–54) is a good example of the difficulty in authenticating the deeds of Jesus. Because this miracle story is attested in two sources, John and Q, some scholars argue that it reports a historical event. But close analysis shows that:

1. the illness is uncertain (paralysis in Matthew, a fever in John, unspecified in Luke)
2. neither a direct encounter between Jesus and the sick boy nor the healing technique is reported
3. neither the officer nor the boy confirms that a healing occurred – it is reported only by others (servants or friends or the narrator)

What in fact lies behind the narrative is a religious confession based on the model of the Roman patronage system. Jesus is acclaimed as a healer because he, like the centurion, is viewed as a broker of a higher authority. By asking Jesus to heal his boy (Luke 7:7b) and then describing the patronage system in Roman Palestine (Luke 7:8), the centurion reveals his belief that Jesus occupies a similar mediating function vis-a-vis God as he, the centurion, occupies vis-a-vis Caesar. Jesus is amazed that the centurion has such a sophisticated insight (Luke 7:9). But such reflection on the theological significance of an action means that the narrative has crossed the line from a bare report that something happened to later Christian reflection on the meaning of the deed. As a result, other scholars have concluded that the centurion's boy is neither a miracle story nor a report about the historical Jesus, but, in light of the saying in Luke 7:9 ("I tell you, not even in Israel have I found such faith.") is a creation of the early church to justify its mission to the Gentiles.

In the judgment of the Jesus Seminar, therefore, it is methodologically unsound to begin with the deeds in reconstructing the historical Jesus because this material is stylized and cannot get us back any further than early Christian reports about Jesus' actions – though one would need at some point to account for the fact that in the oral tradition Jesus was perceived to be a divine man with the accompanying powers to heal and exorcise demons.

The distinctive voice of Jesus

Thus far I have been addressing the conservative critics of the Jesus Seminar who believe that the reports of Jesus' deeds are the place to begin the Quest. But, having argued on methodological grounds that we cannot get behind these reports to the historical Jesus, I must now address the critics on the other side who share the same skepticism with respect to the sayings of Jesus. They remind us that there were no tape recorders in the ancient world and that all reported speeches were composed by later authors on the basis of what they were told the speaker said or even what they thought the speaker should have said under the circumstances – a convention used to report speeches in Thucydides' history of the Peloponnesian War as early as the fifth century BCE. For example, German scholar Philipp Vielhauer has demonstrated that Paul's speech in Athens (Acts 17:22–31) was a composition which Luke placed on the lips of Paul, but which has little if anything in common with Paul's thought as reflected in his letters.[20] And thus it is that in the passage cited above, Bornkamm lumps words together with the deeds of Jesus in expressing his doubt that "the bare facts of history" can be recovered in either case. The burden of proof is thus on the side of those who argue that either words or deeds are authentic. (The fact that the Jesus Seminar started with the assumption that at least some of the Jesus materials can be authenticated – as opposed to those who would vote every item black – indicates that it is a rather more conservative project than is portrayed in the popular press!)

It is at this point in the argument that the criterion of dissimilarity becomes important. It was utilized by Norman Perrin and others as a way of distinguishing Jesus' message both from the message of his predecessors, like John the Baptist and other Jewish reformers, and from the message of his successors, like Paul and the Evangelists. Proponents of the so-called Third Quest have charged that this criterion produces a non-Jewish and a non-Christian Jesus.[21] But the point is not to separate Jesus from his social world. The criterion of dissimilarity was formulated to discriminate the voice of Jesus from the many voices that surrounded him. Just as in a crowded room we may isolate one voice and block out the rest because of its distinctive sound, so, by analogy, if Jesus proclaimed a distinctive message, that message should be recognizable in his authentic sayings, even if those sayings have been paraphrased or abbreviated in the process of oral transmission.

Thus, the vote that at least 18% of the sayings are authentic does not mean they are the actual words of Jesus, but that they preserve the gist of Jesus' message in a way that makes those sayings recognizable as deriving from him and not from the early church or the Evangelists. In order to indicate that this criterion was being used to isolate Jesus' message and not to separate him from his social and religious context, the criterion of dissimilarity has been nuanced by the Seminar in order to detect the distinctive features of Jesus' speech. As noted above, lengthy discussions of this redefined criterion of distinctiveness are contained in the introductions to the Red Letter Edition of *The Gospel of Mark* and *The Five Gospels.*

The distinctive message of Jesus is reflected in both the novel form of Jesus' sayings, parables and aphorisms, and in their radical content, a new vision of how human activity is qualified by virtue of its divine horizon. In order to be able to recognize this distinctiveness, however, one must have a significant sample of authentic sayings which are coherent in both form and content.

By analyzing the history of individual sayings in isolation from other sayings, one could produce a collection of allegedly authentic sayings that are not coherent. As a result, the test of coherence must be added to the criterion of distinctiveness: after a collection of sayings has been evaluated using historical critical methods, those sayings must then be compared to determine whether they are consistent and thus could have come from the same speaker. This question of coherence is now being tested by the third phase of the Jesus Seminar. Having established a database during the first two phases, can different scholars, using that database, now create profiles of the historical Jesus which harmonize with one another and also account for the variety of Jesus traditions which emerged during the first century? In many ways, the interesting work of the Jesus Seminar is just now beginning as the collated data are tested against the resultant profiles.

Implications for a profile of Jesus

This is not the place for me to present my own profile of Jesus, but I do want to conclude with a few comments on the distinctiveness of Jesus' sayings which suggest that we are close to the actual voice of Jesus with the red and pink items in *The Five Gospels*. First, though other ancient rabbis used parables, the narrative parables of Jesus are immediately recognizable because they are short stories which begin with a realistic scene, are transformed into metaphors by means of a surprising, unrealistic twist in the middle, and invite hearers to act on the basis of this new, but not fully defined, vision of reality.[22] Jesus' one-line parables are also distinctive because their vivid images are inverted cultural symbols: leaven, for example, was a symbol of sin in ancient Israel; Jesus makes it a symbol of God's domain.[23] Similarly, Jesus' aphorisms do not repeat collective, ancestral wisdom, but articulate his own personal and unconventional insight about the really Real.[24] Beginning one's profile of Jesus with his distinctive speech, and not the reported deeds, forces one to rethink Schweitzer's view that Jesus was an apocalyptic preacher.[25] As one who lived during the escalating crisis of first-century Palestine, Jesus was familiar with the apocalyptic outlook of the Essenes and evidently shared their negative evaluation of history, though he usually expressed it as a protest against conventional wisdom rather than in cosmic terms. But his solution to the crisis shows that his message was not an apocalyptic one for he offered parables as gateways to the kingdom of God rather than mythical descriptions of a future holocaust.

Second, in order to fathom their metaphors, one must view the parables as wholes, rather that allegorizing their parts. Jesus is saying that what is going on in the parables hints at what it means to live in the presence of God ("The kingdom of God is like . . ." followed by the parable). This formula suggests that functioning as metaphors, the parables refer to a symbol (kingdom of God), yet in the juxtaposition of their narrative content with that symbol they deconstruct and reconstruct the meaning of the symbol.

In *Jesus and the Language of the Kingdom*, Norman Perrin recognized that the term kingdom of God is a symbol and not a political term for a new theocracy.[26] He demonstrates that the kingship of God was a symbol of domination drawn from the ancient near eastern creation myth and later transposed by the apocalyptic imagination into a mythical scenario for the conquest of evil in the near future. But he does not clearly show how the meaning of this symbol is subverted by Jesus when he juxtaposes it with parables like the mustard seed. If the mighty cedars of Lebanon represented royal power, then comparing the rule of God to a puny mustard plant shows that for Jesus, at least, the kingdom was not about conquest and domination and that God's rule would not be established as the result of a cosmic conflict between the military forces of good and evil. In short, Jesus' use of parables to announce the arrival of God's presence separates his message clearly from the mythical scenarios of the future contained in the Qumran War Scroll and the Apocalypse of John.

Could such a message get one crucified? Perhaps not, if one takes the modern view that "talk is cheap," that words don't matter. In this context, one would need to begin with a subversive deed like overturning the tables of the Temple moneychangers or the plotting with one of the revolutionary groups like the Zealots in order to account for Jesus' fate. But if one dwelt in a world in which language was potent, a world in which words could move the gods to change their plans (a world of prayers and curses) and word-pictures could enlighten and empower marginalized peasants, then in fact the integrity of Jesus' vision as expressed through his sayings could have threatened the authorities and resulted in his execution.[27] One has only to think of Socrates and John the Baptist to realize that in the ancient world offensive words could get a teacher or prophet executed. In the world of the first century it is both possible and methodologically necessary to start with sayings and then move to deeds as a way of reconstructing the historical Jesus and accounting for both his message and his destiny.

Jesus
A Sketch

Marcus J. Borg

The story is told that the great Rabbi Hillel, was asked by a Gentile to explain all of Judaism to him while standing on one foot. The invitation to write a quick and concise description of how I see Jesus feels a bit like that. I have written book-length and chapter-length treatments of Jesus, and I have taught thirty-hour, three-hour, and one-hour versions. But writing the fifteen-minute version is a new challenge.

The resulting sketch of Jesus is drawn with five broad strokes. Each stroke is a short phrase that identifies a central characteristic of Jesus. But first, I begin with some notes about sources and context.

Sources

Our primary sources are the early layers of the synoptic gospels of Matthew, Mark and Luke and the Gospel of Thomas (but not John). The earliest layer of the synoptics is Q, a collection of Jesus' sayings. There is also early material in Thomas, another sayings collection. For narrative material (individual stories, such as healing stories, as well as the narrative structure as a whole), we are essentially dependent upon a single source, Mark, the earliest of our present gospels (written about 70 CE).

Context

The context for interpreting our sources is everything we can know about the social world of Jewish Palestine in the first third of the first century. Our picture is the product of two factors: data produced by the

129

study of documents and archaeology, and models that enable us to constellate the data into coherent wholes. Three types of cross-cultural and interdisciplinary models especially illuminate the social world of first-century Palestine and help us interpret the words and actions of Jesus: those of peasant societies (pre-industrial agrarian societies), purity societies (societies organized as a purity system), and patriarchal societies (andro-centric and hierarchical).

Jesus

My understanding of Jesus has been very much shaped by the interplay between historical Jesus scholarship and the much more comprehensive discipline of religious studies. When I began my study of Jesus some twenty-five years ago, the education I received included no exposure to other religious systems, but concentrated exclusively on the Jewish-Christian tradition. In the decades since, my teaching assignments have included courses in non-western religions, religious experience, religion and psychology, and religion and society.

From this broader exposure to religious studies, particularly the phenomenology of religious experience and a typology of religious figures, I have learned much of great value for constructing an image of Jesus. Each stroke in my five-stroke sketch of Jesus corresponds to a type of religious figure known in many cultures: the ecstatic, the healer, the wisdom teacher, the social prophet, and the movement initiator.

I will spend a disproportionate amount of time on the description of Jesus as ecstatic. This is central to my construction of an historical image of Jesus; within the scholarly community it is the most distinctive element of my historical reconstruction. Though other scholars do not necessarily deny that Jesus was an ecstatic, few make it so centrally important.

Ecstatic or mystic

The word ecstasy simply means separation from one's ordinary state of being. A religious ecstatic or mystic is a person who frequently experiences non-ordinary states of consciousness which are felt to be disclosures of another, deeper, or "more real" level of reality than that known in ordinary states of consciousness.

The range of ecstatic religious experiences is broad. *Visions* involve seeing into another level of reality, and *shamanistic experiences* add to this a sense of journeying into another level. *Unitive or mystical experiences* involve a strong sense of connectedness (union or communion) with "what is." They can be introverted experiences ("eyes closed") or extroverted ("eyes open," as in nature mysticism) and can occur in meditative solitude or in the midst of activity in the world. *Encounter experiences* include a vivid sense of the sacred becoming present (sometimes, but not always, in visionary form), and are marked not by connectedness as much as by confrontation with "otherness," challenge, and sometimes commissioning.

The varieties and nuances of ecstatic religious experiences (as well as the broad sense in which I define the notion) are suggested by the various phrases used to characterize them: Rudolf Otto's experiences of the numinous which is also the *mysterium tremendum et fascinans*, Abraham Maslow's "peak experiences," R. M. Bucke's "cosmic consciousness," Abraham Heschel's "radical amazement," and Martin Buber's "I-Thou/I-You" moments which contrast sharply with the "I-It" (subject/object) quality of our ordinary experience. These experiences also include such widely differing states as the "shamanic state of consciousness" described by cultural anthropologists, and the "enlightenment experience" of the Buddha. Jewish thought and history includes such phenomena as the "throne mysticism" of a mystical tradition preceding the time of Jesus, the "call visions" of the classical prophets, the "other-worldly journey experiences" lying behind at least some of the apocalypses, a nature mysticism which seems to lie behind characterizations of the world as "filled with the glory of God" (radiant presence), and the reported trance-like state of some Jewish healers of Jesus' time.

All of these forms of ecstasy share an experienced sense of "the sacred," of "what is," of "the ultimate," of "the way things really are." For ecstatics – those with intense or frequent episodes of this sense – "the sacred" is not an article of belief, but an element of experience.

Such people know God. This statement, provocative and possibly problematic, leads to a final comment about ecstatic religious experience. Scholars studying the phenomenon report that persons having such experiences consistently describe them as a state of knowing, not just as a state of feeling. William James spoke of such experiences as having a *noetic* quality: not just feelings of joy and ecstasy, but a cognitive sense of *knowing* something one didn't know before. Abraham Maslow identified the same quality as "B-cognition," a somewhat unhappy term, sounding like a class of cognition inferior to some first-class "A-cognition." Peak experiences, according to Maslow are not only affective "highs" but include a strong sense of knowing. What is known is Being-itself; "B-cognition" thus means "cognition of Being". Whatever the terminology, the point is the same: for ecstatics, the experience of "the sacred" carries with it a vivid sense of epiphany – a strong subjective sense that what one has experienced is indeed a disclosure of reality.

For ecstatics, religious conviction is not the result of strong belief in "secondhand religion" (William James' term for religious beliefs one learns about from others). Cognition is the product of firsthand religious experience. Ecstatics are those who can say, as did Job at the climax of his divine epiphany, "I had heard of thee by the hearing of the ear, *but now my eye beholds thee.*" (Job 42:5). God becomes an experiential reality, and it is in this sense that an ecstatic knows God.

Jesus seems to have been one of these ecstatics. He was a Jewish mystic. The conclusion seems inescapable when one realizes that there really are people who have experiences like these; that the Jewish tradition has many such figures at its center (including the patriarchs, Moses, Elijah, the classical prophets, and others); and that so much in the gospels points to his being a Jewish ecstatic: the language of "Spirit," the tradition that Jesus had visions, the reports of him engaging in long hours of prayer (best understood as meditation or contemplation), and his healings (about which I will soon speak). Moreover, such experience seems the best explanation of what else we see in the traditions about Jesus: the foundation of his subversive wisdom, the ground of his passion and courage as a social prophet, and the source of his radical social vision.

I do not think we know enough to be specific about the kinds of ecstatic religious experiences Jesus had. I have hunches, though I cannot fully support them. I think he was a "religious quester," which seems the best explanation of his going to the wilderness to John the Baptizer. I think he had visions, though I don't know whether we have an account of any of them. (I am prepared to see the baptismal and wilderness ordeal visions as community products, yet one can make a reasonable case that at least the former reflects an experience). I have a hunch that he had experiences of nature mysticism (like Heschel's "radical amazement"); this would be consistent with his sense of the immediate presence of God. Such experiences seem to be reflected in a number of sayings, including the great line from the gospel of Thomas which speaks of the Kingdom of God as spread out upon the earth, only people do not see it (Thomas 113); we, in our ordinary state of consciousness, do not see that reality even though it is *here*. I suspect that Jesus had an experiential sense of the reality of God in his prayer life, which I assume included some form of meditation.

As mentioned earlier, I have emphasized Jesus' ecstatic religious type because it seems foundational to what else is in the traditions about him, as healer, wisdom teacher, social prophet, and movement initiator.

Healer

Some ecstatics become healers. Though I know of no estimates from studies, it would seem that only a very small percentage do. Many ecstatics are "simply" visionaries, or mystics, or prophets. But some become healers, a religious type known across cultures in both ancient and modern times. We know of many such persons near the time of Jesus, both in the broader Mediterranean world and within Judaism, perhaps the best-known of whom was Haninah ben Dosa.

Within this cross-cultural framework of ecstatic healers, I am persuaded that the gospel traditions about Jesus as healer and exorcist reflect historical happenings. I do not think he did any of what are often called "the nature miracles," but I think he effected healings that struck people as remarkable, and performed what both he and his contemporaries experienced as exorcisms. It seems likely to me that one reason he attracted attention and a following was his reputation as a healer.

Let us further clarify: drawing from the work of medical anthropologists, some scholars make a strong distinction between healing illness and curing disease. Illness, it is argued, is the social meaning placed upon a physical condition, while disease refers to the organic condition itself. Healing pertains only to removing the social meaning (and thus social consequences) of illness.

So, one might then ask, "Did Jesus simply heal illness, or did he also cure disease?" Whatever complexity of psychosomatic relationships might be involved (I am not inclined to engage in psychosomatic "reductionism"), I think he did both. Not only does the gospel tradition indicate that, but it is difficult to imagine that simply healing illness (without organic, physical cure) could have made much of an impression within a peasant milieu.

Wisdom teacher

The forms and contents of his teaching indicate that Jesus was a wisdom teacher. As an oral teacher, he most frequently spoke in parables and aphorisms. Both are wisdom forms of speech: parables are short stories, and aphorisms are "great one-liners." Both forms of teaching are not only memorable, but invitational: they invite a new way of seeing very different from acculturated ways of seeing. Content is integrated with this invitational form. The content of Jesus' wisdom subverts conventional wisdom, and is an invitation to an alternative way or path, which may be spoken of as the eye of the needle, the narrow way, the road less travelled.

It seems likely that an enlightenment experience was the source of the transformed way of seeing reflected in Jesus' alternative wisdom. An enlightenment experience is a particular kind of mystical or peak experience in which the cognitive aspect is especially strong. Combining such mundane factors as the personality type of the recipient with his or her natural intelligence and gifts and modes of expression, we get an enlightened teacher. Such was Jesus, and in this respect he was like Lao Tzu, the Buddha, and Socrates.

Social prophet

Here the model for the religious type comes from the social prophets of the Jewish tradition, especially Elijah, Amos, Hosea, Micah, Isaiah of Jerusalem, and Jeremiah. They were all ecstatics with a vivid experiential sense of the reality of God, and they all passionately criticized the urban ruling elites who exploited an oppressed peasantry and at the same time legitimated their place in society with religious ideology and ritual.

The model of a peasant or pre-industrial agrarian society mentioned earlier is crucial for seeing this. This type of society lasted in ancient Israel from the rise of the monarchy in the tenth century b.c.e. through and beyond the time of Jesus; the only significant change was the addition of foreign ruling elites to native ones. In the time of Jesus, the peasant society was structured as a purity system or a "politics of purity," which was the ideology of the ruling elites; in that sense it was the "dominant consciousness" of his social world. The society was manifestly oppressive. The governing class, the top one percent of the population, received about fifty percent of the wealth. The top ten percent (the governing class plus retainers and merchants) received about two-thirds. The remaining ninety percent (mostly peasants) produced most of the wealth, yet retained, due to taxation and land ownership by the elites, only about one-third of their production.

As a social prophet, Jesus was an ecstatic who championed the cause of the poor and indicted the urban ruling elites. We see this in his use of prophetic forms of speech: the lament, the threat oracle, the woes, aphoristic indictments, and parables with a socio-political edge (so that one may even speak of "indictment parables"). We see this also in the content of his indictments: they are directed against wealth, religious ideology, the purity system, hierarchy and patriarchy, the temple and Jerusalem itself – not as the center of Judaism, but as the center of the urban ruling elites, who were also the temple and purity elites.

Indeed, the most plausible understanding of Jesus' arrest and execution is that he was perceived as troublesome by the elites. It was not "the Jews" or "the Jewish people" who rejected Jesus; rather, it was some of the Jewish aristocratic elite, who are more accurately seen as oppressors, not representatives, of the Jewish people.

Movement catalyzer

Choosing "movement catalyzer" rather than "movement founder," I hedge my language a bit. In previous publications, I spoke of Jesus as a movement founder. By that, I meant to emphasize a negative point: he was not the founder of Christianity (in the sense that he intended to generate a new religion) but was the founder of a Jewish movement whose purpose was a social and religious transformation within Judaism.

I continue to think this negative point is important, but I am no longer sure it is useful to speak of him as "founding a movement" during his life time. I doubt that there was a moment when Jesus said or thought, in effect, "I hereby establish a movement." Moreover, his public activity was very brief; and there was no institutionalization (the creation of leadership structures, community rules or boundaries, etc.) until quite some time after his death.

Speaking of Jesus as a movement catalyzer means two things. First, I do not think his vision was individualistic; rather, I think his teachings and actions contain an alternative social vision, not just social criticism. Secondly, I think that during his lifetime there was already an embodiment of this social vision in his characteristic actions and in the company of those who took him seriously. This is especially so in his meal practice – what John Dominic Crossan calls his "open commensality" and what I and others have called his inclusive table fellowship. His social vision is seen too in his subversion of the sharp social boundaries created by purity and patriarchy, and in the centrality given to compassion as the core value of a life lived in faithfulness to God: "Be compassionate as God is compassionate." By speaking of him as a movement catalyzer, I am affirming that his social vision was not a discarnate ideal, but was already, in embryo, incarnate in his following during his lifetime.

It seems likely that Jesus' alternative social vision also came out of his ecstatic experience. There is a kind of ecstatic experience that radically minimizes cultural distinctions by disclosing their artificial character: the distinctions are a humanly created grid imposed on reality, and not an order built into reality itself (that is, not decreed by God). Yet on another level, those distinctions do matter, for they are one of the central causes of human suffering throughout history. Because their artificial character is apparent, they are even more intolerable. Almost (but not quite) paradoxically, these distinctions are relativized even as they become the target of passionate indictment and compassionate creation of an alternative vision.

Finally, further to characterize this sketch of Jesus, he was non-apocalyptic. Jesus did not expect an imminent divine intervention in which the objective state of affairs would change so dramatically that everybody would have to say, "Yes, the Kingdom of God (or the Messianic Age) has arrived." I intend this characterization of apocalyptic eschatology to be sufficiently broad to include the scholarly tradition running from Johannes Weiss and Albert Schweitzer at the beginning of this century through Rudolf Bultmann and Gunther Bornkamm in the middle third of this century to E. P Sanders in the present. This is not what Jesus expected. To think that he could have held such a dogmatic and literalistic view of the future when he had such an enlightened view of the present is difficult for me to imagine. Perhaps I don't want to believe that Jesus was a proclaimer of "The end is coming soon!" But more than that, I find it hard to believe that such eschatological literalism could be part of the consciousness of an enlightened one.

My five stroke sketch of the pre-Easter Jesus is complete. With the appropriate expansions, I would be willing to reduce it to a three stroke sketch. He was an enlightened one, by which I mean a teacher of an enlightened wisdom whose source was ecstatic experience; a healer whose powers were similarly grounded in ecstatic experience; and a social visionary who saw both that the source of much of human misery lies in exploitation and the solution is a vision of human community grounded in the inclusive compassion of God.

Gender and Class in the Teaching of Jesus
A Profile

Kathleen E. Corley

Certain scholars explain the presence of women followers in Jesus' retinue on the basis of his teaching of the Kingdom of God: Jesus' message would have been clearly understood as an explicit challenge to the patriarchal bias of his culture. Elisabeth Schüssler Fiorenza calls this aspect of his message a "critical feminist impulse that came to the fore in the vision and ministry of Jesus."[1] Both John Dominic Crossan and Marcus Borg see Jesus' message of the Kingdom similarly and cite his "radical egalitarianism" in the midst of a culture that devalued both women and the poor peasant underclass.[2] Yet little in the sayings generally considered authentic merits such elaborate claims insofar as women are concerned. Although his teaching demonstrates a clear awareness of poverty and a critique of class inequity in ancient Palestine, it does not show an equivalent critique of patriarchy, nor a similar interest in gender concerns. Thus, although there is reason to describe aspects of his message concerning the Kingdom of God as "egalitarian," this egalitarianism does not extend to the concerns of women, nor was it aimed at a clear social program geared towards major social change for women.

Women in the parables of Jesus

The parables of Jesus have long vexed New Testament scholars. Only recently freed from centuries of misleading allegorical interpretations, the parables continue to attract the attention of many serious commentators, and books on the subject have become legion. Most scholars now agree that the parables were not intended to be complex allegories containing several points of reference, but are stories that create their own narrative world. The allegorization of Jesus' parables began early in Christian tradition, a tendency that can be seen in Mark's version of the parable of the Sower (Mark 4:3–20) or Matthew's version of the parable of the Banquet (Matt 22:1–14). Other parables went through a process of alteration either in oral retelling or in written redaction. In spite of this, the parables remain the bedrock of historical information concerning Jesus, as well as the defining center of his proclamation of the Kingdom of God.

Since the parables use images drawn from everyday Palestinian life, women and women's activities occasionally figure as the point of comparison to the Kingdom of God. This leads certain scholars to posit an anti-patriarchal or egalitarian ethic for Jesus' teachings overall. Upon closer analysis, however, the images and roles of women in Jesus' parables are unexceptional. Stories involving women simply reflect the presence of women in Jesus' social environment; they are told to make points about the Kingdom of God, not the status of women. Activities such as kneading bread, carrying grain jars, sweeping floors, and grinding meal not only reflect traditional roles of women in ancient society, but their juxtaposition in the gospels over against typical male roles such as planting seeds, shepherding sheep, parenting sons, and reclining on couches for meals reinforces gender roles rather than challenges them. This arrangement of parables in gendered pairs is arguably secondary to the tradition and reflects either the legal interests of a document like Q, or simply the tendency in that social environment towards a gendered division of labor among peasants and the lower classes. Such images reflect everyday situations from ancient Palestine and force the hearer to active thought concerning either the Kingdom of God or the situation described in the story itself.

Recent feminist analysis has drawn attention to the feminine imagery of Jesus' parables, which can be viewed in either a positive or negative light. However, in spite of the tendency among certain feminist scholars to characterize Jesus' overall teaching as anti-patriarchal, the evidence of the parables reveals that Jesus was part of the patriarchal society in which he lived and that he evinced similar patriarchal biases. For example, as Nicola Slee has pointed out, among Jesus' parables and sayings in the Synoptic gospels, of the 104 in Matthew, 47 involve human actors, with 85 characters in all. Of the 85, 73 are men and 12 are women – 5 of whom are foolish maidens. In the 94 parables and sayings in Luke, 51 concern human actors, with 108 characters. Of those 108, 99 are men and 9 are women. Slee is right to caution that the predominance of male characters in Jesus' parables and sayings by itself suggests that Jesus, like other speakers and writers of his day, was by nature predisposed to re-imagine in his narratives a world dominated by men and their concerns and shows little interest for women and women's concerns.[3] There are in fact only five parables now arguably considered authentic which utilize images of women: the Leaven (Matt 13:3/Luke 13:20–21/Thomas 96), the Lost Coin (Luke 15:8–9), the Empty Jar (Thomas 97), the Unjust Judge (Luke 18:2–8) and the Prodigal Son (Luke 15:11–32). And of these only four focus upon actions of women, since in the last case women are mentioned only briefly as the prostitutes upon whom the Prodigal Son squanders his money (Luke 15:20). Indeed, the Empty Jar from the Gospel of Thomas has only recently been considered in these discussions – a fact which reflects the increasing tendency to include evidence for Jesus' teachings from Thomas as equally significant for reconstructions of the historical Jesus.

In spite of the presence of images of women in these parables, it is difficult to argue that the first three demonstrate any subversion of gender roles. Rather, the parables of the Leaven, the Lost Coin and the Empty Jar underscore common gendered roles from antiquity by creating images of women engaged in everyday activities. Further, the feminine activities described in these parables are not themselves referents for the Kingdom of God.

The parable of the Leaven is assuredly an authentic parable of Jesus. Since Thomas has introduced a contrast of the small amount of the leaven with the large size of the leavened loaves (Thomas 96), the version found in Luke 13:20–21/Matt 13:33 (Q) is arguably the earliest. The original parable thus compares the Kingdom of God (or Heaven) to leaven which a woman takes and hides in a very large amount of flour until the leaven spreads throughout. The use of "to hide" is surprising in combination with leaven. The verb "to knead" is more to be expected (cf. Hos 7:4, LXX). Scholars have suggested various interpretations of the parable by emphasizing the smallness of the beginnings of the Kingdom in contrast to its later size, the mysterious nature of the Kingdom's growth, the reversal of expectations of the nature of the God's reign, the culmination of the Kingdom of God in Jesus' ministry, or the domestic work of women as an example of the activity of God. In any case, however, the parable clearly highlights the images of the leaven and the meal as the point of comparison for the reign of God, rather than the woman herself. Thus, even though the image is one of women's domestic work, the focus is still the leavening, not the woman. Since leaven was regarded in Judaism as a symbol of corruption (Exod 12:15; Mark 8:15; 1 Cor 5:7), Jesus' comparison of leaven to God's Kingdom is very provocative. Indeed he quite reverses the expectations of his hearers. What appears to be the activity of corruption – the overproduction of leavened bread – is essential and characteristic of divine activity, the reign of God. Thus, the parable turns not on the fact that this is a woman's activity, but rather on the unexpected comparison of leaven to God's activity – a possible allusion to the presence of lower classes and outcasts in Jesus' close circle of followers.

The Lost Coin (Luke 15:8–10) contains what may be a similar story of domestic incompetence followed by the surprising joy of rediscovery. A woman loses one drachma of the ten she has, searches for it, and upon its rediscovery rejoices with her women neighbors. This parable is coupled in Luke with the parable of the Lost Sheep and followed by the parable of the Prodigal Son. In Luke the parable concerns the joy in heaven over human repentance, an interpretation that is widely considered secondary. The image is again unexpected. A woman searches diligently for something that on the face of it is of limited intrinsic value. A drachma was a Greek silver coin equal in worth to a denarius, which was a day's pay for a male fieldhand. Of course the drachma may be worth considerably more to her, since women workers made barely half as much as men for the same amount of manual labor. The single drachma is thus enough for roughly two days of subsistence level support for one person. Some interpreters have proposed that the money was part of the woman's dowry, but nothing in the text suggests this. And given Luke's context and interpretation, it is difficult to consider the woman a feminine image for God or Jesus. As Dominic Crossan has said, there is no tradition comparable to John 10:11, "I am the good shepherd," declaring "I am the good housewife."[4] Still, such a reading remains popular, essentially following the Lukan interpretation in which the shepherd, the woman and the father all represent images of insistent divine activity. Apart from its Lukan context, however, this parable further associates the reign of God with the unexpected. What appears to be of little value is highly prized, and the kingdom is again associated with the poor, and one might add, the incompetent.

The parable of the Empty Jar contains yet another image of womanly inattention or incompetence (Thomas 97). The Kingdom of "the Father" is compared to a woman carrying a full jar of meal:

Jesus said: The [father's] kingdom is like a woman who was carrying a [jar] full of meal . While she was walking along

[a] distant road, the handle of the jar broke and the meal spilled behind her [along] the road. She did not know it; she had not noticed a problem. When she reached her house, she put the jar down and discovered that it was empty.[5]

In the gospel of Thomas, the Empty Jar is set between the parables of the Leaven (Thomas 96) and the Assassin (Thomas 98). The image of the woman is also one of domesticity and failure. Although hardly a clear image of uncleanness simply due to her femaleness, the woman does not notice when her jar is broken and thus loses all of her grain, the basice means of subsistence for the poor in antiquity. The tension inherent in this story is underscored by a well known parallel in the Hebrew Bible, the story of the widow of Zarephath (1 Kgs 17:8–16). In a time of famine Elijah is told to go to the widow of Zarephath who has been commanded to feed him. When Elijah finds her, she tells him that she has nothing prepared and only a small amount of meal and oil. Miraculously, the grain in her jar does not run out and she, her child and Elijah subsist on cakes baked from her supplies for many days. Thus, the Empty Jar parable reverses the story of the Elijah and the widow Zarephath. No prophet comes to the woman's aid; her jar remains empty. Once again, expectations for the reign of God are reversed. The images of women in these three parables are hardly complimentary. One loses a coin worth two days sustenance, another spills her grain without noticing it, another overproduces bread; the point of the parable is made at each woman's expense.

The final authentic parable which employs the image of a woman is usually called the Unjust Judge (Luke 18:2–8). Although occasionally named after the widow in the story, the main character in the story is the man. In this engaging story, a woman receives justice at court, not because her cause is just, nor because the judge she approaches is just, but because she is persistent to the point of threatening the judge with a black eye ("she will wear me out," lit. "give me a black eye" or "bruise". The image is striking to the point of being humorous. The contrast between the social and economic circumstances of the two characters in the story is stark: the judge would be a member of the urban elite, the woman of the urban poor. Further, in a long history of Jewish tradition, widows belonged to a category of persons who needed special protection from God: "widows, orphans and foreigners." Israelites were commanded to protect these classes. Just as God protected the Israelites while they were in bondage in Egypt, so he is the patron of the most needy of the Israelite community. Indeed, the treatment of widows, orphans and foreigners amounted to a gauge for determining the faithfulness of the Jewish people.

Many commentators see the parable in terms of an analogy between the judge and God: if a widow can get justice from an unjust judge, how much more likely will God respond to persistent prayer? Luke's appended interpretation encourages this reading (Luke 18:6–8), but is probably secondary. Read without this Lukan interpretation, the parable takes on a quite different meaning. The emphasis falls upon the woman's unflagging insistence for vindication, not upon the action of the judge whose motive is self interest. The parable thus portrays a disadvantaged widow gaining justice by her own means, without reliance upon God. It might fittingly be likened to Luke's parable of the Unjust Steward (Luke 16:1–8), in that the overwhelmingly aggressive and even insubordinate behavior the widow achieves her intended result. Her actions border upon harassment. Jesus' description of this woman, although hardly complimentary, is in marked contrast to the images of domestic failure in the parables of the Leaven, the Lost Coin, and the Empty Jar. Such a story surely reinforces shrewd, calculated and resistant behavior on the part of the oppressed and is not merely a metaphor for the continuation of the kingdom. Still, since the internal monologue is that of the judge, the story reflects not the woman's perspective, but the man's.

Open commensality and the Parable of the Feast

Insofar as gender issues and women are concerned, the above parables do not substantiate modern feminist claims for Jesus. Rather, they suggest a male-centered outlook that tends to portray women characters in less than complimentary ways. Nor do these parables focus on the acceptance of women as women into the kingdom, but rather on their status as members of a larger class of outcasts whose acceptability as God's children underscores the unexpected nature of the reign of God. One parable, however, when read in conjunction with the tradition that Jesus welcomed "tax collectors and sinners" to his table does seem to suggest the invitation of women to the Kingdom of God, and that is the parable of the Feast (Matt 22:2–13; Luke 14:16–24). Here the theme of the unexpected nature of the Kingdom of God has its clearest expression. In this parable Jesus overturns ancient social paradigms of honor and wealth in a depiction of a Feast for the lowly and the derelict, rather than one for the customary guests of rank and privilege. Borg, Crossan, and Schüssler

Fiorenza all focus on the message of the parable of the Feast and Jesus' table practice as a sign of his egalitarian ethic.[6] Both Borg and Schüssler Fiorenza see Jesus as opening up the banquet of the Kingdom to the unclean: Jesus overturns purity regulations by eating with women.[7] Dominic Crossan and Luise Schottroff see Jesus' egalitarianism as reflective of a peasant mentality or a consequence of impoverishment. Jesus' parable of the Feast thus portrays the Kingdom of God as a large inclusive meal to which are invited people from all levels of society, including women (Luke 14:16–24; Matt 22:1–14; Thom 64:1–12).[8]

Such arguments require some nuance. First, the argument that Jesus here challenges purity regulations is unlikely since, as was note earlier, Jews may not have been overly concerned with purity outside of the Temple, and because Rabbinic sources emphasizing purity issues post-date the New Testament. Recent reconstructions of the Qumran community suggest that even the purity-conscious sectarians at Qumran could have allowed women to join certain ritual meals. Thus concern over Jesus' table practice is more likely to have been a matter of propriety than purity. Second, the point of the parable of the Feast does not hinge on the issue of gender, but on that of class or rank. Any application of the parable to the situation of women would therefore have been strictly secondary. One could argue that women are invited as those among the poor, the sick, and the street people, but the point of the parable is not to invite *women* to the Feast, but the underclasses. Jesus here does not defend the right of women to join him at table. Given the strong likelihood that Greco-Roman culture pervaded Palestine, and with it the customary presence of women at meals with men, it seems more plausible that inclusion of women at Jesus' meals reflects progressive (although controversial) cultural practices found throughout Greco-Roman society and in Hellenistic Judaism, rather than a peasant egalitarian ideology or Sophia-inspired prophetic vision.

In fact, later gospel portrayals of Jesus at meals do not show him taking a particularly radical stance. For example, in the story of his meal with Mary and Martha (Luke 10:38–42), Jesus does encourage Mary, who is seated at his feet. However, although such a position does indicate that Mary is receiving instruction, her posture reflects a more conservative, matronly role, and she remains silent throughout the scene. The more radical stance would have been to invite Mary to recline with him like an equal on a banquet couch, as Jesus does with Salome in the Gospel of Thomas (Thomas 61). In these Lukan stories Jesus does not appear radical in his relationships with women; it is the women who are bold, not Jesus.

In order to derive from the Feast parable an egalitarian meaning, it must be read in conjunction with one other piece of evidence from the

Jesus tradition, the accusation that Jesus dined with "tax collectors and sinners" (Mark 2:15; Q 7:34). This accusation reflects typical characterizations of those known for banqueting with tax collectors, pimps and prostitutes. The very imagery of disreputable banquet behavior calls to mind the presence of lewd women, slaves, and courtesans – the kind of women present in a typical Hellenistic banquet scene. This accusation should thus be seen as a standard charge of Hellenistic rhetoric, and not necessarily indicative of the occupations or morals of Jesus' actual table companions. Both Mark and Q imply that Jesus is eating with women, and thus a participant in the social progressivisim of his day.[9] Again, however, the force of this tradition maintains between Jesus and his dining companions a distinction that remains one of class, not necessarily sex-differentiation. Jesus is here accused of dining with those who are beneath his station. Dennis E. Smith writes:

> The strongest evidence for the open commensality theme in the Jesus tradition is the theme that Jesus dined with tax collectors and sinners. Yet, this theme only works best if Jesus is not of the same social level with tax collectors and sinners. If all parties involved, including Jesus, are peasants, then the motif fails, for there is no experience of social stratification at table.[10]

If Jesus or all of his followers are of the same low social class, then the force of the insult leveled against him is lost. Smith argues that John Dominic Crossan, although having made a good case for an egalitarian table ethic in Jesus' movement, undercuts his proposition by turning Jesus into a peasant.[11] Still, it is possible to maintain a lower social location for Jesus as long as it is recognized that there would have been those even beneath his social station in ancient Palestine, particularly slaves. The Feast parable would then reflect Jesus' resistance to authority on behalf of those beneath his station, including perhaps women of the lower classes, even though they are not the focus of the Feast parable proper.

That said, it is still possible to identify one tradition considered by some scholars both early and authentic, that suggests Jesus himself defended the presence of women among his followers by deflecting slander leveled against them. Probably going back in some form to Q[12] is the statement of Jesus that links women to both his movement and to John the Baptist's:

> Truly I say to you, the tax collectors and the harlots go into the kingdom of God before you. For John came to you in righteousness, and you did not believe him, but the tax col-

lectors and the harlots believed him; and even when you saw it, you did not afterward repent and believe him (Matt 21:31b–32; RSV).

Here Jesus calls the women entering the Kingdom of God "whores." As I have suggested, taken as a repeated form of slander leveled against Jesus and his table companions, rather than as a social description of some of his followers, this would indicate that he was well aware of the controversial nature of his group, including the presence of women. He accepted the label of the women around him as "whores," possibly in bitter jest, even as the basis of a bitingly sarcastic riposte. His opponents accused him of consorting with "tax collectors and whores," but those so labeled will enter the Kingdom of God first. To claim an insult robs it of its power. Of course, Jesus' use of snide humor implies discomfort as well as acceptance. By using the gender stereotypical label of "whores" for the women in his group, Jesus identifies the underlying cause of the tension aroused by the presence of women among his followers – their difference. So employed, humor seeks to relieve tension through laughter, while at the same time serving to incorporate women in a predominantly male group. In sum, this saying does not identify the women in Jesus' group as actual prostitutes, but merely repeats a slander leveled against women whose bad reputations are due either to their socially progressive behavior, or to their low social status. That Jesus could have expressed his discomfort with the presence of women in his company by means of snide humor suggests either the resistant attitude of lower class peasants, or a wit informed by the currents of Greco-Roman philosophy present in first century Palestine, or both.

Thus, the parable of the Feast in combination with the typical characterization of his dining companions as "tax collectors, sinners and whores," suggests that Jesus' teaching on open commensality was inclusive of women and those beneath Jesus' station, such as domestic servants and slaves. Yet the critique of Greco-Roman ideals of rank and privilege (and by extension the system of slavery) remains central to the Feast parable and this theme can be shown to be far more significant than gender within Jesus' overall message.

Slavery, ethics and the Kingdom of God

Although obscured in most translations due to the use of terms like "servant" and "steward," slave imagery abounds within the parables and sayings of Jesus far more than feminine imagery. For example, Jesus' parables use terms like "slave" (Matt 18:23; Luke 14:17; Matt 21:34/Luke

20:10; cf. Thomas 65; Luke 19:13/Matt 25:14), "steward" (Luke 16:1), as well as "vinedresser" or "gardener" (Luke 13:7), "tenant" (Matt 21:34/Luke 20:10; cf. Thomas 65), "worker" (Matt 20:1), and "hired laborer" (Luke 15:17). Josephus makes clear references to servants who are real slaves, not simply hired laborers, and he does not distinguish between Jewish slaves and non-Jewish slaves – both are slaves.[13] Although not as crucial to the economy as elsewhere in the Roman empire, the presence of slaves as workers, especially as domestic workers or even debt slaves should be assumed for first century Palestine. The use of tenant farmers and sharecroppers was more common, but slaves were used in both agricultural contexts and in the trades. The so-called "Servant" parables of Jesus and several of his sayings are thus better understood within the context of the institution of Greco-Roman slavery. As Crossan has pointed out, a total of nine parables from the gospels have servants as central characters and involve a "master-servant relationship and a moment of critical reckoning therein."[14] Two parables usually considered authentic illustrate Jesus' attitude toward slaves and the servant/master relationship: the parable of the Dishonest Steward (Luke 16:1–8) and the Unmerciful Slave (Matt 18:23–24).

The parable of the Dishonest Steward continues to puzzle commentators. In this story the manager of a rich man's estate is dismissed for supposed financial mismanagement. Following his dismissal, the steward calls in his master's debtors and reduces the amount of their debts to his employer with the understanding that in return they will care for him in his time of need. He is subsequently praised by his master for his shrewdness. The original parable probably ended at this point (16:8a), as the lord here easily refers back to the lord in vv. 3 and 5. The three appended explanations to the parable in Luke demonstrate the difficulties of its interpretation even in antiquity. In past years many scholars saw the meaning of the parable centered on the prudent behavior of the steward during a time of crisis, a course of action analogous to the appropriate response to the preaching of the Kingdom. More recent scholars have questioned an apocalyptic interpretation, and rightly refocus upon the social word evoked in the parable itself. The audience of the parable would have assumed that the steward was a slave or freedman. The steward is dismissed from his post, and faces the prospect of hard manual labor (Luke 16:3). In quick response, the steward acts to protect his own interests. The difficulty of interpretation lies in the master's praise for a servant, who has in effect twice defrauded him of large amounts of money.

Mary Ann Beavis has proposed that the best context in which to understand the steward is in his resemblance to Aesop the crafty, trickster slave of the *Life of Aesop*.[15] In episode after episode, this Greco-Roman picaresque hero finds himself in similar crises, in trouble with his master or mistress, takes quick action to protect himself – usually by means of his quick wit, and subsequently gets the better of his superiors. Seen against this backdrop, the story of the Dishonest Steward would be both funny and familiar. The steward is in trouble with his master, he acts to remedy the situation behind his master's back, and then succeeds and receives the praise of his master for doing so. The charges leveled against the steward may be exaggerated, as a character like Aesop is often quickly punished on the basis of false accusations without the opportunity to defend himself. In any case, the sympathy of the hearers of this parable, especially those from the lower classes, would have been with the steward and the other debtors, not the master. The story thus has a subversive function, in that it praises the self-interested, resistant actions of a slave or freedman steward, whose actions help him survive in economically threatening circumstances. Neither the institution of slavery nor economic exploitation is directly challenged; rather the survivalist actions of the steward are praised.

The parable of the Unmerciful Servant (Matt 18:23–35) is found only in Matthew's gospel where it concludes the discourse on community discipline. As Matthew presents it, the parable concerns the nature of the Kingdom of Heaven, the mutual forgiveness required in the community, and the subsequent judgment in light of moral failure. Interpreters have generally argued that the connective "therefore" and introductory formula "the kingdom of Heaven is like" (v. 23a) are Matthean, as is the final reference to judgment at the end of the parable proper (v. 35).

The story hinges on the intricate relationships between patrons and their clients among the upper classes. The servant in this case is clearly a slave (v. 23) as is demonstrated by the king's ability to sell not only the servant, but his wife and children (v. 25). His entire family is owned by the king, although this particular slave has obviously risen to a high level within the court bureaucracy. The forgiveness of the slave's unimaginably large debt by the king is the most surprising feature of the story (v. 27), as one would expect the king to keep the debt in place as a means to exert control over his well-placed underling. For this reason Herzog's suggestion that the king's action is meant to recall the messianic jubilee has merit. However, it is clear from the story that the actions of a king are not sufficient to initiate the jubilee; persons within each level of the bureaucracy must also be willing to forgive the debts owed to them. As Jeremias has suggested, the story is thus a negative example of discipleship[16] and its message comports with Jesus' exhortation to pray for mutual forgiveness of debts (Matt 6:12; Luke 11:4a–b). High levels of indebtedness led inexorably to increased enslavements of the lower classes, who could be forced to sell themselves or their children in order to meet the terms of outstanding loans. The parable of the Unmerciful Servant thus suggests to Jesus' hearers the surprising solution of the forgiveness of debts, even those among the lower classes, who should not merely wait for a coming messianic jubilee.

Since other servant parables attributed to Jesus are less unsettling in their implications, gospel traditions that attempt to reverse the implications of these parables by picturing slaves behaving in expected and obedient ways are thus rendered historically suspect. In later traditions slaves watch eagerly for their returning master (Mark 13:34–27), are punished accordingly for good or bad behavior (by dismemberment Matt 24:45–51/Luke 12:42–46), and should not expect their master to wait upon them upon his return (Luke 17:7–10). Moreover, it must be explicitly stated at a later point that slaves are not above their masters (Matt 10:24; John 13:16). This trajectory in the gospel tradition suggests that later gospel writers needed to temper Jesus' authentic teachings in order to deflect the controversial nature of earlier traditions concerning slavery and slave/master relations.

In light of Jesus' interest in his parables to challenge his hearers to consider slave/master relations, I would like to introduce into this discussion two traditions that have gone unnoticed for their probable significance for Jesus' social interests: the welcoming of "children" into the Kingdom of God (Mark 10:14/Matt 19:14/Luke 18:16) and the cryptic reference to those who make themselves eunuchs for the Kingdom (Matt 19:12). Both suggest Jesus maintained a subversive attitude towards slavery. In Mark 10:14–15 Jesus says,

> Let the children *(paidia)* come to me, do not hinder them; for to such belongs the kingdom of God. Truly I say to you whoever does not receive the kingdom of God like a child *(paidion)* will not enter it.

Virtually all commentators assume that Jesus here refers to children, and refer at some length to the low familial and social status of children in antiquity. Children are those last who shall be first (Matt

20:16; cf. Mark 10:31; Matt 19:30; Luke 13:30; Thomas 4). However, children were not the lowest in prestige in ancient society unless they were slaves. Further, free children were not marginalized in antiquity, and were involved in many rites and festivals of public and private life. Indeed, in Mark servitude is the model for discipleship, not childhood. Mark clearly identifies the "last" in prestige as slaves or servants. Whoever would be first must become the slave of all (Mark 10:44); whoever would be first must be last and servant of all (Mark 9:35). In light of these observations, the saying probably has a quite different meaning, especially in Mark. The cognates *pais* and *paidion* have another meaning that goes unnoticed here. Both can mean slave or young slave, and can include boys, girls and handsome young men. This meaning is well attested in both Hellenistic literature, including Josephus and Philo,[17] and in papyri contemporary with the New Testament.[18] It is eminently reasonable, then, to propose that Jesus' hearers are told to identify themselves with the enslaved or those in positions of servitude. In fact, the reign of God belongs especially to them. Given that according to Mark Jesus is scolded by his disciples for blessing *paidia* brought to him (Mark 10:13), Jesus' saying makes more sense if it refers to slaves, not children. Surely the statement that young slaves were of God's kingdom would have been met with surprise or even shock by his hearers, especially the free, even if they were poor. Any who had been forced to sell children into servitude, however, would have appreciated Jesus' subversive speech.

The Eunuch saying carries this admonition to an even further extreme (Matt 19:12a). One of the most difficult of Jesus' sayings, it is probably authentic. Since it can be easily detached from its Matthean setting, it probably circulated separately from the discussion concerning divorce (Matt 19:4–10). It is usually assumed that the reference here is to a celibate lifestyle, a recommendation which would have been hard to accept. However, eunuchs were not necessarily celibate, merely sterile. In fact, eunuchs were often castrated as young boys in order to maintain their appeal as sex objects. Hence, I would like to suggest an alternative interpretation. Not only were eunuchs in a category segregated and devalued in Jewish life but virtually all eunuchs were slaves or freedmen, having been cruelly emasculated before puberty. Although like all slaves eunuchs could rise within estate and royal bureaucracies, they were still the objects of derision and scorn. Thus in a clear use of hyperbole, Jesus declares that some will "castrate themselves for the sake of the kingdom of heaven" (Matt 19:12) – i.e., they will become like slaves. What could this mean? I would like to suggest that it be understood in light of the kind of self-sacrifice recommended in 1 Clement:

> We know that many among ourselves have given themselves
> to bondage that they might ransom others. Many have
> delivered themselves to slavery, and provided food for oth-
> ers with the price they received for themselves.[19]

This would place this saying well within the context of other ethical statements of Jesus found in other well known sayings: lend without
interest (Thom 95:1–2/ Matt 5:42b; Luke 6:34–35), always give to beggars (Matt 5:42/Luke 6:30), offer the other cheek, give the shirt off your
back, walk that extra mile (Matt 5:39–41) and sell all you have and give
to the poor (Mark 10:21). The first shall be last and the last shall be first
(Matt 20:16; cf. Mark 10:31; Matt 19:30; Luke 13:30; Thomas 4); whoever would be first must become the slave of all (Mark 10:44); whoever
would be first must be last and servant of all (Mark 9:35). Jesus' could
be espousing either a radical Hebrew ideal of charity or a Hellenistic
philosophical ethic. The social environment of Palestine and the Galilee
allows for both. Thus, both the Eunuch and the Young Slave sayings are
highlighted by a saturnalian inversion of rank, and encourage this behavior as an ongoing altruistic ethic in the Kingdom of God. Mark interprets Jesus' ideal of service in terms of his suffering and death, an ideal
which the Markan community should emulate during times of persecu-
tion (Mark 10:45) and in positions of leadership (Mark 10:35–45). John
portrays Jesus as actually performing the service of a slave by washing
the disciples' feet at a meal (John 13:1–20).

Conflicts in the family

Such teachings inevitably created social conflicts, their nature and
intensity depending in considerable part on the social class of the hearers. Contemporary dissension over Jesus' teachings has certainly left its
mark on the gospel record in the form of an anti-familial theme and an
emphasis on the primacy of a heavenly Father, not an earthly one. Jesus'
true relatives are not his real family, but those who do the will of the
Father (Matt 12:48–50/Thomas 99; cf. Mark 3:33–35/Luke 8:21); one
must be ready to hate one's own family for the kingdom (Luke 14:26;
cf. Thomas 55; Matt 10:37/Thomas 101); and in Luke those who come
after Jesus must revoke "father and mother and wife and children and
brothers and sisters" (Luke 14:25–27). Certain scholars have argued that
Jesus' remarks concerning both the family and God's true fatherhood
reflect an anti-patriarchal ethic in his teachings.[20]

However, it is highly unlikely that family disruption in families caused by Jesus' movement can be explained on the basis of a direct challenge to the inequality between men and women in the family. Peasant families and marital relationships are characterized by their gendered division of labor. Further, the family conflict described in the two following passages derived from Q is clearly generational, not gendered:

> "For henceforth in one house there will be five divided, three against two and two against three; they will be divided, father against son and son against father, mother against daughter and daughter against her mother, mother-in-law against her daughter-in-law and daughter-in-law against her mother-in-law. (Q 12:52–53).

And again:

> Whoever loves father and mother more than me is not worthy of me; and whoever loves son or daughter more than me is not worthy of me (Matt 10:37).

Thomas' version of the first saying, which is no doubt an earlier form, omits the reference to women altogether, and keeps the conflict strictly between father and son (Thomas 16). Further, conflict between mothers-in-law and daughters-in-law is customary in extended families, since the daughter-in-law is not tied to her new family by blood, and mothers-in-law generally rule over their daughters-in-law sternly. This underscores the secondary nature of Q 12:52–53 and makes it more likely that someone unfamiliar with women's intimate relationships – a scribe, perhaps – has expanded the saying on the basis of Micah 7:5–6. The Lukan counterpart of Matt 10:37 has likewise expanded the familial conflicts to include those between men and women, as well as those between parents and children: one must "hate his own father and mother and wife and children and brothers and sisters" (Luke 14:25–27) (RSV). The Lukan version, omitting the reference to wives and children and requiring hatred of the family, is probably more authentic.

This anti-familial theme in the gospel record suggests that women and men did leave their families to follow Jesus; their usual household concerns became secondary to their commitment to his vision. This caused dissension, divisions, and probably separations. The potential for family crisis is clear from the fact that for members of the working classes and the peasantry, survival depended on close interdependence between husband and wife. Jesus' teachings on marriage show sensitivity to this reality of lower class life. Thus, although Jesus acknowledged the family dissension and divisions caused by his message, he seems to have upheld the marriage and family bond between men and women by restricting divorce and remarriage.

Marriage and divorce

Jesus' teaching on divorce occurs in three separate strands of early Christian tradition: Mark (Mark 10:5–10/Matt 5:32), Q (Luke 16:18 / Matt 5:32), and Paul (1 Cor 7:9–11). This triple attestation makes it likely that Jesus made a pronouncement on divorce. Unfortunately, the great discrepancy among the three traditions makes Jesus' actual words irrecoverable. Matthew has added the exception clause for cases involving adultery or fornication (Matt 5:32, 19:9), an addition that is widely considered Matthean. The unqualified moral prohibition found in Mark is probably earlier. Both Mark and Paul assume that either the man or the woman has the legal right to initiate a divorce; Q assumes that right is only the man's. The significant variations in wording found among the divorce sayings suggest early Christians found Jesus' teaching on marriage and divorce difficult. It is best then to conclude that Jesus did prohibit divorce and remarriage. The Markan version will be a convenient point of departure, since it is the earliest of the Synoptic versions.

Mark sets Jesus' comments on divorce in the context of a dialogue with Pharisees who have questioned him about divorce. Jesus responds by challenging Mosaic law (Deut 24:1–4), which allows a man to dissolve his marriage by simply presenting his wife with a certificate of divorce. Portrayed here as a point of contention with Jewish authorities on the Law, Jesus' teaching may be viewed in terms of the debate between the schools of the conservative Shammai and more liberal Hillel. The use of Genesis to support the security of the marriage bond sounds strikingly similar to discussions found in the Dead Sea Scrolls, which seem to prohibit both polygamy as well as remarriage.[21] The dialogue between Jesus and the Pharisees ends with an aphorism: "Therefore what God has joined together let no one separate" (Mark 10:9). Such aphorisms are characteristic of Jesus' authentic words. In an aside to his disciples, Jesus categorically prohibits divorce and remarriage (Mark 10:10–12). Here Jesus' views are reminiscent of Malachi 2:10–16. His comments also suggest that both men and women could initiate divorce proceedings, and thus be equally culpable of adultery. Although many scholars argue this saying assumes Roman and not Jewish law, it is clear that some Jewish women did sue for divorce in first century Palestine.[22] It is also the case, however, that Cynic-Stoic philosophical writers were similarly supportive of marriage, and therefore probable that we have here another theme in Jesus' teaching which reflects the multi-cultural environment of first century Palestine.[23]

One could argue that in his affirmation of the sanctity of marriage Jesus reinforces the main hierarchical relationship between the sexes in ancient society rather than disrupts it. Whether this prohibition of divorce would be restrictive of women depended on their individual situations. It may have limited some Jewish women, by denying them a legal right they enjoyed; others, dependent on their husbands for their equal share in the economic unit of a peasant household, may have welcomed it. Nor should it be forgotten that such a proscription would have been even more restrictive of men, since first century men enjoyed a high degree of sexual freedom as well as legal access to divorce. The fact that Jesus spoke to the matter at all suggests that divorce and separation were facts of life among his followers.

Jesus' teachings thus contain an anti-familial theme and suggest that family divisions and even marital separations occurred within the families of those who responded to his message. However, there is little evidence that Jesus challenged family solidarity on the grounds that the family was inherently patriarchal or was characterized by the inequality between sexes; rather it seems to have been the case that the radical commitment required by his teachings diminished the relative importance of other matters. The proof of this is twofold: he did not attack marriage, the central hierarchical relationship between a man and a woman in his society, and the divisions caused by his message were primarily between the generations, not the sexes. Finally, Jesus seems to have been critical of the reverence children accord fathers, or even parents. Jesus' ideal family requires husbands and wives, but it does not include fathers: Jesus' true relatives do the will of the Father in heaven (Matt 12:48–50/Thomas 99; cf. Mark 3:33–35/Luke 8:21). Yet even this appears to reflect not an anti-patriarchal theme in Jesus' teaching, but a Hebraic reaffirmation of the fatherhood of God, a faith that had ramifications for relationships between the generations, rather than between women and men.

Call no man on earth Father

Few dispute that Jesus addressed God as Father. Based on the work of Joachim Jeremias, many Christian scholars have affirmed the special nature of Jesus' relationship to God on the basis of this title and have argued that Jesus' use of the term *abba* set him apart from both

Hellenistic Judaism and the early church.[24] Robert Hammerton-Kelly further asserted the anti-patriarchal nature of Jesus' theology in the wake of feminist critiques of the use of titles like "father" for God.[25] Certain feminist scholars followed Hammerton-Kelly's example in their reconstructions of the message of Jesus.[26] Mary Rose D'Angelo has documented this discussion, and successfully called all aspects of it into question.[27] Jewish texts in first century Palestine, most notably from Qumran,[28] give evidence for the use of the term "father" as an address to God both in general declarative statements, and in prayer. Further, linguistic analysis of the use of the Aramaic *abba* does not support a specialized meaning conveying the intimacy between father and child.[29] Rather, the title "father" evoked the power, divine authority and kingship of the Jewish God in the face of Roman Imperial propaganda.[30] D' Angelo argues that presupposing as it does the superiority of men within society, it cannot convey an anti-patriarchal meaning. "Father" is the highest title of authority only within a social system in which privileged men have power over women, children, and such lesser males, as slaves, freedmen and clients.[31] Therefore, if Jesus addressed God as his father, he did so within the context of a Hellenistic Judaism that revered its God as king in an empire that demanded fealty to the emperor (cf. Mark 12:17/Luke 20:25/Matt 22:21; Thom 100:2–3).

Yet the evidence that Jesus applied the title "Father" to God is slight. It is limited to Mark 14:36 when Jesus prays to God in the Garden of Gethsemane, the Lord's Prayer in Q (Luke 11:2b/Matt 6:9), and also from Q the so-called "Johannine Thunderbolt" (Luke 10:21–22/Matt 11:25–27).[32] But only with great difficulty can one ascribe to Jesus the use of "*abba*" for God in Mark 14:36, given that it occurs in a section of Mark which is undeniably Markan composition. For one thing Jesus is alone; no one can witness to his words. Second, Mark casts Jesus as one in a line of Jewish martyrs.[33] Further, since "abba" was used liturgically in the early church (the spirit causes believers cry out "Abba, father!" [Gal 4:6; Rom 8:15]),[34] the use of Aramaic does not suggest that here we have Jesus' actual words. Thus, the cry of Jesus in the Garden of Gethsemane almost certainly does not go back to Jesus. Similarly, Jesus' claim of a special relationship with the Father in Luke 10:21–22/Matt 11:25–27 reflects Q's identification of Jesus with the figure of Wisdom, and is therefore not likely to represent Jesus' understanding of God or himself. The Lord's Prayer, derived from Q, thus remains the only identification of God as "father" that can reasonably be attributed to Jesus himself. Yet there is no compelling reason to assume that the Aramaic "Abba" lies behind this address. No recensions of the Lord's Prayer read

"Abba," nor is there any evidence that the Lord's Prayer was composed in anything but Greek. Given that "Father" appears as an address in Jewish prayer of the period, D'Angelo is right to conclude that it is not surprising to find Jesus employing in prayer "an address to God that called Caesar's reign into question and made a special claim on God's protection, mercy, and providence."[35]

Still, D' Angelo's discussion accounts neither for the absence of fathers from Jesus' ideal family nor for the generational nature of the dispute fostered by Jesus' message. The context of a Jewish anti-imperial theology does not by itself explain either Jesus' address of God as father, or the incidence of family conflict created by his message.

However, another controversy within Judaism could well explain Jesus' interest in God as the true father. In Judaism, as in other religions of the ancient Mediterranean, there existed a complex of family rituals surrounding the burial of family members; it is commonly referred to as the cult of the dead. This family cult was usually dominated by women, although within Judaism men were also active in mourning rites. Ceremonies included funeral liturgies and feasts, frequent visits to the burial place, and the offering of foodstuffs to the deceased, who was thought to be in need of sustenance following death.[36] These practices were condemned by a number of Jewish prophets and assailed in other biblical writings. The Deuteronomist, for instance, declared that such practices were in conflict with Yahwism and centralized worship of Yahweh in the Jerusalem Temple. Laceration of the flesh, practiced by the prophets of Jezebel (1 Kgs 18:28), is condemned in Deut 14:1.[37] Elsewhere we find denunciations of the customs of leaving food in tombs and funerary feasting with the dead.[38] Isaiah denounces the continued invocation of the spirits of the dead, as well as other related customs such as eating with the dead in tombs.[39] Neither Jeremiah nor Ezekiel participated in funerals; Ezekiel did not even mourn the death of his wife.[40]

In Jesus' day care of the dead included rites of reburial; after the body of a loved one had decayed, the bones were carefully placed in a bone-box called an ossuary, which was then placed in a niche in the family tomb. Rather than being restricted to a particular group of Jews, such as the Pharisees or the upper classes, such reburials are now considered to have been performed more generally. Even the High Priest Caiaphas and his family were re-buried in ossuaries. Inscriptional evidence for the naming of children after family members rather than popular biblical figures may reflect Hellenistic influence, but it clearly shows an interest in Jewish ancestral lines among Palestinian Jews of the Second Temple period.

The veneration of special prophets and patriarchs was a well established practice in first century Palestine. Extant at the time of Jesus were tombs dedicated to the Patriarchs and Matriarchs, Rachel, the Maccabean martyrs, the prophetess Hulda, the prophet Isaiah, the prophet Zechariah ben Judah and a necropolis of kings near Jerusalem. Making pilgrimages to these tombs and monuments is precisely the custom that is being criticized in Q 11:47–51(Luke 11:47–51/Matt 23:29–36). Several of these special tomb monuments, such as Zechariah's, are still standing in the Kidron valley. In Bethlehem a tomb monument to Rachel still remains. Depictions of these tombs of the special dead can be found as ossuary decorations, further attesting to their popularity during the first century. Jewish writers are found debating the efficacy of prayer to prophets and "fathers." Deborah is portrayed in the first century *Biblical Antiquities* as saying right before her death: "Do not hope in your fathers," an exhortation which correctly – if ironically would discourage veneration of her as a dead prophetess and matriarch.[41] In Second Baruch the writer envisions a future in which such prayers to the ancestors and prophets will cease.[42] John the Baptist warned his contemporaries not to depend on Abraham as their Father (Matt 3:7–10/Luke 3:7–9).

Within this context I would like to place a series of sayings attributed to Jesus which suggest both a generational dispute over burials and disapprobation of practices involving veneration of the dead:

> To another (Jesus) said, "Follow me." But he said, "Lord, let me go first and bury my father." But he said to him, "Leave the dead to bury their own dead; but as for you, go and proclaim the kingdom of God (Luke 9:59/Matt 8:21).

> Where the corpse is, there the eagles with be gathered together (Luke 17:37/ Matt 24:28).

> Become passersby (Thomas 42).

> Woe to you! for you are like unmarked graves, and people who walk over them do not know it (Luke 11:44/Matt 23:27).

> Woe to you! for you build the tombs of the prophets but it was your fathers that killed them (Luke 11:47/Matt 23:29).

> Call no man your father on earth (Matt 23:6–11).

The saying on the dead burying their dead is usually considered authentic. Since burial rites for parents were a special responsibility, this saying would have been particularly offensive to many. Accordingly, most scholars have interpreted this saying to mean "let the (spiritually) dead bury the (physically) dead." However, Byron McCane has argued persuasively that this saying refers not to initial burial, but to reburial, particularly the practice of reburial in ossuaries. Jesus would then be saying, "let the dead (in the tombs) re-bury their own dead," and thus denouncing special attention to the dead as contrary to his teaching of the Kingdom of God.[43] The saying from the Gospel of Thomas can also be read to betray a similar critique of the over attention to graves: "Become passersby" may well allude to the phrase "passersby" common in ancient grave epitaphs. The point would be to keep on walking. The saying on eagles and corpses seems to express a similar distaste for burials; vultures were birds of carrion, in the same class with ravens and crows.[44] This teaching of Jesus is the most likely to foster a family generational dispute, as it denies the legitimacy of burial practices traditionally owed to parents by their children. Excessive concern with tombs, corpses, and burials – to one's "fathers" or ancestors – was regularly censured by biblical writers and prophets as being at odds with true Hebraic monotheism. Jesus' concern was similar.

But this does not fully explain the witty harshness of these sayings, which fit better in a Hellenistic context. Cynic, Epicurean and Stoic philosophers also considered such solicitude for the dead superstitious, and were fond of quoting Theodore the Atheist to Lysimachus who was threatened with death without burial: "What matters it if I rot on the earth or under it?"[45] Socrates, of course, was also notable for his lack of concern for his own burial. When asked how he would like to be buried, he replied, "However you please, if you can catch me."[46] Other philosophers, especially Cynics, expressed a similar lack of concern for the disposal of their remains.[47] Thus, Jesus' saying has a clear Hellenistic flavor to it, although the underlying concern is Hebraic, not Greek.

Likely enough, Jesus also rejected the practice of venerating the dead at tombs. The woes against the Pharisees involving graves and the tombs of the prophets should be reconsidered as evidence for the historical Jesus. Many scholars reject these sayings because they betray the influence of a Deuteronomic view of history and therefore tend to presuppose the situation following Jesus' death.[48] While that is certainly the case for Luke 11:49–51/Matt 23:34–36, there are several reasons to consider the less complex sayings in Luke 11:44, 49/ Matt 23:27, 29 as authentic. First, Q 11:47–48 is not so obviously Deuteronomic, and is detachable from Q 11:49–51.[49] Second, O. H. Steck has argued that by the first century CE two themes in prophetic thought had coalesced: 1) the Deuteronomic view of history which assumed that God's judgment was precipitated by Israel's disobedience to God's law, and 2) the notion that prophets were habitually killed by Israel (cf. Neh 9:26). According to Steck this blended theme was an oral tradition, widespread in Palestinian Judaism between 200 BCE and 100 CE [50] Hence Jesus' words in Q 11:47–48 do not presuppose his death, and may make good sense for the situation following the death of John the Baptist. It is therefore not necessary to consider the entire section of the woes against the Pharisees in Matt 23:27–36/Luke 11:44–51 inauthentic. Jesus could well be reproaching the Pharisees for participating in a documentable and popular institution from first century Palestine, the veneration of popular prophets and patriarchs at special tombsites. This scenario accords well with the widespread view that Jesus was a prophetic figure who defended a strict view of Hebraic monotheism.

Clearly, Matthew so understood these imprecations. As a precursor to the woes against the Pharisees, he quotes Jesus as saying:

> Call no man your Father on earth, for you have one Father who is in heaven (Matt 23:9) (RSV).

This is a Matthean addition to Mark 12:37b–40, the question concerning the greatest commandment, which Matthew connects to one of the Q passages in which Jesus attacks the popular veneration of the prophets (Q 11:47–48). This suggests a concern not for family, marriage, or patriarchy, but for monotheism. Here, emphasizing and expanding on a theme that I suggest was fundamental to Jesus' own teaching, Matthew reasserts Hebraic monotheism according to classic prophetic style: God sends prophets who preach repentance, but Israel persecutes and subsequently kills them.

Jesus' concern for the veneration of prophets at tombsites readily comports with the saying "let the dead bury their own dead," which criticized the reburial of "fathers" as contrary to the vision of the Kingdom of God. Both would reflect an ongoing concern within Judaism going back to Exilic times. The presence of such a prophetic theme in Jesus' teaching would best explain the repeated characterization of Jesus as a prophet without denying the Hellenistic flavor of many of his sayings. Further, according to Q Jesus taught that the judgment would come unnoticed in the midst of everyday activities (Luke 11:26–32/Matt 24:37–39; Luke 17:34–35/Matt 24:40–41). That is, most would not notice that there was anything amiss. Similarly, burial customs were so much a part of the culture it is easy to imagine that few would have considered them objectionable.

That Jesus repudiated extravagant burial practices for parents and the veneration of patriarchs and special prophets at tombs makes better sense of his omission of fathers from the ideal family (Mark 3:33–35) and the generational nature of family divisions fostered by his message as found in Q (Luke 12:52–53/Matt 10:35–36; Luke 14:25–27; Matt 10:37). Burial customs are essential to the workings of any culture, and Jesus' challenge to traditional practices, even ancient practices considered at odds with Jewish monotheistic tradition, would have been highly offensive and caused deep divisions within households. This theme of Jesus' teachings demonstrates both the Hebraic aspects of his message, and its Hellenistic flavor, reflecting as it does both prophetic monotheistic interests and the often mordant wit of Hellenistic aphorisms expressing a lack of interest in burial. The easy intertwining of these two influences in Jesus' message should warn us against glibly characterizing him as either a prophetic character or a Cynic, but it does allow for his assimilation in the culturally eclectic environment of Palestine and Lower Galilee. Further, this interpretation of Jesus' message does not permit an anti-patriarchal characterization either for Jesus' emphasis on the fatherhood of God or for the absence of fathers in the ideal family. Rather, Jesus' interest was focused on other matters entirely, particularly the fatherhood of the one God within his kingdom.

Gender, class and Jesus: Some conclusions

Women obviously joined the Jesus movement, although interest in that presence is largely absent from Jesus' teaching itself. A few women belonged to the Jesus movement just as they were present in small numbers among the Cynics, Epicureans, Pythagoreans, Stoics, Therapeutae, the Zealot group led by Simon son of Gioras, the disciples of John the Baptist and the sectarians at Qumran. So why were women in Jesus' movement? Why did they join? Their presence no doubt reflects the fact that women then, like women now, had diverse interests. It is inappropriate to stereotype first century women in such a way that we cannot imagine the true diversity of their experience. For example, wealthier women could have been attracted to Jesus' challenge to the ancient notion of rank, having experienced the often close relationship between women and their house slaves (Q 14:16–24; Thom 64:1–12). Poor women might have been attracted to Jesus' saying, "Blessed are the poor"

(Q 6:20). Both girls sold into debt slavery and their parents might have been attracted to his declaration about the forgiveness of debts (Q 11:2–4; see also Matt 18:23–34). Some working women would have been attracted by the motif of lower class resistance to authority explicit in parables such as the Unjust Judge and the Dishonest Steward. Others may have responded, as did a number of men, to Jesus' criticism of traditional burial practices and his emphasis on God as Father. Although women's particular interests are secondary to such concerns, it can be argued that the social resistance inherent in Jesus' reign of God, and the enactment of that resistance in the context of open commensality and renewed emphasis on the Fatherhood of God must have contributed to women's interest in becoming disciples of Jesus and in joining early Christian communities.[51]

Jesus as a Mediterranean Jewish Peasant

John Dominic Crossan

In the straitened Mediterranean, the kingdom of Heaven
had to have something to do with food and drink.

Peter Brown

One central issue in constructing a portrait of Jesus out of the
gospel sources is the relationship between the parables and the miracles.
Another way of putting this problem is: Did Jesus have an ecstatic vision
of an ideal world, as the parables suggest, or did he also have a practical
design for a social program, as the miracle stories indicate?

In this article, I examine a number of important texts in arriving
at my own conclusion: The heart of the original Jesus movement was a
shared egalitarianism of spiritual and material resources. Its material side
and its spiritual aspects, the fact of it and its symbolic representation,
cannot be separated. This article makes use of a few of the most important texts in illustrating the process – the method of sorting out the versions in the attempt to recover something akin to the original.

Ecstatic vision

The parable of *The Feast* is found in two independent sources (see
box for a chart of sources), *The Gospel of Thomas* and the *Sayings Gospel Q*,
both dating from the fifties or sixties of the Common Era. *The Feast* is of
course reproduced in both Matthew and Luke, who make use of the common source, Q. Each evangelist has edited the parable to suit the view-

point of his gospel. However, my interest lies not in how Thomas, Matthew, or Luke edit the parable, so much as in the reconstructed plot-structure of the parable as Jesus employed it. Of course, to get to the original plot-structure we must closely compare and contrast the surviving versions.

I begin with Thomas 64. There are three parables in Thomas 63–65 with very similar openings and very similar warnings against ordinary worldly concerns, which is one of the themes important to Thomas. The middle parable in the group of three, *The Feast*, records that Jesus said:

> A person was receiving guests. When he had prepared the dinner, he sent his servant to invite the guests. [1]The servant went to the first and said to that one, "My master invites you." That one said, "Some merchants owe me money; they are coming to me tonight. I must go and give instructions to them. Please excuse me from dinner." [2]*The servant went to another and said to that one, "My master has invited you." That one said to the servant, "I have bought a house, and I have been called away for a day. I shall have no time."* [3]The servant went to another and said to that one, "My master invites you." That one said to the servant, "My friend is to be married, and I am to arrange the dinner. I shall not be able to come. Please excuse me from dinner." [4]The servant went to another and said to that one, "My master invites you." That one said to the servant, "I have bought an estate, and I am going to collect the rent. I shall not be able to come. Please excuse me." The servant returned and said to his master, "Those whom you invited to dinner have asked you to be excused." The master said to his servant, "GO OUT ON THE STREETS, AND BRING WHOMEVER YOU FIND TO HAVE DINNER." *Buyers and merchants [will] not enter the places of my Father.*
>
> Thomas 64 [my numbers, italics, & emphases]

The first thing to observe is that the author of Thomas has added the two italicized items to emphasize his understanding of the Christian life: buying a house and working as a merchant do not go with the ascetic life recommended by Thomas. The first addition raises the number of excuses from three to four, while the second addition drives home the parable's world-negating interpretation. These elaborations can therefore be set aside.

What cannot be set aside is the instruction set in caps. For the servants to execute that order they would have to create an open and shared table, a meal in which poor and rich, female and male, single and married, slave and free, gentile and Jew, might all end up eating together. And that as anyone knows, in the first as in the twentieth century, is no way to have a meal, no way to give a party.

The second version of *The Feast* appears in the Sayings Gospel Q. Matthew and Luke have drastically rewritten the Q text in order to produce their own versions. And they have surrounded the parable with interpretative contexts (Matt 21:33–46; Luke 14:12–15), just as Thomas placed the parable in the middle of a group of three in order to interpret his version of *The Feast*. These interpretative contexts are again not our direct concern. In the parallel versions reproduced here, the words and phrases Matthew and Luke presumably derived from the Q source are italicized.

Matt 22:1–10 The reign of the heavens is like *a man*, a king, who *gave* a wedding feast for his son. *And he sent out his servants to summon* those who had been invited to the wedding feast, but they did not want to come. Again he sent out other servants saying, "*Tell those who have been invited:* Behold, I have prepared my dinner, my oxen and fat calves are killed and everything is *ready.* Come to the wedding." But they made light of it and departed, one to his *farm,* another to his business, and the rest seized his servants, abused them and killed them. *The* king *was angry* and dispatching his troops he destroyed those murderers and razed their city. Then he says *to his servants,* "The wedding feast is ready, but those who had been invited were not worthy; go therefore into the byways *and* invite as many as you find to the feast." And those servants *went out into the roads* and gathered everyone they found, both evil and good. And then when they all sat down, the wedding hall was full.

Luke 14:16–23 A certain *man gave* a large banquet, and he *summoned* many and *he sent out his servant* at the hour of the banquet to *tell those who have been invited:* "Come, for it is *ready.*" And they began one by one to make excuses: The first said to him, "I have bought a *farm* and I must go to inspect it. I ask, have me excused." And another said, "I have bought five yoke of oxen, and I am going to examine them. I ask, have me excused." And another said, "I have married a wife and therefore I am unable to come." And the servant came and told this to his master. Then *the* householder *was angry* and said *to his servant,* "Go out quickly into the plazas and alleys of this city *and* bring the poor and maimed and blind and lame here." And the servant said, "Sir, what you commanded has been done, and still there is room." And the master said to the servant, "*Go out onto the roads* and hedges and compel them to enter, so that my house will be full."

Take note of the replacements who are to substitute for the original guests.

Luke has a double set. The first set is specified as the disenfranchised, "the poor and maimed and blind and lame," which is the same fourfold designation that appears earlier in Luke 14:13: "the poor and maimed and lame and blind." These are very likely Luke's categories. The second set is left unspecified.

Matthew does not have a double set; he has only a double mention of the one set. In Matthew, the servants are instructed to "invite as many as you find" to the feast; then the servants went out and "gathered everyone they found, both evil and good." These two statements serve the same function as Luke's doubling: they allow Matthew to specify the replacement guests as "both evil and good."

In the Q source, as in the Gospel of Thomas, the replacement guests are simply anyone the servant finds on the streets. And this was probably the point made by Jesus when he spoke the parable.

In the first century, as in the twentieth, a person might give a feast for society's outcasts as a special event. That could easily be understood in the honor/shame ideology of Mediterranean society as the act of a benefactor, an event with high visibility. But if one gave such feasts persistently and exclusively, there would undoubtedly have been some very negative social repercussions. To invite outcasts to a dinner as a special event is a less socially radical act than to invite anyone found on the streets and to do so repeatedly. It is the indiscriminate character of that "anyone" which negates the social function of the table, which is to establish a social ranking by what one eats, how one eats, and with whom one eats. It is the random selection of guests and the open table that is the most startling element of the meal depicted in the parable. At this feast, one could easily have classes, sexes, ranks, and grades all mixed up together.

The social challenge of an egalitarian table is the radical threat posed by the parable and is the content of Jesus' ecstatic vision.

The parable is only a story, of course, but it is a story that focuses its challenge on the heart of society, the table, the place where persons meet to eat, the place where they establish and confirm the social order.

Social program

The vision of Jesus comes to expression in *The Feast* and in many other parables and aphorisms. But was there also a correlative social program that can be traced back to the historical Jesus?

Jesus did have a social program, in my view – a conclusion I base on three independent sources, Thomas, Q, and Mark.

First, two warnings about the texts we will be examining. These texts belong to what is sometimes referred to as "the missionary discourse." That designation can be very misleading. I ask you not to think of the Christian mission as we know it historically, or even to think of Paul's so-called missionary efforts in the middle of the first century. I am thinking rather of the "mission" of those healed by Jesus to heal others. Jesus assumed no personal monopoly on exorcizing or healing. Furthermore, I am assuming as the background of this material the kind of information medical anthropologists can provide us about healing among indigenous peoples rather than what Christian apologetic theology can tell us about miracles as evidence of Christ's divinity.

We may begin again with Thomas. The four questions posed about fasting, prayer, alms, and diet in Thom 6:1,

> His disciples asked him and said to him, "Do you want us to fast? How shall we pray? Shall we give alms? What diet shall we observe?"

are appropriately answered in Thom 14:1–5:

> Jesus said to them, "If you fast, you will bring sin upon yourselves, [2]and if you pray, you will be condemned, [3]and if you give alms, you will harm your spirits. [4]When you go into any country and walk from place to place, when the people receive you, eat what they serve you and heal the sick among them. [5]For what goes into your mouth will not defile you; rather, it is what comes out of your mouth that will defile you."

The key text is v. 4: in this text healing has become a part of the tradition received by Thomas since Thomas shows no interest in it elsewhere in his gospel. And in Thomas healing is linked with eating. It is the reciprocal relationship between what is given and what is received, between magic and meal, curing and eating, free healing and open table that is important. And this reciprocity can be traced in our other two independent sources, Q and Mark.

The Sayings Gospel Q can once again be discerned behind Matt 9:37–38, 10:7–15 and Luke 10:2–12. The common source can be isolated in the two versions by noting the words and phrases italicized in each version. I have added parenthetical numbering in the two versions to make it easier to identify the common phrases, since Matthew has greatly changed the sequence of items. The numbers should not be confused with verses. The order in Luke is taken to be the original order, so the numbers in Luke run from 1 to 7. In Matthew, who conflates Q with Mark 6:7–13, the items are given in the order 6, 1, 4, 5, 3, 2, 7.

> Preach as you go, saying [6]*"The reign of* heaven *has come near."* *Heal the sick*, raise the dead, cleanse lepers, exorcise demons . . . Take [1]*no gold or silver, nor copper in your belts, no knapsack* for your journey, nor two tunics, *nor sandals*, nor a staff [4]*for the worker deserves his* food. [5]*Into whatever city* or village *you enter*, determine who in it is worthy, and [3]*stay* with that person until you depart. As [2]*you enter the house*, greet it. *And if* the house *is* worthy, let *your peace* come *upon* it; *but* if it is *not* worthy, let your peace return to *you.* And [7]*whoever does not welcome you* or listen to your words, as you *go out* of that house or *city* shake off the *dust* from your *feet.* (Matt 10:7–8a, 9–12, 14)

> Carry [1]*no purse, no knapsack, no sandals*; and greet no one on the road. Into whatever [2]*house you enter*, first say, "Peace be to this house!" *And if* a child of peace *is* there, *your peace* shall rest *upon* him; *but if not*, it shall return to *you.* And [3]*stay* in the same house, eating and drinking whatever they have, [4]*for the worker deserves his* wages. Do not go from house to house. [5]*And if you enter a city* and they welcome you, eat what is set before you; and [6]*heal the sick* in it and say to them, "*The reign of* God *has come near* to you." But [7]*whatever* city you enter that *does not welcome you, go out* into its streets and say, "Even *the dust* of your *city* that clings to our *feet*, we wipe off against you; but know this, that the reign of God has come near. (Luke 10:4–11)

The original Q sequence is to be observed in Luke. That sequence involved a balance of positive and negative, of acceptance and rejection, in two locations: first, in the house in [2–4], then in the city in [5–7]. Matthew has obscured that progress by having house in his [2], then city or village in his [5], and finally house or city in his [7].

The negative aspect grows in intensity in the sequence. In Thom 14:4, a negative reception was only a possibility: "if they receive you . . . " In item [2] in Q, the negative reception has become a more explicit possibility, although it is still surrounded by the more positive possibility of a welcome, but by the time we come to [5–7], it is almost as if the negative has taken over; in light of the subsequent verses in Q preserved in Luke 10:12–15, the negative reception had become the norm rather than the exception:

I tell you, on that day Sodom will be better off than that town."[13] Woe to you, Chorazin! Woe to you, Bethsaida! for if the miracles done in you had been done in Tyre and Sidon, they would have repented long ago sitting in sackcloth and ashes.[14] But it shall be more tolerable on the judgement for Tyre and Sidon than for you.[15] And you, Caphernaum, will you be exalted to heaven! You shall descend to Hades!"

The move from the rural houses and hamlets of lower Galilee to the urban towns and "cities" such as Chorazin, Bethsaida, and Capernaum may reflect the move from the historical Jesus to the Q community twenty or thirty years later.

The fundamental point, however, is the reciprocity of open healing and open eating, shared miracle and shared table: both were clearly present in Q, although they are now refocused quite differently in Matthew and Luke.

The third and final source is in Mark 6:7-13. In this version notice that the healing injunctions that are represented as instructions given by Jesus are given as part of the narrative framework in Mark.

He called the twelve and began to send them out two by two, and gave them authority over the unclean spirits. He ordered them to take nothing for their journey except a staff, no bread, no bag, no money in their belts; but to wear sandals and not to put on two tunics. He said to them, "Wherever you enter a house, stay there until you leave the place. If any place will not welcome you and they refuse to hear you, shake off the dust that is on your feet as a testimony against them." So they went out and proclaimed that all should repent. They cast out many demons, and anointed with oil many who were sick and cured them.

Mark 6:7-13

It is worth noting that in Mark the only place mentioned is the house; there is no mention of town or city.

Further, in Thom 14:4 there is mention of eating; in the Q texts from Matthew and Luke, there is talk about staying and eating; in Mark mention is made only of staying.

Yet in all these texts, the same basic point appears: things are shared in common. There healers are not to receive alms or handouts, let alone payments or wages. They bring with them a free, open, and shared healing. In return they are to receive a free, open, and shared eating.

And that explains, of course, the two items of dress code on which Q and Mark agree: Jesus' followers are not to carry either money-purse or bag. They do not need a money-purse because they are not to receive alms in the form of money. And they do not require a bag because they are not to receive alms in the form of food. For Jesus, in other words, sharing was not just a strategy for supporting the mission. That could have been achieved by the use of alms, or wages, or charges, or fees of some sort. It could have been done, for instance, by begging in the fashion of Cynic philosophers who wandered around the Greco-Roman cities. Sharing was rather a strategy for building or rebuilding the peasant community on radically different principles from those undergirding an honor/shame society, a society based on patronage and clientage. Jesus' strategy was based on an egalitarian sharing of spiritual and material power at the most grassroots level. For that reason, dress and equipment were just as important as house and table.

To sum up, Jesus had both a vision and a program, which were designed originally to move from peasant to peasant among the houses and small villages of lower Galilee. And what is still visible, even in sources written down years later for circumstances quite different from those under which Jesus labored and for circumstances that differed from Christian community to Christian community, is the clear evidence that we are not dealing originally with mere begging and almsgiving, but with a common table and open sharing. The disciples do not carry a bag because they do not beg for alms or food or clothing or anything else. They share a miracle and a kingdom and in return they receive a table and a house. Here, I think, is the heart of the original Jesus movement, a shared egalitarianism of spiritual and material resources. I emphasize this as strongly as possible and I insist that its material aspects and its spiritual aspects, the fact of it and its symbolic representation cannot be separated. The mission we are talking about is not, like Paul's, a dramatic thrust along major trade routes to urban centers hundreds of miles apart. Yet it concerns the longest journey in the Greco-Roman world, maybe in any world, the step across the threshold of a peasant stranger's home.

Jesus in the
Company of Sages

Hal Taussig

"The Cynic's only shield is his self-respect. If he doesn't use
that (and that only), he'll find himself naked and disgraced
in public. This is his house and his front door, the attendants at his bedroom door, and his protective night-time
darkness. He ought to have nothing of his own that he
wants to hide. Otherwise he's gone off, he's destroyed the
Cynic that was, the public figure, the free man, he's started
to be afraid about externals, he's begun to feel the need for
concealment. And he couldn't keep anything concealed
even if he wanted to. Where or how could he possibly hide
himself?"   Epictetus, 111. 22.14–16

"May nothing fine remain unseen. May it be brought into
the clear light of the shining sun."
                                      Philo, *De Somniis* 11.282

"There is nothing veiled that won't be unveiled or hidden
that won't be made known.   Jesus in Luke 12:2

The profile of the historical Jesus is recognizable from most angles.
It is the profile of a sage. Like most profiles, the sage profile of Jesus is
recognizable because it is similar to other figures within view.

The profile of Jesus resembles in particular two sub-categories of
the sage outline: Jesus looks like an aphoristic sage of hellenistic Jewish
wisdom, and he fits the basic outline of popular Cynics of the hellenis-

169

tic Mediterranean. That evidence of both these sub-categories exists in Jesus' Galilean milieu hastens recognition of Jesus' profile within the gestalt of Jewish and Cynic wisdom that made sense to both him and those around him.

For the most part, then, the profile I propose is not an innovative one. Rather, this profile aims to underline the ways those portions of the works of F. Gerald Downing, John Dominic Crossan, Leif Vaage, Marcus Borg, and Burton L. Mack in which they provide a clear, historically rooted image of Jesus. Similarly this profile attempts to demonstrate that the already well-elaborated profile of the historical Jesus as a Jewish aphorist influenced directly by popular Cynicism makes the most sense of the Jesus Seminar votes and data. Although my position differs somewhat from Downing, Crossan, Vaage, Borg, and Mack, the differences are occasioned principally by these scholars' departure from the profile of Jesus as aphoristic/Cynic sage. That is, I shall differ from those who have promoted associations of Jesus with aphoristic and Cynic wisdom only in that I mean to locate him more precisely in terms of these established parameters than they have.

My approach, then, will be to review briefly the case for Jesus as aphoristic/Cynic sage as it has been made by the above mentioned scholars, and to extend that proposal in several areas which either have not been attended to or in which scholars have departed from the aphoristic/Cynic profile.

Recognizing the similarity of this profile to that of generally recognizable figures in first century Galilee has its consequences for situating Jesus of Nazareth's significance in history. Following this vein I will conclude with proposals to relativize and reduce the historical Jesus' significance a few degrees more than has already been suggested by the Seminar's work.

The case for Jesus as aphoristic/ cynic sage

The correlation between Jewish aphoristic wisdom and itinerant Cynic philosophy is striking. Although hardly the same, these two intellectual movements were complementary in so many ways that this hybrid identity of the historical Jesus is easy to integrate. Both movements eschewed reference to sacred literature as authority. Both focused on everyday human experience as the primary frame of reference. Both drew on nature as authoritative. Neither viewed ritual, socio-economic status, or family as important in and of themselves. The views evident in

his core sayings suggest that living in an area where both these movements were in evidence must have strongly influenced Jesus to draw on
and combine their precepts in his own understanding.[1] In his study of
first century Galilee, Martin Hengel concludes that the "affinities
between Gospel tradition and Cynic religious and social criticism go
right back to Jesus himself," adding, "Why should not the craftsman
Jesus, who grew up in the neighborhood of Sepphoris, have made contact with Cynic itinerant preachers . . . ?"[2]

To be sure, in the complicated mix of Jew and gentile and the
wealthy, merchant, and peasant classes of Galilee, Jesus seems to have
interacted primarily with peasant and merchant Jews to the exclusion of
most gentiles and wealthy persons. But this does not mean that he was
unaware of the culture of the wealthy or such gentile traditions as popular Cynicism. Jesus drew from both Jewish aphoristic wisdom and popular Cynic philosophy to articulate his point of view.

Crossan has summarized this Jesus as belonging to a "peasant,
oral, and popular philosophical praxis of what might be termed, if adjec-
tive and noun are given equal weight, a Jewish Cynicism . . . It involved
practice and not just theory, life-style and not just mind-set in opposition to the cultural heart of Mediterranean civilization, a way of looking
and dressing, of eating, living, and relating that announced its contempt
for honor and shame, for patronage and clientage . . . They were hippies
in a world of Augustan yuppies. . . . The historical Jesus was, then, a
peasant Jewish Cynic."[3]

Crossan's summary, with its attendant in-depth background in his
major volume, The *Historical Jesus*, appeared as a kind of culmination to
a burst of similar articulations by Vaage, Downing, Mack, and Borg
between 1986 and 1992.[4] Mack, Borg, Vaage, and Crossan have all published follow-up works on this emergent profile of Jesus, the sage. Even
Ben Witherington, the long-time opponent of the Jesus Seminar, has
joined the chorus with his large volume, *Jesus, the Sage.*

The first decade of proposal and debate[5] on these proposals has
produced a relatively finely drawn picture of an aphoristic/Cynic Jesus.
The distinctions now available within the profile of Jesus as aphoris-
tic/Cynic sage are summarized by David Seeley: "According to Eddy,
'to claim that Jesus' use of aphoristic wisdom and biting wit is best
understood within the context of Hellenistic Cynicism is to miss the
most plausible context: Jewish wisdom" (460). But no one has said that
Jesus' use of Cynic thought kept him from using Jewish thought as well.
Downing says that Jesus fashioned a "marriage" of Cynic ideas "with his
own native Judaism," and that "Jesus the Jew must also be seen as Jesus

the Cynic." Burton Mack says that Jesus' speaking style is "very similar to the Cynics' way with words." To be similar to one thing still allows for being similar to something else. In fact, Mack has explicitly stated that he sees Jesus as using Jewish wisdom:

> "One might imagine Jesus doing at a popular level what many Jewish intellectuals did at a more sophisticated and conceptual level, namely combining Jewish and Hellenistic traditions of wisdom in order to make critical judgments about the times and to propose a religious ethic held to be in keeping with Jewish ideals."[6]

Jesus as this kind of Galilean sage fits well within what we know about ancient near eastern wisdom movements. Such movements are best understood through the contemporary term "learning." Wisdom in its near eastern forms was characterized by a devotion to and enthusiasm for the learning process itself. Wisdom movements promoted the uncovering of understanding. The heart of these efforts was in the learning of, not just the passing on of, material. This passion of near eastern wisdom for the process of learning itself is perhaps most poignantly illustrated by the Hellenistic Jewish sage in Wisdom of Solomon 7:17–21:

> God it was who gave me sure knowledge of what exists, to understand the structure of the world and the actions of the elements, the beginning, end and middle of the times, the alternation of the solstices and the succession of the seasons, the cycles of the year and the position of the stars, the natures of animals and the instincts of wild beasts, the powers of spirits and human mental processes, the varieties of plants and the medical properties of roots. And now I understand everything, hidden or visible, for Wisdom, the designer of all things, has instructed me. (New Jerusalem Bible)

Ancient near eastern sages were first of all enamored by the ways their world changed through learning, and only derivatively devoted to the teaching of what they knew to the next generation. This preference for learning over inculcation in ancient near eastern wisdom is perhaps most easily seen in the often haphazard organization of wisdom literature. The sages seem more interested in proceeding to the next insight than in ordering the old learnings.

Wisdom/learning expected that the life and the world could be known, and that such knowledge would change people. Aphoristic wisdom became more sophisticated in its approach to ordinary human experience by being sensitive to the exceptions, the wrinkles, and that which was not immediately obvious. Cynic wisdom – as a form of aphoristic wisdom – was willing to risk challenging social convention and power brokerage in order to learn that which was not seen on the surface of things.

Marcus Borg, John Dominic Crossan, Gerald Downing, and Burton Mack have made strong cases that associate the historical Jesus with this deep devotion to wisdom, indeed that show his teachings united in their devotion to the process of learning. Wisdom/learning – when it becomes an energized program, as generally in ancient near eastern wisdom movements and specifically in the case of the historical Jesus – is at once subversive, prosaic, gracious, humorous. Its energetic receptivity to knowledge can occasion both active challenges to existing assumptions and gracious contexting of that which is obvious. A broadly attested and even more widely cited logion of Jesus summarizes this devotion to and confidence in learning: "There is nothing veiled that will not be unveiled, or hidden that won't be made known" (Luke 12:2, Thom 5:1–2, Thom 6:5–6, Matt 10:26, Luke 8:17, and Mark 4:22, POxy 654:5).

It seems strange that despite this logion's almost proverbial familiarity few scholars have given it any serious study. In passing, David Tiede, Frederick Danker, Sharon Ringe, and William Hendrikson have asserted that it is a something like a "wisdom saying" (Ringe, 176), but have not treated it in any depth. Little scholarship has examined this saying of the hidden being revealed in the way this essay will: as a summary of the calling of the Hellenistic sage. No doubt this stems largely from the lack of attention scholarship has paid to wisdom modalities, and partly from the possibility of seeing this text as an apocalyptic prediction.

But an apocalyptic reading contradicts its contexts. Most important, its double appearance in the anti-apocalyptic Gospel of Thomas would require explanation. Both Thomas 5 and 6 have versions of it in distinctly non-apocalyptic contexts. The Oxyrhynchus papyrus 654 also reflects a non-apocalyptic intention. Even Mark, who tends to take wisdom sayings and read them apocalyptically does not do so with this text, instead paralleling it to removing a light from under a cover (4:21–23).

Perhaps most striking is the parallel between this Jesus logion and the above-quoted Wisdom of Solomon text which sets forth the lengthy curriculum of the Hellenistic sage, and describes the accomplishment of this learning as understanding "everything, hidden or visible." The comparison with Luke 12:2 (and parallels) is unavoidable. Both Wisdom of Solomon 7 and this Jesus logion celebrate both that "everything" will be learned, and that learning itself is the uncovering of the "hidden."

In short, Jesus employs the standard wisdom vocabulary of his day to announce his calling to learn, his readiness to participate in the collective process of wisdom and the uncovering of that which is not obvious. In doing so, he identifies himself as a sage.

Jesus as aphoristic/cynic sage and major currents in historical Jesus research

As Downing, Crossan, Vaage, and Mack have noted, recognizing Jesus as a Cynic-influenced aphoristic sage links together a number of broad-based conclusions about the historical Jesus. The following four strains of historical Jesus research bedrock connect in the sage profile:

1. *The meals of Jesus.* The widespread agreement that Jesus' work involved meals in a primary way accents Jesus' sage profile, since in the hellenistic Mediterranean world meals were a primary venue for teaching. In both Jewish and Greco-Roman settings it was at meals where schools often met, where philosophers discussed, and where religious leaders taught.[7]

The works of James Breech, Crossan, and Mack all emphasize the prominence of meals in Jesus' work. For Crossan and Breech meals were a central part of Jesus' programmatic strategy. Mack, while emphasizing the role of meals in the Jesus movements as "itself the sign and substance of the new order of things"[8] sees them as mostly the occasion for conversation and learning. While Mack recognizes the full significance of Jesus' commensality, he is silent as to whether Jesus himself saw the meals as the sign of the new order.

The clear profile of Jesus as aphoristic/Cynic sage can act here as an important caution about the historical Jesus' role at meals. The major problem I find with Jesus using meals for anything other than an occasion for teaching is the thorough-going resistance of all the texts except the clearly mythologized last supper to picture Jesus as a leader at the meals. All accounts agree that Jesus never presided at meals in houses. He was always a guest who came to speak, a common role for teachers in that society. Even the mythically framed outdoor meals (the miraculous feedings) for which Crossan has proposed some historicity – at least as peasant meals of bread and fish with Jesus[9] – show Jesus not as the convenor of the meal, but as a reluctant respondent. Given the unanimity of the texts in portraying him as guest or reluctant convenor, it is very difficult to imagine this same Jesus convening, organizing, and interpreting meals as a major part of his program.

The broadly held position that Jesus somehow organized eating with outsiders or the socially undesirable suffers from the similar problem that we have no texts which show Jesus planning or convening a meal with such a diverse or scandalous constituency. Although not one such story exists, many scholars continue to make this a part of their profiles.[10]

In some contrast to both of these positions, I return again to the clarity of the peasant sage profile. Jesus was regularly a guest sage at meals. The resonance of the texts concerning Jesus' disreputable table companions comes from the honor and shame codes concerning the company one kept, rather than from any strategic or programmatic initiative Jesus could have taken as leader or host at meals.

2. Jesus' "missional" instructions to his followers. It was with the missional instructions that Vaage and Downing seemed to have started in uncovering the extensive parallels[11] between the teachings of Jesus and those of the Cynics. Both Mack and Crossan also provide extensive parallels in the apparel and public behavior of Jesus (and/or the subsequent Q following) and Cynic teaching. Robinson, Koester, Rhodes, and Betz[12] have discounted some of these parallels, but interestingly enough mostly by arguing that the descriptions of the apparel are not exact parallels. Given the books full of parallels cited by Vaage and Downing, and the acute analysis of Crossan and Mack, these criticisms may appear in the larger perspective as confirmations that the Cynics and the historical Jesus looked very much (but not exactly) alike. The profile of Jesus as an aphoristic/Cynic sage goes a long way toward explaining these extensive parallels.

3. The iconoclastic character of many of Jesus' core teachings. Both Jewish aphoristic wisdom and Cynic teachings had a critical edge concerning the conventions of family, religion, the marketplace, and honor and shame codes.[13] Of the red and pink sayings at least 33 of the 91 are direct challenges to one of these conventions. Of course, one can say[19] that it is the prophetic tradition which challenges these same conventions, but one can also find the term prophet being applied to late first-century Christian itinerants.[20]

I would suggest that the categories of sage and prophet seem substantially merged in hellenistic Judaism. The latter-day prophets no longer addressed themselves to the nation, but to groups (households, synagogues, churches, marketplaces) in which they were active. The profile of the aphoristic/Cynic sage is not essentially from that of the ethical prophets in post-national Judaism. The debate in Didache 11 and 12 about how to treat the "prophets" is the same debate countless groups had about how to relate to troublesome sages.

4. *Jesus' association with "tax collectors and sinners."* Popular Cynics thrived on being associated with those who were considered outsiders, and made a point of citing disreputables as their authorities. The relatively strong textual case[15] to be made for Jesus being castigated for associating with those without honor corresponds to the dishonor with which Cynics were treated (the name Cynic comes, of course, from these individuals being called "dogs"). The profile of an aphoristic/Cynic sage comports nicely with the Jesus whose honor was called into question by virtue of his associations.

Re-configurations of Jesus occasioned by a thorough-going sage profile

In addition to making sense of these commonly held dimensions, contemplating Jesus as a sage also allows the re-configuring of his message to make his individual sayings and deeds more coherent both with one another and with the larger social role of a sage. This re-configuration involves two major aspects of Jesus' teaching and one part of his activity:

Re-configuring the teachings about the "basileia" of God

Jesus' teachings about God's domain, kingdom, or imperial rule make most sense within the categories of wisdom and learning. Subsuming these basileia teachings under the cohesive category of wisdom gives them more consistency as elements in the corpus of Jesus' sayings and as an historically identifiable rubric. Both hellenistic Jewish wisdom and Cynic wisdom employ reigning and kingship as primary images of how wisdom/learning works. The thematic underpinning of the Wisdom of Solomon is that the sage is like King Solomon insofar as he/she understands the world. Cynic wisdom is replete with the same image.[16] The governing thought in both hellenistic Jewish wisdom and Cynic thought was this: a correct understanding of one's self and the world allowed one to act like a king. The Cynics almost always added the following indications of understanding being realized in action: 1) to control one's self is a sign that one is king, and 2) acting free from obligation to social convention also demonstrated the understanding that made one king.[17] So the sage can speak as King Solomon.

> I esteemed wisdom more than sceptres and thrones; com-
> pared with her, I held riches as nothing . . . in her company
> all good things came to me . . . What I learned diligently, I
> shall pass on liberally . . . those who acquire this win God's
> friendship, commended to him by the gifts of instruction."
> (Wisdom of Solomon 7:7, 11, 14)

Given the dominance of the basileia metaphor for the process and fruits of learning in both sage movements reflected in Jesus, it seems odd that scholars generally privilege the metaphor of kingdom/basileia over that of wisdom. It is true that by the fifth century the metaphor of kingdom had prevailed over wisdom in theological discourse, but this seems highly influenced by the Roman imperial appropriation of Christianity in the meantime. I would therefore suggest that two other factors – the cultural situation of Christians "ruling the world" over the past three centuries, and a sublimated messianic agenda – have further influenced modern scholarship to subsume wisdom under kingdom, rather than vice versa. Profiling Jesus consistently as a sage among sages asks that the basileia teachings of Jesus be understood as a subset of the wisdom dictum and strategy that "nothing hidden will not be made known."

Ironically it may very well have been a similar misunderstanding of Jesus' basileia teachings that resulted in his death. Seen from the outside, the way Jesus' basileia teachings actively parodied the Roman empire may not have been quite so obviously the rhetoric of a sage. The Romans could well have understood the basileia proclamations of Jesus not as exhortations to a spiritual kingship for those who understand, but as a call to create some kind of social design counter to the existing government. Certainly a good aphoristic/Cynic sage would not disabuse them of their misunderstanding, since their conclusions had betrayed them as dullards. The tragic scenario was envisioned by another sage, Epictetus:

> If you want to be crucified, just wait. The cross will come. If
> it seems reasonable to comply, and the circumstances are
> right, then it's to be done, and your integrity maintained.[18]

Reconfiguring Jesus' hyperbolic instructions on behavior

Some of the Seminar's reddest sayings are not aphorisms as such, but rather instructions on behavior which employ radical hyperbole. The exaggerated character of their injunctions, as Robert Funk has clearly detailed, is intentional. Turning the other cheek, going the extra mile, loving the enemy, and giving up the coat one is wearing "are not prescriptive. They are suggestive of behavior that undermines the intent of the initial act."[19]

These exaggerated instructions were not meant to tell people how to live, but to help them learn the true character of those they had to deal with. In each case, following Jesus' recommendation unmasked the flawed and/or pretentious conduct of an opponent. In other words, these actions were ways to wisdom and learning about difficult people. What was hidden by their rank, patronage, or honorable status was unveiled so that the sage and his hearers could see the situation for what it was. Jesus was not so much a prescriber of righteous behavior as a teacher of wisdom.

Re-configuring Jesus' relationship to the Baptizer

The aphoristic/Cynic sage profile for Jesus helps bring his teaching activity into clearer relationship to his participation in the movement of John the Baptizer. Here the recent work by Leif Vaage on the substratum of Q is crucial to this re-configuration. Complementing his earlier work on the way the Baptizer's clothing and habits are reminiscent of Cynic behavior, Vaage finds in this substratum a clear and consistent set of references to John as a Cynic. He concludes: "John appears in (Q) 7:24b, 26, 28a, 33 as a "serious" Cynic, critical of those around him and the cultural habits they displayed. For John's critics at this stage, the man's main mark of divinity was just the demon in him. His admirers, however, recalled John as "the greatest man ever born." Here certainly was no "softie" like the sycophants at Herod's court, no toady of the local tyrant. Like the Q people, John was rather to be found in the desert, on the social margin, aggressively pursuing another "better" life. Jesus emerges in the memory of Q's formative stratum as a more convivial, though no less demanding Cynic."[20]

Vaage's work allows a further re-configuration. In an aphoristic/ Cynic perspective, baptizing itself could have been a clever satire on prescriptive ritual washings. Baptism would then have been a creative dislocation of *mikvah* requirements from the temple precincts to the wilderness of the Jordan. Moving the bathing rite to a wilder, more natural setting would have both made light of the conventional ritual and transformed its significance by suggesting a cleansing from the corruption of the marketplace and temple organization. No wonder Jesus could emerge from such a movement with a wink in his eye and a readiness to teach.

Elaborations of Jesus as sage

There are two substantial sets of red and pink material which have received practically no attention in recent profiles of the historical Jesus, but which – once considered – fit nicely into the profile of Jesus as aphoristic/Cynic sage. These are Jesus' prayer and his common wisdom teachings.

Jesus and prayer

Jesus as aphoristic/Cynic sage offers opportunities to integrate the prayer life of Jesus into a coherent picture. The praying of Jesus has played an enigmatic role in his recent portraiture. Although eight texts and five different "fragments of prayers"[21] were voted red or pink by the Seminar, there has been little discussion of Jesus praying. Despite the strong support for the five prayer fragments, the treatment of Jesus at prayer has tended either to be absent or to rest uncritically on conventional notions of piety without probing the specific character of Jesus' prayer in relationship to his milieu and his teachings. This major lacuna in the portraiture of the historical Jesus may be occasioned by contemporary scholarly embarrassment about prayer, or by the curious character of the prayer texts of Jesus which have emerged from the Seminar's work.

The following sustained look at the character of these red and pink prayer texts points to their rather fluid integration into the profile of Jesus as aphoristic/Cynic sage.

The Seminar's voting red and pink on five sentences from the so-called Lord's Prayer, gray on another, and black on three others seems at first curious, but on closer examination displays internal coherence and consistency. The Lord's Prayer displays strong literary structure[22] in its Q, Matthean, and Lukan forms.[23] These rather tight literary unities are strong indications of post-oral redaction/composition of the prayer as a whole. In addition, Q, Matthew, and Luke all contain particular petitions which clearly belong to situations after Jesus' death.[24] In short, the "Lord's Prayer" is best seen as composed by Q and elaborated by Matthew and Luke.

Given this later textual provenance, the Seminar chose to vote on the authenticity of the individual sentences which comprise the prayer. These votes depended on the notion of "prayer fragments" which would have been spoken independently of one another by Jesus.[25] Examination of the ways these "prayer fragments" cohere with Jesus's aphoristic/Cynic teachings helps situate the prayer of Jesus as a part of his overall profile.

Abba / Father (Luke 11:2 / Matt 6:9)

Placing the prayer phrase "Abba/Father" in the context of the other ninety authentic sayings of Jesus points toward a posture in which one called traditional dependencies into question and cast oneself on the care of God. The life style of a Cynic sage flaunted its independence, and looked to the manifestation of a deeper order and freedom in nature. Instead of dependence on the conventions, Jesus' teachings invoke trust in the basic fabric of life that God provides as evidenced in nature.

> Don't fret about your life – what you're going to eat or drink – or about your body – what you're going to wear. There is more to living than food and clothing, isn't there? Take a look at the birds of the air . . .   (Matt 6:25–30)

Such teachings enjoining fundamental trust were companions to those that challenged dependency on wealth (such as Luke 6:20 and Mark 10:25), family (such as Luke 14:26 and Matt 12:48–50), scholarly prestige (such as Mark 12:38–39), or religion (such as Mark 2:27-28 and Luke 18:10–14).

An intangible and fluid source of strength and nurture is often implicit in the core teachings of Jesus. Sometimes it was associated with the "reign/rule/domain" of God, and even occasionally with God directly. But this was not a God who was enmeshed in and allied to systems of wealth, family, and religion. This was an "Abba/Father"[26], a God invoked over against the conventions of wealth, family, nation, empire, temple, and clan.

Since Jesus seldom spoke directly about God and did not come close to mandating that the title of "Abba/Father" be used all the time, this appellation most likely emerged as a clever dimension to his challenge of family privileges and conventions. Note, for instance, the way the traditions of family are juxtaposed with the "Abba/Fatherhood" of God in this core saying of Jesus:

> My mother and my brothers – whoever are they?. . . Here are my mother and my brothers. For whoever does the will of my Father in heaven, that's my brother and sister and mother. (Matt 12:48–50)

For Jesus, reliance on traditional family ties was an impediment to a lifestyle that trusts in the God beyond family conventions. Seeing God as "Abba/Father" was a clever combination of challenge to family tradition[27] and evocation of a new trust in the divinely sustained fabric of life itself. Calling out to God as "Abba/Father" replaced one's reliance on family systems of privilege, inheritance, and honor. Such a prayer relinquished these conventions and expressed Jesus' dependence on a less tangible dynamic. So praying to "Abba/Father" belonged to the life style of a Cynic sage who loved to give an aphoristic twist to his utterances. As prayer, "Abba/Father" was far from pious; it was a taunt to the conventional systems of support; it was part of the fabric and consciousness of a clever sage, who sought to reveal the hidden through a vigorous learning process. Learning uncovered the open-ended interactions of God, humans, and nature – and it prompted an occasional invocation of the "Abba/Father" underneath, around, and/or above the obvious.

"Your name be revered" Luke 11:2d (Matt 6:9d)

It would have been nearly impossible for Jesus not to have prayed that God's name be revered and honored as holy. "Your name is holy," reads the third of the Eighteen Benedictions repeated daily in first-century Galilee. Two among many similar Kaddish prayers read: "Magnified and sanctified be his great name" and "Your name, O Lord our God, shall be hallowed."[28] So surely while growing up, and probably in his adult life as well, Jesus asked that God's name be revered. He certainly spoke this petition in group prayers (at a meal, at sundown, in a synagogue), and perhaps voiced it when he was alone.

Since no other references to the holiness of God's name appear in the core teachings of Jesus, we have no indication that this was a key idea in Jesus' teachings. More likely it was a part of Jesus' consciousness simply because he belonged to Galilean Jewish culture and prayed together with other Jews.

It is quite possible that this phrase, "Your name be revered," was cleverly joined with Jesus' "Abba/Father" prayer before the Lord's Prayer linked them. Since we do not have any literary evidence between Jesus' oral performance of the two phrases and the Q composition of the Lord's Prayer, it is unclear whether Jesus himself prayed "Abba/Father, your name be revered" or whether the generation after Jesus put these two prayers of his together. Whoever did that was in a humorous mood of discovery, and produced one of the better jokes of early Christianity. It is, unfortunately, a joke that modern readers do not get.

The trope went something like this. When first-century Jews gave reverence to God's name, they were referring to a particular, special, and sacred word that was God's name. That name was thought to be so special and alive with the divine that it was pronounced either rarely, not at all, or with great reverence.[29]

When Jesus or his followers first prayed "Abba/Father, your name be revered," they were in effect giving God an additional name, one in the common Aramaic, and in common every day in every household. That is, it was not in the sacred Hebrew language, and it was not treated as any kind of special name. Associating "Abba" with the very special holy name of God (everyone knew it was "Yahweh," not "Abba") was almost a contradiction in terms. Any first-century Jew would have understood the wisecrack, and either laughed or felt offended.

This ironic association of the common word for father with the revered name of God was certainly as shocking as many of his aphorisms were – like the one that attributed blessedness to the poor and hungry. "The unexpected combination surprised people into rethinking what was and was not holy. As a prayer, it called people to see God and reverence in a much broader scheme; it fit well with Jesus' repeated citation of the poor and children as images of God's reign. Putting together "Abba" with "Your name be revered" opened up the vision of what was important and holy, just as Jesus' parables and aphorisms did. If Jesus did not put these two prayer fragments together, some of his witty followers must have delighted in doing so prior to the later composition of the unaphoristic "Lord's Prayer."

In any case this combination illustrates the character of Jesus' prayer. As we saw in considering the Abba prayer fragment by itself, his prayer was similar to his teaching in seeking to uncover the learnable all around him, and boldly challenging conventional categories which would limit the scope of discovery.

Impose your imperial rule (Luke 11:2e, Matt 6:10a)

A prayer by Jesus asking for God's reign or imperial rule[30] comports with his aphoristic/Cynic teachings in at least four ways:

1. Jesus' teachings reveal his appetite for and fascination with God's reign over the world.

God's "basileia" is a major theme in the teachings of the historical Jesus. Of the ninety sayings that can be traced to him, at least fourteen are explicitly about "God's basileia." At least eight others were later associated by the gospel writers with Jesus' idea of God's imperial rule. So it is quite easy to imagine Jesus saying this sentence prayer almost as a sigh of anticipation: "Come on, God, impose this rule of yours" or "Oh God, just let this reign of yours come."

2. We noted earlier that Jesus' reference to God's "basileia" was typical of the ways hellenistic wisdom associated learning with rule. This

common teaching that a sage held sway or ruled over the world through his/her wisdom situates the "domain" or "rule" of God in Jesus' teachings within a broader range of wisdom proclamations about an intangible reign available only to the one who seeks to understand. As we have noted earlier, the pervasiveness of sages' proclamations of an intangible and elusive reign makes an astonishingly close fit with many of Jesus' parables and aphorisms. Indeed, prayers for the establishment of this reign were common among learners/sages. Such prayer by Jesus must have been at once wry and self-involving. Asking for God's reign as a sage was a way of keeping one's learning quest open-ended and ongoing. Such a prayer by a sage would have been spoken in the delightful and risk-taking self-consciousness that it is through one's own openness to learn that one becomes a part of God's reign.

3. The "basileia" of God in the teachings of Jesus surprises and baffles the listener, especially with its elusive character. Perhaps the saying which best captures its transcendent nature is Thom 113:2–4:

> His disciples said to him, "When will the Father's imperial rule come?" "It will not come by watching for it. It will not be said, 'Look, here' or 'Look, there.' Rather, the Father's imperial rule is spread out upon the earth, and people don't see it."

This divine "basileia" did not fit into the normal patterns of economy or social convention. According to one of the core teachings of Jesus, God's domain is like a vineyard owner who pays all his laborers the same wage, even though some worked three times as long as others (Matt 20:1–15). Even more shocking to a society where having many sons was a sure sign of God's favor, Jesus saluted the men who "castrated themselves because of Heaven's imperial rule" (Matt 19:12). In a world where wealth also was seen as a sign of God's blessing, Jesus underscored the otherness of God's reign by exclaiming: "How difficult it is for those who have money to enter God's domain!" (Mark 10:23). A prayer for God's rule or domain was then an invocation of surprising learning. Staying open to such a combination of surprise and learning is, of course, not easy. A predisposition to discover the hidden world around one involves particular kinds of consciousness and risk-taking. Initiating and maintaining this spiritual openness was the rationale for Jesus' prayer that the comprehensive, elusive, and surprising reign of God come.

4. The Scholars Version translation of "basileia" as "imperial rule" (rather than the traditional "kingdom") has brought to light one of the

key dimensions of both this prayer and Jesus' teachings. Invoking an eternal "kingdom" must have involved both an aphoristic twist and a satirical commentary on the claims and presumptions of the Roman empire. Hence the translation "God's imperial rule" (or in this verse, "your imperial rule") helps accent the ironic character of Jesus' proclamation and invocation of God's reign. The coming and presence of God's reign in Jesus' teachings mocked and pre-empted the more obvious imperial rule of Rome. A prayer for the coming of "your imperial rule" amounted to a self-investment in uncovering this hidden counter-movement of God. Such a prayer deepened and personalized the sage's overall effort to uncover the hidden through learning.

Provide us with the bread we need for the day (Matt 6:11)

Jesus and some of his followers traversed the Galilean countryside, teaching and healing and eating what was given them. The wandering teacher who relied on the hospitality of others was a well known figure in the eastern Mediterranean world. Especially since those who practiced popular Cynic philosophy followed very similar practices, when Jesus either begged for food and/or hoped for a dinner invitation where he could do some teaching, he fit a customary pattern of behavior in his world.

It is most likely in this context that Jesus prayed: "Provide us with the bread we need for the day." Since he seems to have been dependent on others for his food — at least while he was on the road teaching — such a prayer would have been simply that he receive enough food that day.

This simple sentence prayer resembles Jesus' teachings both in that Jesus and his followers, like peripatetic Cynics, cast themselves on the care of God and nature, and also in that it challenged the conventions of family, economy, or accumulated wealth. Jesus' prayer for only the current day's bread fit very well with two other pink sayings. Thom 36:1 reads,

> Don't fret from morning to evening and evening to morning about your food.

And in Luke 12:24, Jesus said,

> Think about the crows: they don't plant or harvest, they don't have storerooms or barns. Yet God feeds them.

As in the previous three prayer fragments, an aphoristic/Cynic ethos provides a coherent context for this prayer. Once the fragment is disengaged from the literary composition we know as the Lord's Prayer, it fits easily into the profile of this kind of sage.

> Forgive our debts to the extent that we have forgiven those
> in debt to us. (Matt 6:12)

Indebtedness was one of the major social and economic problems of first-century Palestine.[31] The peasant farmers and the merchants in the towns and villages were constantly in danger of falling into crippling debt to the landed class and the urban elite. The core teachings of Jesus show him very conscious of debt. A good number of sayings refer to persons in one stage or another of indebtedness. The parable of the shrewd manager who manages the debts of his master (Luke 16:1-8), Jesus' instructions about lending money (Matt 5:42b), and the parable of the unforgiving slave (Matt 18:23-34) all refer directly to the dilemmas of small merchants and peasant farmers racked by debt.

Interestingly enough, whether they are from Jesus or the later tradition, these sayings do not reveal a clear position on a number of problems related to indebtedness. For example, while they show a strong awareness that it exists, they seem to resist a consistent stand against condemning either the debtor or the lender.

The sentence prayer "forgive our debts to the extent that we have forgiven those in debt to us" surely speaks to this grave socio-economic problem in Roman Palestine. This prayer of Jesus asked God to get him or his people out of debt, but not without exploring the hidden side of such a request. The aphoristic and Cynic characteristics of this prayer committed Jesus and his friends to write off whatever anyone owed them in return for the forgiveness of their debts. One could not offer this petition for release from indebtedness through this prayer without forgiving the debts one was owed by others. In effect, the prayer invoked cooperation from both God and the one praying to do away with the plague of indebtedness.

This fits with the only other red or pink instruction about indebtedness. In Thom 95:1–2 (and its pink parallel, Matt 5:42b) Jesus advises:

> If you have money, don't lend it at interest. Rather give it
> to someone from whom you won't get it back.

Going behind the Lord's Prayer to the prayer fragments has produced a more unified profile of Jesus. The fragments show a Jesus consistent with the aphoristic/Cynic sage. Like many of the red and pink teachings of Jesus the prayer as a whole challenged both convention and one's self. It has for quite some time been a conceptual problem for scholars[37] to accommodate the iconoclastic character of Jesus' aphorisms and Cynic-like instructions to a Lord's Prayer meant for personal or liturgical use or even one representing a catalogue of Jesus' concerns. As the above review of prayer fragments has illustrated, breaking the clauses into smaller unconnected units re-connects them with the strongest literary attestations to Jesus, the sage.

Since aphorists and iconoclasts of our day are not much given to prayer, it may be difficult to associate prayer with the kind of teaching reflected in the red and pink sayings of Jesus. But that was not the case in either the Cynic tradition or that of Jewish aphoristic wisdom. There are numerous Cynic examples like that of God being "thanked and praised, trusted, addressed and referred to as Father, God of all, guiding and enlightening individuals for the general good, always forgiving, despite the evident wickedness of humanity."[33] The extensive prayer in the first-century Wisdom of Solomon 9:1–18 is a dramatic example of Jewish wisdom merging the themes of learning and God's reign. However removed contemporary piety may be from the aphoristic temper, Jesus as an aphoristic/Cynic sage stood in an active tradition of prayer.

How then did that particular prayer tradition work in the case of the historical Jesus? To put it briefly, Jesus' particular "style" of prayer as evidenced in these fragments was very much in intense interaction with the people around him and his social settings. Although he most probably also prayed in some rote manner during his life time (e.g. "Your name be revered"), most of the small prayers evidenced in our study seemed to have been almost hyper-conscious of people listening in, either in actuality or by way of their psychological presence in Jesus' mind. It is typical of the aphoristic style that the way he used "Abba," "Abba, your name be revered," "May your basileia come," "Forgive us our debts as we forgive those indebted to us," and "Give us today the bread we need" both assumes and plays off his listeners' responses, so that the prayers themselves seem in large measure defined by the interaction between the one who prayed and those who were listening. I do not mean to imply any hypocrisy on Jesus' part, but rather to suggest that such social interaction could have realized its own unexpected but authentic integrity as prayer in the very fact of its evocative interaction.[34] In this sense the engagement with God in prayer did not in any way exclude simultaneous interaction with people.

Another way of thinking about this style of prayer can be derived from the teaching character of Jesus' activity. When the prayer leader purposefully creates interaction with those around him/her, a dynamic we have discovered underlying the Lord's Prayer, we quite easily recognize the mentality of an aphoristic teacher. From this angle, one could say that the aphoristic teacher Jesus brought that teaching/learning dynamic to his prayer; indeed, he does not seem to have been able to turn off the teacher/learner interaction in his prayer. The performative character of Jesus' teachings seem to be applicable as well to his prayer. The search for wisdom's social dimension seems to have been a primary shaper of his prayers, and they were animated by the faith that there was nothing hidden which could not be discovered. These prayer fragments thrived on exposing the one praying and those listening to new levels of disclosure, both of themselves and their overlapping milieux. This kind of disclosure, discovery, and learning is, in fact, characteristic of God in the wisdom literature.[35]

By associating Jesus' prayer with his teaching, I do not mean to suggest that Jesus taught his followers specific prayers. Downing's summary of Cynics at prayer seems to make best sense of the way Jesus' teaching and praying mixed. Downing notes that the Cynics were not at all shy in praying, but were equally insistent that prayers not be taught.[36] Jesus as an aphoristic sage prayed in evocative and socially interactive ways that taught implicitly, as aphorisms do. Obviously this sort of prayer tended to elicit responses from the persons listening, not to invite rote repetition. But like his sayings, Jesus' prayers were often striking enough to be remembered, elaborated, and probably imitated. Their memorable quality easily explains why a number of prayer fragments would be remembered and repeated by his followers.

The highly interactive style of prayer evidenced in the prayer fragments stands in some contrast to the descriptions of Jesus alone in prayer found in the gospels, passages voted gray and black by the Seminar, but advocated by some contemporary scholars[37] as representing a primary practice of the historical Jesus. It is, of course, not impossible that both styles of prayer were used by Jesus. The remarkable difference in style, however, does seem to corroborate the various literary grounds on which the Seminar saw fit to reject the historicity of such passages as Gethsemane, the temptation in the desert, and the time alone after the first miracle of the loaves. Concerning the question as to whether Jesus spent substantial times alone in prayer as suggested by these passages, I would simply say that we have no credible evidence to say that he did or did not.[38]

Once the notion of pre-Lord's Prayer "prayer fragments" is established, it is easier to evaluate how narrowly or broadly the historical Jesus' prayer life was focused. The five (or six, depending on how one is counting)[39] prayer fragments demonstrate a wide range of concerns and contexts, including food (Give us today . . .), response to some kind of Cynic on-the-roadness (Give us today . . .), indebtedness (Forgive us . . .), family relationships (Abba . . .), God (Abba . . ., May your name . . .), politics (Impose your rule . . .), religious convention (Abba, may your name . . .), education (Impose, your rule . . .), sex (Impose your rule . . .), and economics (Impose your rule . . .). Although there is no way of determining how frequently Jesus prayed, this large range of issues evoked by the prayer fragments (along with the intensely interactive or "public" character of his prayer which emerges from its aphoristic character) indicates that he prayed in a wide variety of settings about a broad spectrum of issues.

The intensely social presence of Jesus in prayer and the broad range of issues he addressed in prayer again underline the coherence of these data with his activity as an aphoristic/Cynic sage. The aggressive agenda that there is nothing hidden or veiled that cannot be discovered and learned about seems to have permeated the prayer life of Jesus.

Jesus and common wisdom

One of the major advantages to keeping an understanding of Jesus well within the profile of a hellenistic sage is that this accounts for the more mundane and unremarkable characteristics of Jesus' teaching reflected in the work of the Seminar. The Seminar declared authentic 13 sayings in 35 different texts, all of which report proverbs or common wisdom. Even though there was often an explicit Seminar bias against the authenticity of common wisdom in the teachings of Jesus,[40] almost 15 percent of the red and pink sayings fall in this category.

From proverbs like "no servant can be a slave to two masters" (Luke 16:13a and four parallels) through injunctions like "you must be sly as a snake and as simple as a dove" (Matt 10: l6b) to example stories like the assassin who tried out his strength at home before using his sword against someone powerful (Thomas 98), the Seminar often to its own surprise found strong (mostly technical) reasons to associate various common wisdom sayings with the historical Jesus.

It seems likely that a more consistent stance by the Seminar on whether Jesus taught common wisdom would have resulted in finding more like 20 or 25 per cent of his authentic sayings derived from common wisdom. For instance, the common saying, "Anyone here with two good ears had better listen," (voted gray by the Seminar) is attested in at least 19 different early Christian texts in at least four separate traditions. It is the most multiply attested saying in all of the literature on the sayings of Jesus. The agreement among the variety of texts is close enough to be considered performancial by Crossan who considers it to be a "classical example of oral sensibility."[41] Of course, in some of the parallels the saying could be an editorial "intensification" as Rudolf Bultmann claims.[42] But the overwhelming diversity of attestation makes it unlikely that all of them are later accretions. This is clearly a common saying of a number of sages that Jesus almost certainly also said, perhaps one too many times for some of his hearers with ears.[43]

Keeping the historical Jesus strongly within the profile of a sage helps us understand how these rather mundane and only occasionally profound proverbs cohere with the more remarkable and ingenious sayings of Jesus. Even the most remarkable sages or teachers speak (or misspeak) the obvious and the trivial with some regularity.

Bultmann, the father of the criterion of dissimilarity – which is generally used to discredit the historicity of Jesus' common wisdom – showed a rather profound ambivalence on this issue. At one point, he wrote, "Why could he (Jesus) not have used the saying about serving two masters in his sermon if he knew it already as a proverb."[44]

The Gospel of Thomas plays a crucial role in the possibility of re-integrating Jesus' common wisdom[45] into the larger picture of Jesus as aphoristic/Cynic sage. Thomas has provided a number of independent parallels to common wisdom sayings in the synoptics, so that they must be moved back from the levels of written composition and redaction to the oral sensibility Crossan has described.

Jesus as teacher of common wisdom fits the overall aphoristic/Cynic sage profile in two ways.

Common wisdom and aphoristic wisdom were on the same continuum of learning. They were both ways of ascertaining hidden patterns in the ways things are. They both examine life, seeking to discover an unseen order below the surface of events. Common wisdom often, of course, overstated the pattern in ways that obscured the point or missed the exception. Aphoristic wisdom, in trying to identify the subtleties and include the aberrations, is a refinement of common wisdom. A sage almost always had first to discover both the power and limits of common wisdom in order to develop an aphoristic approach. The aphorism was born in the unveiling of both the experience itself and the failure of the proverb. From this point of view, then, common wisdom had to have been part of the methodology of an aphoristic sage.

One can observe this continuum between common and aphoristic wisdom in both important Jewish and Cynic hellenistic sages.[46] In direct correlation, for instance, to Jesus' use of the common proverb about two masters, Dio Chrysostom 66.13 reads "Every slavery is hard to bear, but think of someone who happens to be slave in a household with two or three masters." And, Philo, in discussing the contrast between love of external things and moral virtue wrote: "It is quite impracticable for the former to agree to share a common home with the other."[47]

At least as important in situating Jesus' common wisdom within the larger profile of aphoristic/Cynic sage is the way Jesus' teachings regularly referred the learner/listener to everyday life. The way the parable of the mustard seed played off the majestic cedar of Lebanon by consigning the reign of God to the common mustard plant illustrates Jesus' typical strategy of grounding wisdom in the ordinary. Jesus' aphoristic approach contained within itself the assumptions of common wisdom. His aphorisms regularly projected the search for wisdom into the marketplace, the household, and agriculture.

The discounting of common wisdom belonging to a profile of Jesus has generally held that such sayings are "not particularly distinctive and so could have been said by any sage" and consequently, do "not tell us much about Jesus."[48] I would suggest that these common wisdom sayings tell us quite a bit about Jesus, precisely because they could have been said by any sage. That so much far from earthshaking common wisdom ended up in the Seminar's data base for the historical Jesus is a major indication that Jesus was not entirely unique. Integrating the widely attested common wisdom of Jesus into this sage profile is one element of the larger twentieth century challenge to the notion of the absolute uniqueness of Jesus.[49] It is crucial for the overall profile of Jesus that he was not always brilliant, original, or radical. That Jesus' teachings were also sometimes ordinary, second-hand, and conservative tells us a great deal about who he was. Especially in the context of the Christianity of the last thousand years, there is a major difference between a teacher who is always brilliant (a legend and a god) and one who is often brilliant but sometimes ordinary (a sage).

Jesus and healing

By almost all accounts the typical hellenistic sage did not heal. Downing searches in vain for Cynic parallels, concluding almost plaintively: "We have no tales of Cynic healing to match the list in 'Q'. However, there is considerable (if traditionally Greek) stress on physical well-being as a sign of the teaching's value. It is not impossible that a Cynic trusting he shared the royal power of Zeus might expect to be able to heal."[50] Both Crossan and Downing have shown that the ancient world's most vividly and extensively described lifestyle corresponding to the core teachings of the historical Jesus is that of the popular Cynics. That these descriptions do not include healing is telling. The absence of healing from the Cynic corpus loosens the connection between healing and the practice of a sage like Jesus. Jewish wisdom texts also seem to lack any linkage of healing and teaching. In a manner completely coherent with the Cynic literature, the injunctions to the sage and the sage's followers in Proverbs, Ben Sirach, Baruch, and the Wisdom of Solomon include no encouragement for the sage to heal. Indeed, the idea that a sage might heal does not even occur in this literature.

Ironically one of the strongest cases for Jesus as healer and Jesus as teacher being contradictory categories is in a work strongly and complexly arguing the case that Jesus was a healer. In his 1995 book, *Jesus, the Healer: Possession, Trance, and the Origins of Christianity*, Stevan Davies maintains that the ideas of Jesus as teacher and Jesus as healer are contradictory. To support this contradiction of the modes of healing and teaching, Davies proposes that in the history of scholarship "the paradigm of Jesus the Teacher has proven itself to be very problematic." Having substantiated the problematic character of a teaching healer, Davies then suggests that "it may well be that the very idea that Jesus was primarily a teacher came into being only after his death." (He concludes and documents thoroughly with both ancient sources and contemporary anthropological studies that "the ruling metaphor, or paradigm, that does work, that does reveal an historical Jesus who did pretty much what the New Testament said he did, and who is *not* (Davies' own italics) a social type never before or since heard of in the world…is the metaphor of Jesus the Healer." In drawing this conclusion Davies is simply taking seriously the fact that "healer and teacher" is an unlikely combination.

Yet while I submit that Davies' rigor and his insistence that the modalities of healer and teacher not be a-historically mixed provide an important compass, I do not agree with his conclusion. I concur with Davies, Downing, and Crossan's perception that healers and teachers don't mix in the ancient world, but draw the opposite inference: since Jesus as healer and teacher appears to be an anomaly, I conclude that Jesus was not a healer but only a sage.

That the gospel stories of Jesus' themselves show Jesus' healing to be symbolic of a greater meaning only underlines the strong possibility that the motif of Jesus as healer was added after his death. I do not ground this in nineteenth and twentieth century positivism, which holds that healings are impossible. I do follow Davies, Crossan, and the Jesus

Seminar in maintaining that modern anthropology has adequately demonstrated that such healings occur, especially in exorcistic contexts. I also think that such exorcistic healings happened in early Christianity, and that the teachings of the historical Jesus about the immanent realm of God inspired other early Christians to do exorcistic healing, as both Q and the Acts of the Apostles propose. It was these early Christians' healings and their effects which made it so easy to posthumously associate Jesus himself with healing.

Crossan, whose use of anthropological data from other periods and literary analysis of the Jesus traditions is clear and energized, admits in his summary that the jump from Cynic aphorist to healer is chancy and unsubstantiated: "We are forced, then by the primary stratum itself, to bring together two disparate elements: healer and Cynic, magic and meal.[51] Crossan's attempt to bring healer and sage together is an intellectual effort of Herculean proportions, but flies too boldly in the face of the larger historical patterns Davies takes seriously.

Here then, in holding closely to the larger historical logic of the sage profile, is my only substantial departure from the voting results of the Seminar. While agreeing with the socio-anthropological data which validated a variety of healing traditions similar to those in the gospels, and while acknowledging that there were probably early Christian healers, I suspect that no such Christian healers were teaching sages. The detailed correspondence of Jesus with the extant profiles of sages, as outlined in this essay, strongly cautions against a departure from that coherent, historically grounded portrait.

Conclusion

It is both the strength and the Achilles heel of the historian's discipline to describe the past using concepts and categories indigenous to the era being studied. Painting a continuum in which all the elements cohere with one another is the way historians try to do their craft, and by doing so to make sense of seemingly disparate data. Admittedly, this methodology rules out a priori the possibility that something "completely other" can be historically understood. But epistemologically, staying within the historical process allows the historian to honor both the character of other epochs and the relativity of post-modern consciousness. I have attempted to stay clearly within the discipline of the historian in this profile while yet addressing data with the longest track record for claims to the "totally other."

The Jesus who emerges as aphoristic/Cynic sage was a person of some importance to his region. He was a sage of superior ability, and probably the best-known in the Galilee of the first century. From within the larger wisdom traditions of his time, he challenged a number of conventions and sketched an intangible domain where, if one kept open to learning, everything hidden could be understood. Largely by implication and allusion, he described this abstract realm as a part of God's reign that could be participated in through courageous and persistent learning. An incurably interactive person, he experienced the realms of society and nature as full of occasions for wisdom. In this same search for wisdom, he prayed in ways that tweaked learning from himself and those listening. In all this he belonged to the larger social and intellectual momentum of the eastern Mediterranean wisdom movements.

The religious and intellectual significance of this historical Jesus is consistently overstated.[52] Even after demythologizing Jesus, it is important to stay grounded in the historically relative place he had in the development of Christianity and western consciousness. Neither his teachings, nor his prayers, nor his deeds can claim a central place in contemporary meaning schemes. When placed in the larger movements of history (first the wisdom movements, then the early Christian movements, then the history of Christianity, then the breakdown of western consciousness), some significance for the historical Jesus can be asserted, but it is clearly secondary to the significance of the theological and mythical Jesus(es).

A common challenge to this position is how to account for the dramatic emergence and sustaining power of the Christianity that grew up in the ancient Mediterranean. That, of course, is another topic. But the way to an answer can be stated both historically and theologically. Historically, Christianity's emergence needs to be seen as the product of a complex set of socio-historical developments. That is, the birth of Christianity can be accounted for by looking more carefully at the complex historical forces of the first five centuries, not by some magical Christian destiny or some heroic gestures by a founding figure. The recent works of Burton Mack, Karen King, and Rodney Stark indicate diverse ways of understanding the historical vectors of Christianity's first five centuries. Theologically, Christianity's emergence needs to be seen in the character of Spirit being fully present in widely diverse historical settings and social interactions. From this perspective, Christianity can be viewed not as manifest destiny, but as one example among many others of how Spirit unfolds new phenomena from the fabric of life itself. The works of Thomas Berry, Bernard Lonergan, Marjorie Suchocki, and John Cobb are signs of this exploration.

Dirt, Shame, and Sin in the Expendable Company of Jesus

Stephen J. Patterson

The Gospel of Jesus

What did the followers of Jesus experience in his company that moved them to claim that in his words and deeds they had come to know who God is? What was the goodness they saw in his deeds? What was the good news – the "gospel" – they heard in his words? And how did some people find such ultimate goodness in Jesus, while others experienced him quite differently? Indeed, not everyone experienced Jesus as *good* at all. For some, Jesus was an enigma, an odd ball; what he said and did was to them meaningless nonsense. And among those who did understand him, the meaning of what he said and did was not all the same. For some he was interesting, perhaps even amusing in his novelty. For others, Jesus was a threat, a danger to be dealt with, a voice to be silenced. But for some, what Jesus said and did meant something good. His words were heard as good news, as "gospel." Their experience of him was redemptive, liberating, empowering. And for some, this experience of Jesus gave meaning to their lives in a way that only something ultimately real and authentic can do, and they gave themselves over to it. In Jesus they had seen God. What was it that these first followers of Jesus experienced in his company that moved them to say that in this person they had come to know what God is really like?

History and theology

In what follows, I will focus primarily on things Jesus is said to have done; his sayings and parables I have treated elsewhere. But focus-

195

ing on the so-called "deeds" of Jesus poses some peculiar – some would say intractable – difficulties for the historian. When the Jesus Seminar began its work, it inherited a number of methodological principles from earlier generations of historians in quest of the historical Jesus. But most of those methods were designed to help identify authentic *sayings* of Jesus. When we tried to apply them to things Jesus is said to have done, we soon found that they were not very useful. For example, many sayings of Jesus are attested independently in multiple early Christian sources. Such multiple attestation is usually taken as a sign that a saying is very old, and perhaps goes back to Jesus himself. In dealing with things Jesus is said to have done, we soon found that very few deeds of Jesus were multiply attested. Unless we were to assume that Jesus was a person who talked a lot, but did little, we were forced to conclude that there was something about the way early Christians talked about the deeds of Jesus and passed these traditions on that was different from the way the tradition of Jesus' sayings was transmitted. We did not (and still do not) fully understand these differences. But we knew that the methods of earlier questers were coming up short as we explored this new territory.

Perhaps the best provisional solution to this problem is to say simply that the deeds of Jesus present us with the creative memory of the early church. In the Jesus Seminar, it was seldom that we could assert, even tenuously, the historical accuracy of any particular event or occasion as it is depicted in the gospels, or in fact, that such and such an event ever occurred at all. But we did notice that certain types of events are depicted with great frequency in the Jesus tradition, and across a variety of sources and forms. Things like healings and exorcisms, associating with the unclean and the shamed, conflict with his family – such things began to emerge as "typical" of Jesus in the widespread memory of the early church. Such "typifications," as Bob Funk began to call them, became the basis for a general description of the sort of things Jesus probably did, even though the historicity of any single story in the gospels was always hard to demonstrate. It seems, then, that we have inherited from earliest Christianity the creative memory of what people experienced in Jesus' ministry, and a collection of stories to illustrate and give form to the memory of that experience. The gospels seldom give us what might be described as an historical event. Rather, we have stories born of memory, impressions of what Jesus was like. The limits of ancient history are considerable, indeed.

Needless to say, then, everything in this chapter is said with an implied "probably" affixed to it. But this is true of most writing of history. The work of the historian can normally offer only probability, not exactitude. History is not science; it belongs in the Humanities building, not Natural Sciences. It can offer no quantifiable data, whose meaning would be self-evident to anyone. There is not even any clear starting point for the historian. History is always somewhat circular in its methods. One looks at the past through the memories of those who experienced it, gathering together the impressions left by events on the lives of people. In the end, the historian must try to render a 'reading' of this collective mass of information. She or he must try to assemble it in a way that makes historical sense. She or he must attempt a reading of this amorphous collection of evidence that is fair and unprejudiced. But there are no guarantees. There can be no objectivity in history. We are all much too involved in the subject matter of history – human existence itself – to claim objectivity. At best the historian can strive only to be fair, unprejudiced, and self-critical in looking at the past. Certainty always lies beyond the historian's grasp. But this should not be viewed as a loss, a deficiency of history. To the contrary, it is its very nature and strength. For we look to history not out of idle curiosity, but to ask about the relevance of the past for our own present. History does not ask a scientific question, but an existential one. One cannot observe history; one can only encounter it.

For some, this lack of objectivity makes history an inappropriate medium for engaging in theological reflection. For me, it makes it the most appropriate medium. Like history, theology also does not ask a scientific question. To be sure, the age-old longing for certitude of faith, the desire to know beyond a shadow of a doubt the ultimate secrets of the universe, anxiety about death and the quest for security, all make it tempting to transform theology into a science. This is the impulse behind the dubious concept of "Creationism," which reduces the Bible to a pseudo-science with a false offer of scientific credibility. But the biblical text itself, a mixture of history and its interpretation, will not allow such an easy escape from the existential question posed to us by both history and theology: the question of meaning. What does human existence mean? The answer to this question is never automatic or self-evident in the way that answers to scientific questions might often be. Answering this question with authenticity is infinitely more difficult than answering any question of science, for it always involves a subjective commitment to seeing the world in a certain way. One cannot calculate the answer to an existential question like a mathematical equation. One must reflect on existential questions. One must ponder them. Answers do not come quickly or automatically. They must be tested in the living of them.

For someone who believes in God, human existence means something because there is a God who gives life its ultimate meaning. To believe in God is to believe in a transcendent reality running through and beyond all things, a fundamental reality in which existence itself is grounded. Faith in God is an act of trusting in this reality, and risking a life that is oriented to it. Thus, as Schubert Ogden has rightly argued,[1] the question of faith in God always in reality involves two simultaneous questions posed at once: Who is God? and Who must I become if I choose to give myself over to this God? Finding meaning in life always involves venturing an answer to both of these questions. To be serious about the God question is to ask about that ultimate reality without which life can mean nothing. Answering it seriously involves moving beyond any abstract ideas about what God is like, and giving oneself over to the ultimate reality that is God. That is the risk of faith. When earliest Christians risked faith in Jesus, they were venturing an answer to this most pressing two-fold question: We have found God in the words and deeds of this person, Jesus, and, we really are who he says we are to become. Who was Jesus? And what did he say or do that earliest Christians experienced as this kind of ultimate reality, a reality to which they could give themselves fully? This is to ask what Jesus *meant* to people. It is the question asked by both history and theology.

The Basileia of God

How did Jesus describe what he was doing? The gospels typically depict him speaking of his activity as the *basileia* of God. Jesus announces the presence of this *basileia*; his parables illustrate this *basileia*; he calls prostitutes, tax collectors, children, and beggars into this *basileia*. In the synoptic gospels this term is used over a hundred times. Jesus is depicted as speaking all the time about the *basileia* of God.

Quite naturally, then, this way of speaking has worked itself into the language of Christian faith. The common way of translating this term into English is to use the word "kingdom." That is how you will find it in the old King James Version and its descendants, like the Revised Standard Version and its recent revision, the New Revised Standard Version. That translation tradition was highly influenced by the olde King's English, in which one speaks of sovereignty using "kingdom." But that translation long outlived the King's English from whence it came. It survives today as part of that special antique vocabulary one finds only in the Bible. Now people are beginning to translate it differently, for example, using the neologism "Kindom," removing the androcentrism

of the word "king" — and that is right and good. Some people are translating it as "Reign," reverting to a Latin base that is at least less recogniz-
ably sexist than the English word "kingdom." Others are using the word
"Rule." Religious terminology always demands this sort of careful attention.

But how would an ancient person listening to Jesus have heard
this term, *basileia*? When this word appears in a non-biblical text from
the ancient world it is usually translated as "empire." It is a very political
term. It is the word ancients used to refer to empires, or more precisely
in Jesus' day, *the* empire: Rome. There is only one empire in Jesus' world,
and that is Rome. Jesus took this very political term and attached to it
the words "of God." This was unusual. The term Empire of God
(Kingdom of God), contrary to common assumptions, does not really
appear very often in the literature of the Roman imperial period. But
this is understandable. To speak of "empire" is to speak of Rome. And
why speak of an "Empire *of God*," that is, an empire as *God* would run it,
if one does not have something critical to say about the empire as 'you
know who' runs it. To speak of an Empire of God is, well, risky, to say
the least. But Jesus chose this very political, very risky concept as the
central metaphor for expressing what he was about. Why?

Rome and the world of Jesus

What did Jesus, a peasant from Galilee, know of Rome? Enough.
Rome was not a distant, abstract reality to people like Jesus who lived in
its provincial districts. Rome dominated Jesus' world. He lived and died
about a century after Rome had taken Palestine by force and made it a
province to serve its larger imperial aspirations. In the past, Western
European historians have tended to give their cultural ancestors the benefit of the doubt on the question of how they came to control so much.
It was, after all, such a gift, the great Roman Peace, the *Pax Romana*.
Augustus himself did not blush to boast:

> I extended the frontiers of all the provinces of the Roman
> people, which has as neighbors races not obedient to our
> empire.

> I restored peace to all the provinces of Gaul and Spain and
> to Germany, to all that region washed by the ocean from
> Gades to the mouth of the Elbe. Peace, too, I caused to be
> established in the Alps from the region nearest to the
> Hadriatic as far as the Tuscan sea. . . .

. . . Two armies were led almost at the same time, one into Ethiopia, the other into that part of Arabia which is called Felix; and large forces of the enemy belonging to both races were killed in battle, and many towns captured. . . . Egypt I added to the empire of the Roman people. . . and all of Cyrene. . . . [2]

His work did not go unappreciated in verses penned by his pet poet, Horace, and sung by a choir of young men and maidens on the occasion of the Secular Games of 17 BCE:

If Rome be your handiwork... then do ye, O gods, make teachable our youth and grant them virtuous ways; to the aged give tranquil peace; and to the race of Romulus, riches and offspring, and every glory!

And what the glorious scion of Anchises and Venus [a.k.a. Augustus Caesar], with sacrifice of milk-white steers, entreats of you, that may he obtain, triumphant over the warring foe, but generous to the fallen! [3]

More recently, however, scholars like Richard Horsley have begun to cast the Roman *Pax* in a different hue. One need only read a little between the lines of an historian not quite yet entirely co-opted by Rome for a glimpse of how Roman advancement proceeded in a place like Palestine. Josephus, writing more than a century after the fact, provides evidence that Jews had not yet forgotten how, in 43 BCE, when the towns of Gophna, Emmaus, Lydda, and Thamma were slow in paying their share of the Judean tribute, Cassius sold all their inhabitants into slavery.[4] Or there was the time when the Roman general, Varus, quelled protests following Herod's death (shortly before the birth of Jesus) by sacking the great cities of Galilee and Samaria. Included among them was Sepphoris, just over the hill from Jesus' native Nazareth. Varus sold its inhabitants into slavery. The protests ended with a public crucifixion of 2000 of the ring leaders.[5] And what became of all those slaves? Rome needed them – for the mines, the great Roman latifundia, the galleys. Rome built its empire on the backs of slaves.

So someone like Jesus would have known about Rome and its great *Pax*, but it may not have looked quite as good to him as it did to Horace. Jesus' sentiments might have been closer to those of Tacitus' fictitious Briton general, who has just experienced the *Pax Romana* at the end of a Roman lance: "To plunder, butcher, steal, these things they misname empire; they make a desolation and call it peace."[6]

Rome organized itself into a great hierarchy. Marcus Borg, drawing on the work of the anthropologist, Gerhard Lensky, has given an apt description.[7] If one were to depict the shape of Roman society graphically, it might look like an old fashioned oil can, one of those with the long thin spout, turned up-side down. At the very tip of that spout – or perhaps hovering just above it – was the Emperor. The empire was his to do with as he pleased. This may seem incredible in our own era of government "by the people, of the people, and for the people." But Romans, as with many pre-modern agrarian cultures, subscribed to a proprietary theory of the state, wherein the state is regarded as a piece of property. The wealth and produce of the empire, at least in theory, belonged to the emperor and those to whom he delegated its benefits and privileges. The emperor controlled the means to life.

Below the emperor, in that gossamer thin span of spout leading down to the funnel, were his subordinates, "retainers," as anthropologists would call them: religious and military officials, local client kings, significant land holders, large scale merchants. They benefited directly from the Emperor and in exchange, supported his claim to power. As one reaches the broader part of the funnel, one might find a few more merchants, traders, a small "middle class" who supported those above them. But most people would have fit into that broadening, large open end of the funnel, a vast majority of persons who lived as peasants, that is, at a daily subsistence level. Most people in the empire lived like this – perhaps 80% of the population – on the very margins of existence. That is how Rome managed it. Rome's purpose, especially in the provinces, was to suck up as many of a province's resources as it could without provoking it into revolt or killing it off altogether. It slowly siphoned the life out of places like Palestine.

This hierarchical Roman order was based on something anthropologists might call a patronage system. A patron (let us say, the Emperor) had clients, whom he supported. They, in turn, supported him. But they also had clients, whom they supported, who, in turn, gave them support from below. And so it went, down through the ever widening social pyramid – a kind of giant Amway scheme – with the means to life trickling down the system in a tightly managed *quid pro quo* system of distribution. John Dominic Crossan describes this system in its totality as the "brokered Empire," wherein the means to life are always carefully brokered from the top down.[8] Such a system, of course, works best for those near its apex. But it works also for those vast crowds of peasants living just at the margins of subsistence. They get just enough – but enough – to live.

But in a patronage system there are always a few – sometimes quite a few – who do not have anything to offer a patron. In the *quid pro quo* system, they have no *quid* to offer for *quo*. In a patronage system, anyone who has nothing to offer someone above them gradually falls down through the social pyramid, and eventually out through the cracks in the bottom of the system. Lensky calls these persons "expendables." They are expendable because they have nothing to offer their culture that might be considered of value. These are the beggars and the homeless. These are persons who might do those jobs no one else would do, like tax collecting. These are persons whose person counts for nothing, like prostitutes. With so many people living at the margins of existence, a significant number of expendables were always an inevitability, with persons moving in and out of that status all of the time. Take, for example, the situation of agricultural day laborers. If they are fortunate enough to get a full day's work, then they will receive enough pay to eat for a day. That is what subsistence means. One can earn enough for one day's sustenance, but that is all. There is no savings account put away for a rainy day. When it rains, you beg or you starve. For a peasant living at a subsistence level, expendability is only one day away.

Jesus and expendables

Where did Jesus fit into this pyramidal system of patronage and brokerage? He did not fit. In the gospels, canonical and non-canonical, and in Paul – in the broad memory and praxis of the early church – Jesus is recalled as living outside the system of brokered power and economy of Rome's Empire. He was an itinerant teacher who scrounged for a living and encouraged others to do so as well. Whether he did this as one who chose to opt out of the system, or whether he was himself expendable to it is a matter of dispute, for there is evidence on both sides of the question.

On the one hand, Jesus is depicted in the gospels as inviting people to give up their place in the web of brokerage and become a beggar like him. Consider, for example, Mark's story of the wealthy young man who comes to Jesus asking, "What must I do to inherit eternal life?" (Mark 10:17–22). Initially Jesus gives him the stock answer of his culture: "You know the commandments." But, not wishing to be dismissed so easily, the young man persists until Jesus gives him the *real* answer: "You lack one thing; go, sell all that you own and give it to beggars, and you will have treasure in heaven, and come and follow me." At that, the man turns away, unable to risk removing himself from the security of the web of brokerage and patronage. Originally the story probably ended with something like the saying in Mark 10:23 (an originally independent saying, which the Jesus Seminar designated "pink"): "How hard it will be for those with riches to come into the Empire of God." This story itself is not demonstrably historical, but it fits together with enough similar material in the gospel tradition to appear as an accurate typification of Jesus' ways. Jesus is depicted in all four canonical gospels as an itinerant preacher. He invites people to leave gainful activities to become his followers. In Thomas, he advises, "Become itinerants" (Thomas 42). And from the apostle Paul's itinerant lifestyle, going from place to place as the Spirit moved him, we can see what is likely the continuation of this practice in the activity of the early church. The pattern seems clearly to suggest an imperative: If you are in the imperial web of brokerage and patronage, get out of it.

On the other hand, Jesus not only asks people to risk becoming expendable to the Empire, he seems to be constantly in the company of persons who already are expendable to it, like tax collectors and prostitutes. Jesus most certainly kept company with known prostitutes. It is difficult to imagine that an emergent church, seeking at least some amount of respectability from the world around it, would have created the tradition that Jesus cavorted with prostitutes. It is unlikely, then, that the church can be credited with coining the saying, "Tax collectors and prostitutes go into the Empire of God before you" (Matt 21:31). It is difficult to imagine the church even preserving the tradition, unless, of course, this was crucial to how it had come to understand itself in the followership of Jesus.

Luke has a story that, in this light, appears as an accurate typification of how Jesus related to prostitutes. In this story (Luke 7:36–50) Jesus is having dinner at the table of a Pharisee. Luke perhaps sets it up this way to accentuate the purity concerns raised by this story, concerns represented in Luke's world view by the Pharisaic party. A woman enters, introduced as a "woman who was a sinner in this city," which we may take as circumlocution for "prostitute." If there is any doubt about this, the unfolding scene removes it: "standing behind him at his feet, weeping, she began to wet his feet with her tears, wiping them with the hair of her head, and kissed his feet." Odd as it may seem to modern sensibilities, this business with the tears and dabbing them up with the hair is a detail drawn from ancient erotica, as may be seen, for example, in Xenophon's *Ephesian Tale*.[9] This is what impassioned lovers do. She "comes on" to Jesus. This, quite naturally, alarms the host. He says to himself: "If this man were a prophet, he would have known who and what sort of woman this is who is touching him, for she is a sinner." But Jesus does not reject her. Instead he turns to the host and says (I think one may fairly insert a wink here, and perhaps a coy, slightly mocking tone of voice): "Do you see this woman? I came into your house, and you gave me no water for my feet, but she has wet my feet with her tears and wiped them with her hair. You gave me no kiss, but from the time I came in she has not stopped kissing my feet." In a clever turn about, the unseemly act of a prostitute is received as proper hospitality. She is accepted as she is, doing what she does. Now, Luke's Jesus is no fool. He knows about prostitution, its causes, its hazards, its humiliations. So in the end he says to her, "Your sins are forgiven.... Your faith has saved you; go in peace," which means, I think, "You are no longer a prostitute."

This story is probably not strictly historical. It is offered as a typification for how Jesus regarded prostitutes. They are expendable to the Empire, but they are welcome in Jesus' new Empire of God. So are tax collectors. There persists today the common assumption that a tax collector was someone who, far from expendable, enjoyed a comfortable, profitable niche in the Roman imperial system, as would be illustrated by Luke's well-known story of Zacchaeus (Luke 19:1–9). Though not a popular figure (19:7), Zacchaeus is obviously someone with ample access to the means of life. But Luke calls him a "*chief* tax collector," that is, a tax farmer. He is not the run-of-the-mill collector of tolls and taxes. People like Zacchaeus would typically have engaged subordinates to do the actual work of collecting. Levi, whom Mark depicts as sitting in his toll booth when Jesus comes along and calls him away (Mark 2:14), is such a tax collector. One need only imagine how pleasant a task it would have been to collect Roman tribute from strapped peasants barely making it as it is, to arrive quickly at the profile of such a tax collector. These were persons who could find no other means of making a living. Frequently slaves were purchased for this work. They did not last long. In a sense, one might regard 'tax collector' as the male equivalent to the female role of 'prostitute.' Tax collectors and prostitutes are both expendable in the Empire, but they are included first in the Empire of God. We may add to this list lepers, beggars, the blind, those who could not walk or speak, the mentally ill (possessed) – all of them expendables, in whose company we are apt to find Jesus in the gospels. Thus, "the last will be first, and the first will be last" (Matt 20:16).

What about Jesus himself? Was he also an expendable? He may have been. There is a tradition – well-known and popular, but poorly attested – that Jesus' was a *tekton*, a "carpenter" (see Mark 6:3). In an industrial culture based on the trading of manufactured goods, such a skill would have made Jesus an artisan, part of a class raised slightly above that of the mere peasant. For this reason, many have uncritically assumed that Jesus was part of the ancient "middle class." However, Jesus did not live in an industrial culture, but the pre-industrial, agrarian culture of the ancient world. The basic economic engine in an agrarian culture is the land. Peasants hold land, and can therefore participate in the economy. Without the land, they are nothing. In agrarian cultures the artisan class was usually recruited from among those who had been dispossessed of their land. A skill, a craft, a trade is all that stands between them and starvation. As Lensky has observed, in an agrarian culture artisans generally rank below the peasant class, not above it. So if Jesus was in fact a carpenter, he would have occupied that tenuous narrow band of subsistence hovering just above expendability. On off days, weeks, months, Jesus, like others in his position, would have had to beg for a living.

Jesus knew expendability, he knew expendables, and he invited those who had not fallen out of the Roman system of brokerage and patronage to step out voluntarily and to become part of a new thing, the Empire of God. Why? How did Jesus' words and deeds address the condition of expendability among peasants in provincial Rome? To explore this question we must inquire further into the human experience of expendability. The experience of an expendable person in antiquity included three dimensions, each of which Jesus addressed directly: the experience of being unclean (not clean), the experience of shame (not honor), and the experience of being regarded as sinful (not righteousness).

Unclean, not clean

Expendables in Jesus' world experienced being unclean, not clean. To be unclean is, in a literal sense, to be dirty. Of course, in human culture the distinction between the clean and the unclean is far more complicated than this. Nonetheless, one may perhaps get at this very complicated dynamic by beginning with dirt. Dirt is, to quote Mary Douglas' well-known definition, simply "matter out of place."[10] Dirt in a field is 'soil.' The same stuff on your face is . . . well, 'dirt.' Food on your plate is appetizing. The very same matter on your clothes makes them 'dirty.' Distinctions between what is clean and unclean go to the very basic impulse in every human culture to create order from chaos. Such distinctions, sometimes functional, sometimes not, create order and place. They include not only things, but behaviors as well.

Such distinctions are present across all human cultures, but they are not at all identical. What is clean and unclean can be very culturally specific. For example, in the United States it is generally considered "unclean" to eat a cat, since they do not belong to the category of things called "food." A cat does not go on a plate. They belong to the "pet" category. Cows, on the other hand, do belong to the "food" category, and so can be eaten. In other lands, however, those categories might be reversed. In some parts of India, cows belong to the category of things called "sacred." To eat one would be a religiously unclean act, a sacrilege. And I am told, much to my personal revulsion, that there are places where it is perfectly acceptable to eat a cat. But the revulsion I feel is culturally specific; it must be inculcated in my upbringing. In this way, observance of the basic distinctions between what is clean and unclean can signal one's belonging to a social group; failure to observe such codes can indicate that one does not belong, and so result in ostracizing.

Such distinctions must be learned. They are not automatic. I grew up in a rural part of America, where many children from remote farms and ranches were educated in one-room school houses until the eighth grade, and then sent to town for the high school years. This worked fine most of the time. But occasionally, a child from a remote and recluse family would show up in town for the ninth grade completely unprepared for the society that awaited them there. How to dress, how to act with the other children, how to eat in the cafeteria, tastes, social graces were all a mystery. If the child could somehow overcome the ostracizing that usually resulted, they might eventually learn how to fit in. But the interim period was always very painful. Distinctions between clean and unclean must be learned.

They must also be cultivated. This takes time and resources. Take, for example, the simple matter of clean clothing. It must be washed, which presumes a place to wash and an extra set of clothes to wear while the other is being laundered. Simple things for most people, but anyone who has ever experienced an urban shelter for the homeless in our own culture knows the problem this poses for expendables. Or consider food. Clean food must be purchased and prepared in a clean way. These are luxuries that the destitute do not have. Expendables are always having to accept matter that is not of their own choosing. Beggars rummage through garbage cans for scraps of food. They beg for what they can get. They wear what they can find. Prostitutes disregard their own desires and accept those of others. To be unclean is to have someone else's stuff on you or in you. To be unclean is to feel violated and dirty.

Finally, in Jesus' culture, as in most, there is an explicit connection between being clean and being holy. In our own highly secular culture it is perhaps a bit more difficult to see this connection. But it was not many years ago that the Saturday night bath was a weekly ritual for many families in preparation for Sunday morning worship. This connection between the clean and the holy is also why most people still dress up to go to church or synagogue. In ancient Israel the connection between the clean and the holy was more explicit. Near the end of Leviticus, where the general rules of purity are laid out, the Lord says to the people of Israel:

> If you follow my statutes and keep my commandments and observe them faithfully . . . I will look with favor upon you and make you fruitful and multiply you. . . . I will place my dwelling in your midst, and I shall not abhor you. And I will walk among you and be your God, and you shall be my people. (Lev 26:3, 9, 11–12)

To observe the laws of purity was to insure the favor of God's presence in Israel, to reduce the offense of mortal profane life to God so that God would not "abhor" the Israelites and deign to be with them. The concept is illustrated more graphically in a telling passage from Deuteronomy:

> With your equipment you are to include a trowel. When you go to relieve yourself, you are to dig a hole with it and bury your excrement. For the Lord your God travels along with your camp, to save you and to deliver your enemies to you. Therefore, your camp must be holy, so that [God] may not see anything indecent among you and turn away from you. (Deut 23: 13–14)

God has standards that should not be offended. This is why anyone who is rendered unclean must go outside the camp until such time as they may be cleansed. Sometimes this involves only a short period, followed by a ritual cleansing, as with a nocturnal emission, for example

(Deut 23: 10–11). When the unclean condition has a more permanent or long-term effect, one's ostracizing might last considerably longer, as with leprosy, for example:

> The person who has a leprous disease shall wear torn clothes and have messed hair; they shall cover their upper lip and cry out, "Unclean, unclean." And they shall remain unclean as long as they have the disease; they are unclean. They shall live alone and their dwelling shall be outside the camp. (Lev 13: 45–46)

The idea is clear: God, like most of us, does not want to be with the unclean. I once attended an urban church where, it was explained to me, the ushers were all fairly stout men so that in the event one of the destitute people who inhabited that neighborhood should come in off the street, they could be escorted out of the building. A holy place is a clean place.

Throughout the gospel tradition, Jesus addresses himself to the unclean. It is one of the most common typifications we can identify. Jesus eats with lepers (Mark 14:3). He has conversations with Gentiles (Mark 7:24–30). He welcomes prostitutes into his company (Luke 7:36–50). Jesus and his followers are depicted as habitually eating in an unclean manner. In response to the accusation that Jesus and his disciples do not eat properly, Jesus does not deny the charge, but rather responds:

> there is nothing outside of a person which, by going into them, can defile; it is the things that come out of a person that defile. . . . Do you not see that whatever goes into a person from the outside cannot defile, for it enters not the heart, but the stomach, and then passes on, out into the toilet? (Mark 7:15, 19a)

Mark adds: "Thus he declared all foods clean!" (7:19b), an appropriate remark for Mark's audience, at least some of whom must be Gentiles interested in knowing that Jesus did not condemn eating all their favorite Gentile foods. But the point Jesus makes in the story is really more basic: nothing can defile a person. It is this point that addresses the situation of expendables: their lives render them unclean. Beggars, lepers, prostitutes, tax collectors – they are all unclean because that is what life has dealt them. Jesus disputes this. It is not what happens to you that defiles. "It is what comes out of a person that defiles. For from within, from the human heart come evil thoughts, fornication, theft, murder, adultery...." Mark supplies the conventional list. But the point is made. The power to be clean lies in the character of a person. "Blessed are those who are clean in their hearts, for they shall see God" (Matt 5:8).

Throughout the synoptic gospels, Jesus seems to be on a virtual crusade against unclean spirits. Mark begins the ministry of Jesus with this story:

> And they went into Capernaum, and immediately on the Sabbath he went into the synagogue and taught. . . . And immediately there was in the synagogue a person with an unclean spirit. And he cried out and said, "What business do you have with us, Jesus of Nazareth? Have you come to destroy us? I know who you are: the holy one of God." And Jesus reprimanded him and said, "Shut up and come out of him." And the unclean spirit came out of him, convulsing and yelling. (Mark 1:21–26)

This is an apt introduction to a string of stories in which Jesus casts out unclean spirits. Whenever they see him, they fall down and cry out (Mark 3:11). He exorcises a man with an unclean spirit named "Legion" (Mark 5:1–13); he casts out an unclean spirit from the daughter of a Syrophoenecian woman (Mark 7:24–30); he heals a deaf-mute boy by casting out an unclean spirit from him (Mark 9:14–29). The disciples, also, have authority to do this sort of thing (Mark 6:7). And because of this activity, Jesus himself is said to have an unclean spirit (Mark 3:30). Engaging the unclean casts one into their world. He also heals disabilities and diseases that could render one unclean, like leprosy:

> And a leper came to him pleading, and kneeling he said to him: "If you want to, you can make me clean." Moved with pity, he stretched out his hand and touched him and said, "I do want to. Be clean." And immediately the leprosy left him and he was cleansed. (Mark 1:40–42)

What are we to make of these stories? As a modern person, I do not believe in the existence of spirits and demons. That ancient people did believe in such things helps me to understand the cultural context of these stories and what they mean: Jesus engages in battle the things that render one unclean and outside the company of God and humanity. His ministry meant inclusion for the ostracized. But did Jesus really do such things, or are these simply stories told about Jesus to give form to the memory of his activity of including the unclean? I am undecided. In cultures that believe in demons there are certainly people who are reputed to exorcise them. Jesus could have been such a person. On the other hand, it also belongs to the mythic image of the Son of God that he engages the powers of evil and clears the way for the coming Empire of God. This is Mark's way of thinking about it. His understanding of Jesus' exorcisms presupposes considerable early Christian theological reflection that arose only after Jesus' death. In the end, whether Jesus was a genuine shaman, or whether he simply embraced the company of the unclean, the meaning of his memory is the same: in Jesus we have come to know a God who renders impotent the power of dirt to keep the unclean outside the human community.

Shame, not honor

Expendable persons experience shame, not honor. Honor and shame are two of the basic anthropological dimensions of ancient life. What is honor; what is shame?

One way of understanding honor and shame is simply to extend into the social realm the thinking we have already done around distinctions of clean and unclean. Honor and shame, like distinctions of clean and unclean, have to do with place. To have honor is to have a place, a role, within which one is readily recognized by one's peers, a role whose functions one may competently perform. Like matters of clean and unclean, honor and shame have to do with expectations. One knows what to expect from an honorable person. Honorable people are clear about their role in life; they know what is expected and do their duty. On the other hand, someone who behaves in a way that is inappropriate to his or her role, or to society in general, is a shameful person. Such a person does not behave according to expectations. Their difference is discomfiting. They may even strike one as dangerous. In a peasant culture with only a minimal social infrastructure, honor and shame are the forces that give shape to communal life. In the world of rural antiquity there was no police force, no lawyers, few courts. In such a culture someone who steps out of line must be shamed into conformity. If a person proves impervious to shame and simply will not conform to the expectations of his or her peers, they are regarded as "shameless," and ostracized from the community. In most cultures a set of reliable expectations for various social roles are necessary for the smooth conduct of social life.

Another way of thinking about honor and shame is to consider how honor is acquired. Again, one has honor when one has a place in society, a role, within which one is able to function successfully. Acquiring honor involves three basic steps. First, you must aspire to a role, a place in your culture. Secondly, your peers must recognize you in that role. Finally, once you are recognized in a role, you must now be able successfully to function in that role. If all of this falls into place, you acquire a grant of honor. However, if at any point the process breaks down, you are shamed. If, for example, one aspires to the role of teacher, but no one signs up for the class, one experiences shame for not having been recognized in the role to which they have aspired. Or again, if people come, but eventually walk out in frustration for having learned nothing under their tutelage, one experiences the shame of failure.

Shame is a powerful emotion. It has physical as well as psychological dimensions. Shame is not necessarily a moral category. I am not speaking of guilt, the experience of being *ashamed* for having done something one knows to be wrong. Shame is an existential category. It has to do with self worth, with one's internal image of oneself, with one's sense of belonging and kinship. Here is an example to which most people can relate and recall the very visceral aspects of feeling shamed. Remember the first sock-hop you attended in Junior High School. I can recall it well. As I enter the doors to the gymnasium I can see my classmates dancing and having fun. I marvel at their courage and abandon, how they all seem so natural out there on the gym floor dancing away. I aspire to be one of them, to be a dancer. But doubts subdue my ambition, so I take my place with the others sitting on the side lines, not yet ready to take up the challenge. Finally, I summon the courage to ask the girl sitting next to me if she would like to dance. I am old fashioned. I say, "May I have the *honor*?" May I? Will she recognize my aspirations to be *her* dance partner, or turn me down and shame me back into my place on the side lines? I must carefully calculate this. How popular is she? Can *she* dance? Successfully negotiating the world of honor and shame requires careful attention to place, abilities, expectations. She agrees to dance with me. So far, so good. I have "the honor." But challenges arise. My friends issue cat calls from the sidelines; my honor is in question. I must now successfully function in the role to which I have aspired. If I cannot, I will be shamed and perhaps never summon forth the courage to dance again. Fortunately, these are the 1960s and dancing is quite easy. My honor is retained; shame has been averted, at least this time. But life is full of such situations. Honor and shame are ever-present realities of human existence.

Not everyone pays attention to such things. For example, a person who chooses to disregard the shame of another is called a "fool." Let us imagine that I was unable to dance, so the partner who had risked a dance with me decided to cut her losses and flee, leaving me alone, shamed, on the dance floor. Who will grant me the honor now? Only a fool, who cares little for her own reputation. If such a person exists, she will appear as a hero to me and the all of the shamed, but to the rest of the dancers, she will be regarded as a fool. In the complexities of honor and shame, someone who chooses to ignore the shame of another is a fool. Or let us imagine that, in spite of the fact that I have been abandoned on the dance floor, I ignore the shame I feel and simply continue to dance, incompetently, by myself. People will just shake their heads and mutter, "shameless!" In the system of honor and shame, one who chooses to ignore his or her own shame is called "shameless." Such a person is beyond the pale; they refuse to recognize honor and shame at all. Their behavior has become unpredictable, unreliable. They are dangerous, and must be avoided.

Jesus was remembered as a shameless fool. To spend time with expendables is to be a fool – to refuse to recognize the shame of another. Expendables are by definition shamed. To have honor is to have place, to have a recognized role. This is precisely what expendables do not have. They are expendable to their culture because there is no role in it for them. Beggars must beg with eyes cast down; they are shamed. Prostitutes are worse than shamed – they are "shameless." Forced by their expendability into the sale of their bodies, they must engage repeatedly in behavior against which there are strong societal sanctions and taboos. They must ignore their own shame to survive. One need only recall the story of Jesus and the prostitute from Luke 7 discussed above to see how Jesus was remembered as a "fool," disregarding the shame of another.

There is much opportunity for shame around the issue of marriage and family. In societies strongly oriented to honor and shame, it traditionally falls to the women to guard against shame in the family that might come from extra-marital sex. This is why adultery is defined as the sexual violation of a married woman (but not a man) and treated so harshly in the Ancient Near East (see Mal 2:14–15; Prov 5:15–20; Lev 20:10; Deut 22:22). In conventional texts of John 8 there is found a remarkable story about Jesus and a woman accused of adultery, who is about to be stoned (John 7:53b–8:11). A case for its historicity would be difficult to make, since the origin of this story has become impossible to trace. The earliest and most reliable manuscripts of John do not have it. In some early copies of Luke one finds it inserted after Luke 21:38. We do not even know for sure the gospel with which to associate it. It is what is sometimes called a "floating" tradition – something from the oral tradition that pops up in various places, but whose origin is not known. But the memory of Jesus expressed in it is so remarkably counter-cultural, it must have some claim to authenticity in representing the views of Jesus, even if its claim to historicity is weak.

It presents us with a classic honor-shame confrontation. The woman in this story is accused of violating her given role (wife) and bringing shame upon her entire extended family. In her patriarchal world, her offense is so severe it warrants complete eradication. She must be stoned, a public, communal form of execution featuring the violent disfigurement of the offender. But Jesus defends her with a challenge of his own. He challenges the honor of those wishing to eradicate her shame: "Let him who is without sin cast the first stone at her." And in the magical world of Christian story-telling about Jesus, that ends the matter. Her accusers all skulk away, themselves shamed by Jesus' challenge, beginning with the oldest (the most honorable).

This story gives shape to a powerful memory of what Jesus meant to people who experienced shame. Shame is like dirt: it renders one outside the human community and the company of God. Real shame does not come from within (it is not guilt); it comes from without. One must be shamed by others. But unlike dirt, it is not so easily washed away. Shame stays with you. No ritual ablutions can nullify its power over a person. It works itself into the image of oneself before others, and there remains as a part of one's personal landscape. In stories like that of the woman caught in adultery, early Christians gave shape to the memory that Jesus refused to recognize shame. No one has the power to shame, to castigate and ostracize one from the human community. The point is the same as with distinctions of clean and unclean. Nothing from outside can render one unclean. Only the things that come from the human heart can render one clean or unclean. So also with shame. One cannot be shamed from without. To be sure, one can feel *ashamed*; one can feel guilt and remorse for things done that should not have been done. That is why many of these stories end with the admonition, "Go and sin no more." But Jesus' insight was that it does not lie within the legitimate power of one human being to shame another, and to cast them out of the company of God and humanity.

There are many illustrations of this principle in the gospels. For example, when the blind man, Bartimaeus, calls out to Jesus from the side of the road and is "shushed" by those around him, Jesus stops the entourage and calls him over (Mark 10:46–52). Or when Martha asks Jesus to castigate Mary for stepping out of her conventional role as a woman, Jesus refuses to do so, but acknowledges her in the new role to

which she has aspired: disciple (Luke 10:38–42). This is also the framework within which one ought to understand Jesus' teaching regarding
divorce, a traditional act of public shaming in Jesus' culture. He simply
disallows it (Mark 10:2–12). In Mark 7 there is a most peculiar story
about Jesus and a woman from Syrophoenecia, who asks him to exorcise
her demon-possessed daughter. In Mark's story, Jesus responds to her
request negatively: "Let the children first be fed, for it is not right to
take the children's bread and throw it to the dogs" (7:27). She asks for
something she cannot rightfully have, and so he shames her with a well-
crafted, ancient Near Eastern insult. But she refuses to accept the shame
and retorts, "Yes, Lord; but even the dogs under the table eat the children's crumbs." At this, Jesus repents of his view, capitulates and grants
her request. It is the only story in the New Testament in which Jesus
loses an argument, and learns something in the process. Is this the tradition's way of shaping a memory that Jesus received his insights about
shame from women?

Jesus not only ignored the shame of others, and so was a "fool,"
he also ignored his own shame, and so was "shameless." He did not perform the role to which he was assigned in life. Jesus was a carpenter, an
artisan (*tekton*), or so the tradition presents him (Mark 6:3). But we
encounter him in the gospels as a teacher, a wandering philosopher who
speaks of God, who "preaches." What qualified him for this vocation,
this role? He had no training that we know of. As a peasant artisan, for-
mal study would have been unavailable to him. The leisure and training
to read and write, to study the traditions of Israel, to practice rhetoric –
all of these things would have been lacking in his life. His situation is
rather like that of the Cynic philosophers, railed against and ridiculed
by the ancient writer, Lucian, in his biting satire, *The Fugitives*. Lucian
has become fed up with this upstart philosophical movement he sees as
dominated by untrained artisans, runaway slaves, and women who had
eschewed conventional household duties. What his goddess, Philosophia, says of the Cynics, could well have been said of Jesus and his
followers too:

> There is an abominable class of people, for the most part
> slaves and common laborers, who had nothing to do with
> me in childhood for lack of leisure time, since they were
> performing the work of slaves or common laborers, learn-
> ing such trades as you would expect their type to learn, like
> cobbling, building, taking care of fuller's tubs, or carding
> wool.... Now, to learn all that is necessary for such a calling

would have been a long task, or rather, an impossible one for them. Their trades, however, were petty and laborious, and barely able to provide them with just enough to live.[11]

Lucian is describing the life of an artisan. For such a person it is simply impossible to develop the skills to become a wandering teacher. He calls the Cynics "shameless," and their effort at *philosophia* "counterfeit." In Lucian's elitist tale of social commentary, Philosophia sends Hermes and Heracles as her henchmen to track down a small band of Cynics: three fugitive slaves and a runaway wife. Their fate is tar and feathers.

In the Gospel of Mark there is a story about Jesus coming to his home town to preach and heal as he had done elsewhere. But at home it does not go so well. When Jesus begins to teach in his home synagogue, the crowd begins to object:

> "Where did this person get these things he is saying? What is this wisdom given to him? And what are these miracles done by his hand? Isn't this the carpenter, the son of Mary and the brother of James and Joses, Jude and Simon? And are not his sisters right here in front of us?" And they took offense at him. (Mark 6:2–3)

This becomes the occasion for Mark to insert a famous saying of Jesus, "A prophet is not without honor, except in his own country, among his own relatives, and in his own house." And Mark adds, "He could do no miracles there."

Like other episodes from Jesus' life found in the gospels, we cannot be sure that this one has any claim to historicity. But given what we know about Jesus, it has perfect verisimilitude. The issue here is honor and shame. Jesus aspires to the role of prophet, but his peers, even his family, will not recognize him in that role. They know him too well. They challenge him; they attempt to shame him into accepting his given role among family and kin. But he refuses to shrink back from what he has become in his own mind. He is a prophet now. But to the folks back home, he is shameless. And in the end, he dies a death that would seem appropriate to all but those few who chose to accept Jesus as a prophet. Crucifixion was the ultimate act of shaming. Helpless, exposed to the elements, animals, and passers-by, staked outside the sacred boundaries of the city walls, the victim of Rome's signature form of execution was literally shamed to death.

Sin, not righteousness

Expendables experience sin, or rather, they are regarded as sinful, rather than righteous. With this category we may seem, at least initially, to be on more familiar religious ground: morality. But a closer look at the material reveals that this is not really so. For "sinner," in the ancient world, is not just a moral category; it is a social category as well.

Let us begin with an example from the New Testament to illustrate how the category "sinner" works in relationship to expendability. In the ninth chapter of John, Jesus and the disciples come across a man who was born blind (John 9:1–34). The disciples instinctively ask Jesus: "who sinned, this man or his parents, that he was born blind." Notice the automatic connection between the condition of expendability and the assumption that such a person must be deserving of their predicament. One might be tempted to assign this way of thinking to some bizarre and ancient theodicy. But this is to be resisted. In fact, it is the most natural and psychologically necessary solution to the problem of expendability in any culture. What would one have to admit if no particular shortcoming could be ascribed to persons unable to find a place in the social world we have collectively constructed? The answer would be the deeply disturbing realization that there is something morally wrong about a society, which is itself incapable of living up to its claim to offer a place for everyone. Moreover, *this* moral shortcoming would be one in which everyone who participates willingly in, and benefits from the common social order would be, in greater or lesser degree, culpable. Examples abound from our own modern American social landscape. Women who receive ADC are not seen as persons for whom there is no place in our economy, but as lazy, dishonest, "Welfare Queens" robbing the rest of us of our hard-earned dollars. Kids who deal in drugs to help support their families are not seen as desperate survivors, but as amoral criminals lusting after the latest designer tennis shoes. The governing assumption in such thinking is that if someone operates outside the boundaries of social acceptability, it is not because there is no place for them in the social economy, but because they are somehow deficient in themselves. They are sinners.

This principle can be illustrated in another way from the traditions about Jesus. The following story comes from the gospel of Mark. Like so many other stories from the synoptic tradition, its historicity cannot be proven. Nonetheless, when one thinks about the potentially damaging nature of this story in a world in which the fledgling church was struggling to rise above the suspicions of its neighbors, it is scarcely possible to account for its presence in the tradition apart from some claim to authenticity as a typification of what Jesus was about.

> And as he passed along the way he saw Levi, the son of Alphaeus, sitting in his tax booth. And he said to him, "Follow me." And he got up and followed him. And it happened that he was having dinner at his house, and many tax collectors and sinners were having dinner with Jesus and his disciples (for there were many who followed him). And the scribes of the Pharisees, when they saw that he was eating with sinners and tax collectors, said to his disciples: "Why does he eat with tax collectors and sinners?" And when Jesus heard this, he said to them, "Those who are well have no need of a physician, but those who are sick. I did not come to call righteous people, but sinners. (Mark 2:14–17)

This story is not isolated in the traditions about Jesus. In Q there is preserved an (apparently) common reproach against Jesus: "Look, a glutton and a drunkard, a friend of tax collectors and sinners" (Luke 7:34b). Notice how in both of these traditions a tandem term is created: "tax collector and sinner." We have already discussed the status of tax collectors among the expendables. This sort of front-lines tax collecting was hazardous work, performed by persons with few other options in an economy to which they were expendable. Now this term is placed alongside another, "sinner," as though they were easily interchangeable. And so they were. Tax collectors were not seen as persons doing whatever they could to eke out a living, but as traitors, unworthy of the company of respectable people. Joachim Jeremias identified a number of such occupations in the social world of Jesus that suffered under a similar stigma, including shepherds, dung collectors, tanners, peddlers, weavers, bath attendants, gamblers with dice, bandits and others.[12] Not all of these occupations were despised as notoriously "immoral." Tanners just stank. But all were despised for what they did, scrounging around the edges of Jesus' social world to earn enough to get from day to day. They were all landless expendables.

These are the "sinners" whom Jesus calls into his following. This is clear from how Jesus explains himself at the end of the story: "I did not come to call righteous people, but sinners" (Mark 2:17). There is something missing here, is there not? Luke noticed it, and so adopted Mark's story, but added to the end of this sentence "to repentance" (Luke 5:32). But this changes the meaning of the original story completely. In Mark's version, Jesus does not call sinners "to repentance," he just calls them.

This does not mean that Mark or Mark's Jesus is amoral, for elsewhere he does speak of turning from one's sins (e.g. Mark 1:15; cf. 6:12). Here, however, he is not thinking of "sinner" as a moral category, but a social one. In calling sinners into his following, he recognized the structural nature of expendability in his social world and the illegitimacy of labeling expendables as "sinners" in need of repentance. A tax collector does not need to repent; he just needs land, or a better job. A prostitute does not need better morals, she just needs a legitimate, respectful place to be in the world.

Jesus called sinners. Period. He invited into his company those whose condition rendered them into a category: sinner; unclean; shamed. They all go together in Jesus' world; they are all categories of expendability. Jesus spent his time with sinners, lepers, people with physical disabilities, deaf people, blind people, people who could not walk or talk. He welcomed prostitutes, tax collectors – all manner of expendable people. And he proclaimed for them an empire, the Empire of God, in which the means to life are free and accessible by God's own gracious hand.

The unbrokered Empire of God

Crossan calls this the "Brokerless Kingdom."[13] In contrast to Rome's highly brokered empire, the Empire of God is that place where the means to life are offered freely. Jesus was an itinerant pundit, who by his word and deed called into question the structures of his social world that de-humanized and made expendable so many human beings of God's own making. Indeed, he brought these expendables back into the human community. He regarded the unclean as clean. He treated the shamed with honor. He declared sinners righteous and able to stand in the glorious presence of God. Together they created an empire. Not one in which the means to life are brokered from the top down in a complex hierarchy of *quid pro quo* transactions, but unbrokered, freely offered, like God's own love to all of God's children.

Crossan has argued that this theology of unbrokered access is symbolized most clearly in Jesus' practice of eating with all manner of folk. Let us return for a moment to that story from the second chapter of Mark, in which Jesus' critics question, "Why does he eat with tax collectors and sinners?" (Mark 2:16b) A moment ago we noticed only the company Jesus kept. Now we should also notice what they are doing: eating together. This memory of Jesus eating with tax collectors and sinners is confirmed,

and presented in the worst possible light in the Q tradition that contrasts
Jesus' 'loose' table practices with the ascetic practices of John:

> To what shall I compare the people of this generation, and
> what are they like? They are like children sitting in the mar-
> ket place and calling to one another, "We piped and you did
> not dance; we wailed and you did not weep." For John the
> Baptist came eating no bread and drinking no wine, and you
> say, "He has a demon." The Son of Man has come eating
> and drinking, and you say, "Look, a drunkard and a glutton,
> a friend of tax collectors and sinners!" (Luke 7:31–34)

These words are those of Jesus' followers reflecting on the significance of Jesus and his fate. But in so doing, they preserved what must
have been a common accusation against Jesus and the movement he
spawned: "a drunkard and a glutton, a friend of tax collectors and sinners!" It is presented as the exaggerated and unreasonable, and so, obviously false accusation of the opponents of Jesus. But there must have
been an element of truth to the charge. There are several disputes around
the issue of eating played out in the gospel tradition (see, e.g., Mark
2:18–22; 2:23–28; 7:1–23; and 14:3–9, and their parallels in Matthew
and Luke). One may also point to the considerable reflection in earliest
Christianity around meals and meal-time practices, such as one finds in
Paul's letters (see, e.g., Gal 2:11–21; 1 Cor 8–10; 11:27–34; Rom
14:1–23). All of these examples indicate in one way or another that the
earliest Jesus movement engaged in table fellowship that inspired criticism and conflict over what, how, and with whom one ought to eat.
What is the issue with eating?

Eating together is a basic human activity, the significance of which
can still be seen today if one thinks for a moment about all that goes
into a common dinner invitation. There is always a tinge of anxiety that
accompanies every dinner party. Will the guests accept my invitation?
That is, will those whom I invite see me in the same way that I see them,
as friends and peers? Eating together is a social activity that establishes
group identity and boundaries. What are the boundaries of a meal?
Whom shall I invite? Will so-and-so get along with so-and-so? Will she
want to be seen with him? A meal is an act of social formation. And
what shall I serve? Shall I offer the president of the corporation maca-
roni and cheese? What will show her that I respect and value her company, that I am worthy to be her peer? And what about next week? Will
my invitation be reciprocated, thus reaffirming the common kinship that

I have initiated? Common meals can be social minefields, but once established, the commensality of friends becomes a source of mutual care, affection, and social nourishment. That is why we risk it.

In the ancient world, eating together was perhaps the most common form of social formation. Families, friends, associations of various sorts, religious and ethnic groups, all gathered around their respective tables. The rules, the etiquette, the menu, the company were all tightly managed, just as they are today. Gentiles ate with Gentiles; Jews with Jews. Men ate with men; women with women. Washing preceded eating. Clean hands ate clean food. The host presided, the guests reclined, and the servants served. In the stories about Jesus and his participation in common meals, he is constantly depicted as tweaking these various conventions. He advises that the most highly honored participant ought to prescind from claims to precedence (Luke 14:7–11), and that one's guest list ought not to include one's friends, but the destitute, who could never repay the hospitality (Luke 14:12–14). He and his followers do not wash before eating (Mark 7:1–8; Luke 11:37–41), and Jesus declares all foods clean (Mark 7:14–23; Luke 11:41). There are women at table with Jesus, and he does not chase them away (Mark 14:3–9; Luke 7:36–50). He eats with the clean (Luke 7:36; 14:1) and the unclean (Mark 2:15–17; 14:3). And whether Jesus did so or not, many of his earliest followers felt authorized by his teaching to cross ethnic boundaries and to eat with Gentiles (Gal 2:11–14; Acts 10). Jesus seems to have initiated a very peculiar, open practice of table fellowship.

Crossan thinks that the significance of this very central aspect of Jesus' praxis is captured by the parable of the Great Feast.[14] Here it is in its Lukan form:

> A person once gave a great banquet, and invited many guests. And when it came time for the banquet, he sent his servant around to the invited guests to say "Come, for everything is now ready." But they all, one after another, began to make excuses. The first guest said to him, "I've bought a field and must go out to look it over. Please pass along my regrets." And another said, "I've bought five yoke of oxen and must go examine them. Please pass along my regrets." And another said, "I have just gotten married and so cannot come." So the servant went and reported this to his master. Then the householder got angry and said to his servant, "Go out right away into the streets and alleys of the city and bring in the poor, the maimed, the blind and the lame." And the servant said, "What you have commanded

has been done, but there is still more room." So the master said to the servant, "Go out to the highways and hedges and compel people to come in, so that my house might be filled. For I tell you, none of those who were invited shall ever taste my banquet." (Luke 14:16b–24)

For the most part, this parable is as close to the version Jesus originally told as we can get, with the exception of one critical element. Almost everyone agrees that Luke seems to entertain a special regard for "the poor." In fact, "the poor, the maimed, the blind, and the lame" in Luke 14:21 echoes a Lukan phrase introduced in the story directly preceding this parable in Luke's gospel (see Luke 14:12–14). Thus, the instruction to "Go out right away into the streets and alleys of the city and bring in the poor, the maimed, the blind and the lame," represents a particularly Lukan way of drawing out the significance of the parable: one should practice charity in one's common meals. Luke's interpretation of this parable is admirable, but very conventional. It restricts the parameters of the parable well within the bounds of social manageability. But if this is to be ascribed to Luke, what is left to the original parable's resolution? "Go out to the highways and hedges and compel people to come in, so that my house might be filled." The peculiar and challenging thing about this parable is just this: the doors to the banquet hall are to be thrown wide open. 'Go out to the highways and bring in whomever you might find there.' Men and women. Friend and foe. The clean and unclean. Jews and Gentiles. Princes and thieves. Anyone who dares to respond to the invitation may come inside. This is a table without controls, a table without boundaries. It represents a community in which all are welcomed, into which all may come. This is an open table, a table far less manageable and far more threatening than the charitable table of Luke. In fact, as Crossan so succinctly puts it, "Generous almsgiving may even be conscience's last great refuge against the terror of open commensality." [15]

The Basileia of God

Now, one might say, "All of this is good teaching." It makes sense, especially to poor people, or to persons who are interested in working for a more open and egalitarian society. But is it more than that? Is it more than good teaching? Is it the Empire *of God*? This is to press beyond the question of social formation and ethics. It is to ask a *theologica* question.

Willi Marxsen liked to remind us that not everyone who heard Jesus and experienced him first hand had the same reaction.[16] Some said, "This guy is a nut!" Others said, "This is good teaching. Admirable. Interesting." But others said, "In this person's words and deeds I have experienced God's very own presence in my life." Some people gathered around Jesus' open table and said, "Whoa! I'm never going to do that again. Eating with the unclean – that's just not what God-fearing people do." Others said, "Now that was interesting. Perhaps I'll try it again sometime." But others said, "Around that table I experienced something I would claim as nothing less than the very love and acceptance of God. It is God who calls us to such tables. The words I heard from Jesus were the Word of God." Is this good teaching, or does this activity unveil the fundamental principle of the universe? At such tables do we discover the very ground of all being? That is what early Christians risked believing: that what they learned from Jesus and experienced in his presence was not just a good teaching or way of life, an ethic – though it was all of these. Rather, it was an expression of who they would claim God to be. To them, Jesus was a sign-act of who God is. It is God who offers everyone the means to life, unbrokered, freely given as a gift. Jesus' unbrokered empire is the Empire *of God*. This is what those who chose to follow Jesus experienced as good news, "gospel." The unbrokered Empire of God is the gospel of Jesus.

But is Jesus' unbrokered Empire of God really good news? History, of course, cannot tell us this. It can tell us only that some people did experience it that way, and chose to give themselves over to that reality as a life-transforming vocation. History can tell us what Jesus said and did, within limits. It can even tell us what the followers of Jesus, or later interpreters of Jesus, like Paul or the gospel writers, believed was the real significance of what he said and did. But history cannot tell us if any of this is true. It cannot tell us what we ought to believe. It cannot compel us to risk, as early Christians did, the claim that in Jesus they had come to know who God is. Faith is always a claim, a risk to believe. Historical research cannot minimize that risk, nor should it try. But historical research can clarify the nature of the risk one is asked to take in embracing Jesus' words and deeds as "gospel." To ask about the historical Jesus is to ask just what it was that earliest Christians were confessing when they risked the claim that in Jesus they had come to know God. Was it good news? Is there gospel in the words and deeds of Jesus? This is the risk and the claim that Christian faith invites one to make.

The Gospel of John and the Historical Jesus

Robert T. Fortna

The orthodox gospel . . .

For many Christians, John's gospel is the favorite of the New Testament's four. It alone gives us perhaps the most memorable sayings attributed to Jesus, for example:

> 3:16 God so loved the world that he gave his only son. . . .
> 14:2 In my Father's house there are many mansions.
> 14:6 I am the Way and the Truth and the Life.

Uniquely, throughout this gospel, Jesus himself voices the fully developed Christian conviction about who he is. Consequently this *Fourth Gospel*, as it's often called, came eventually to supply most of the language used by the Nicene Creed of the fourth and fifth centuries to define the second person of the Trinity:

> the only Son of God . . .
> begotten of the Father . . .
> God . . .
> Light . . .
> true God . . .
> through him all things were made . . .
> he came down from heaven . . .
> he became incarnate . . .

By contrast, the three other gospels – the so-called *synoptics* – contributed only the phrases "by the power of the Holy Spirit" and "the Virgin Mary."

(In another way, too, the Nicene Creed is far more *Johannine* than *synoptic*. It says nothing whatever about the life and ministry of Jesus! After " . . . he became incarnate from the Virgin Mary, and was made man" there is simply a period. And it continues: "For our sake he was crucified under Pontius Pilate. . . . " This schema had already been established in the earlier so-called Apostles' Creed: " . . . born of the Virgin Mary, suffered under Pontius Pilate. . . . " John's gospel, of course, contains some material about Jesus' ministry; but unlike the synoptics, John's story is overpowered by interest in the "person" of Jesus, and especially what he has to say about himself.)

So this gospel is the very cornerstone on which orthodox Christianity is based, relying chiefly on the words of Jesus found only here. Therefore it may come as a great shock to learn that in the collective opinion of many scholars and in particular the Jesus Seminar, by clear consensus, *almost none* of the words attributed to Jesus in John is authentic.[1] This is startling to most lay people, and especially offensive to conservative Christians who want to retain the Fourth Gospel as a source for recovering the historical Jesus.

As a member of the Seminar's sub-committee on the Fourth Gospel sayings, I was initially inclined to think that a number of sayings would pass the test of being to some degree historical; but in the end we all came to realize that in almost no case could this be maintained.

Why? Scholars work to distinguish what has long been called "the Jesus of history" from the so-called "Christ of faith." In other words, they recognize the basic fact that *Jesus was not a Christian*. He lived "before Christianity."[2] He was a pre-Christian Jew, and the idea that he was the Son of God, the messiah (in Greek, the *Christ*–a concept obviously basic to *Christ*ianity) was not entertained during his lifetime. Belief that he was the messiah and divine arose only after his death and on the basis of belief in his resurrection.

The Fourth Gospel overwhelmingly presents us with a post-Easter Jesus. And if we believed, with some of the Seminar's critics, that the only "real" Jesus is this Christ of the Gospels, and of the Fourth in particular, we would be committing the Christian fallacy (that is, the heresy, the theological dead-end) of Docetism – denying the historical reality of Jesus the man.

Paul, our earliest writer, probably quoting a rudimentary first-century creed he had received from those who were Christians before him, knows just such a distinction between the pre- and post-Easter Jesus:

> who was descended from David according to the flesh [that
> is, historically, during his lifetime, but later] . . . declared to
> be Son of God . . . by his resurrection from the dead.
> (Rom 1:3b–4)

Despite the impression to the contrary in all the gospels, Jesus did
not expect to be raised from death. To maintain that he did makes a
sham of his fearful but courageous acceptance of the death sentence.
The explicit predictions about the necessity of his death and resurrection, made three times in each of the synoptic gospels and in various
other ways in John, are for the benefit of the reader, who is meant to
understand ahead of time what is still to happen in the story.

So wherever any of the gospels, including occasionally the synoptics, puts on Jesus' lips the Christian claim that he is the Messiah (belief
that is technically called *christology*), we can assume that the author, or
earlier church tradition, has read that christology into the story so as to
make Jesus proclaim himself to be Christ. In fact he made no such statement, held no such belief about himself. Messianic ideas, about anyone,
were evidently of no interest to Jesus.[3] But obviously they were of central interest to later Christians, who sought to trace the roots of their
christological belief back to him.

. . . Jesus' gospel of the Kingdom

What then did Jesus teach? He proclaimed not himself but God's
kingdom, God's "imperial rule" – the new age or condition of life that
he saw dawning in his lifetime. This was the focus of his teaching, especially to those who least expected to hear that it applied to them. And
he called followers to join him in announcing that good news. We
should probably not call this mission during his lifetime "the Jesus
movement," for he was not its focus; rather it was the Kingdom movement. The belief he sought, both from those who became committed
followers and those who simply heard him, was not about who or what
he was (that would be Paul's gospel, and the evangelists', especially
John's) but about the good news of God's kingdom.

After Jesus' death something of his message survived and eventually resurfaced in the synoptic gospels. But for the most part it was soon
drastically changed; after the resurrection the subject of the good news
became no longer the kingdom of God . . . but Jesus himself. As a
famous formula puts it, "the Proclaimer became the one Proclaimed" or,

as Robert Funk has put it, the iconoclast became the icon. In technical terms, the historical Jesus became the kerygmatic Christ [the one preached about and believed in]. And so his kingdom movement almost disappeared.

Paul, writing within ten or fifteen years of his death, knows nothing of that movement or of Jesus' distinctive teaching about the kingdom; Paul gives only a standard first century meaning to the phrase "kingdom of God," and almost never mentions it. It was the author of *Mark*, writing in about 70 CE, who ingeniously reintroduced the memory of what Jesus had said. Until then the gospel about Jesus, as in Paul's case, made no use of Jesus' words. Mark was the first to convey Jesus' message of the kingdom. True, his words are often made to proclaim also the later, Christian message about Jesus as Messiah. But the news that Jesus had preached about the kingdom is still partly audible, and by careful reconstruction it can be lifted out of its present christological reshaping and allowed to speak again much as Jesus intended. Without Mark's gospel it might have been lost altogether. The authors of Matthew and Luke then introduced a great deal more of Jesus' speech (the so-called Q material), but if Mark had not paved the way that material too would probably not have survived.

John a purely christological gospel

Unlike the synoptics, which have authentic teachings of Jesus alongside the christological affirmations put on his lips, the Fourth Gospel has almost totally transformed the Jesus tradition it inherited, and perhaps invented many sayings from whole cloth. Very little of Jesus' original teaching remains; his message has become almost purely christological. Everything Jesus says points to who he is, and does so in very lofty ways. For example: "I and the Father are one" (John 10:30); "No one comes to the Father except through me" (14:6). And so almost nothing of what the Johannine Jesus says can be taken to be historically authentic.

The very form of the sayings in John underscores their late, Christian character. The most distinctive of Jesus' sayings were the *parables* – short, vivid, fictional stories that he told, not about himself or even God but about the kingdom, using circumstances known to his peasant hearers. His parables usually ended with a twist, a question, a startling assertion that forced the hearer to decide what was meant. But nothing of this sort is found in John; there are simply no parables there. In their place, usually set within long monologues, there are riddles and extended metaphors that are exclusively christological ("I am the door . . . the light . . . the vine . . . the shepherd"). Over and over the Fourth Gospel's Jesus explains his relation to God; he says virtually nothing about the kingdom of God.

Alongside the parables, the other characteristic speech-form of Jesus was the *aphorism*, the brief, pithy one-liner that said something memorable and striking about the kingdom of God:

> It's easier for a camel to squeeze through the eye of a
> needle. . . .
> Consider the lilies. . . .
> Blessed are the poor.
> Prophets have no honor in their own hometown.

To be sure, this last aphorism is found in John 4:44, and it is one of the two or three sayings in that gospel that are conceivably authentic. Jesus very likely said it. But it was a common proverb, and while it is consistent with his thought, it is not distinctive.

In the Fourth Gospel there are few aphorisms; instead Jesus makes announcements, usually within long dialogues or monologues, about himself—for example,

> 3:13 No one has gone up to heaven except the one who
>   came down from there – the Son of Man.
> 6:35 I am the bread of life.
> 8:58 Before Abraham was, I am.

Though now found on Jesus' lips as if he once spoke them, it's clear from their consistently christological content that they are actually late first-century statements of Christian belief about him.

Further, there is no difference between words Jesus allegedly spoke and statements about him made by the Fourth Evangelist. In fact, sometimes it's not clear whether Jesus or the author is supposed to be speaking. A striking example is that favorite verse, 3:16, that we noted at the start: "God so loved the world. . . . " Clearly, the Johannine Jesus' words directly reflect the author's point of view. They have been taken from contemporary belief about Jesus and attributed to him as his teaching some sixty years earlier. Whereas in the synoptics there is relatively little of this, John's Jesus speaks almost exclusively this way.

And in the synoptics there is virtually nothing like the baldly christological third-person statements about him that we find, for example, in the Johannine prologue: "became flesh . . . full of grace and truth";

"God the only son in the bosom of the Father . . . has made [God] known" (1:14, 16).

In short, both the words of Jesus in John and the comment of the Fourth Evangelist about him are late. All of this is of course profoundly important for orthodox Christian believers (see conclusion, below), but tells us nothing of what Jesus said or believed.

Events in the fourth gospel

So far we have given primary attention to Jesus' words in John, on the basis of the Jesus Seminar's first volume, *The Five Gospels*. The second phase of the Seminar's work, examining the reported events of Jesus' life, has appeared as *The Acts of Jesus*.[4] What does it tell us about the historical accuracy of the deeds material in John?

1. Some of the *miracle stories* find parallels in the synoptics (for example, the feeding of the five thousand, the healing of the lame man); others have perhaps a faint connection to synoptic material (water into wine, Lazarus raised). But as they stand, none of them can be taken as factual. In every case they are performed by Jesus not out of concern for human need and thus as reflections of God's kingdom—their import in the synoptics—but rather in order to display Jesus' divinity. They are the messianic "signs" of who he is, the kind of deeds that according to the synoptics Jesus summarily refused to perform (see for example Mark 8:12). These signs are purely christological, designed to evoke Christian faith in Jesus as Messiah. (In the first three gospels, the *result* of a miracle, as shaped by the author, may be faith in Jesus, but that is seldom portrayed as Jesus' intent.)

2. Jesus' *itinerary* in John, with several visits to Jerusalem, is very likely more representative of his life than the single, fateful visit recounted in the synoptics. But if so, its accuracy is accidental, since the Fourth Evangelist has created this alternation between Jerusalem and (usually) Galilee for schematic, theological purposes, with no basis in fact—possibly by re-working a source that had no such complex itinerary.

3. The Johannine account of Jesus' *last supper* with his disciples (which, incidentally, lacks all mention of the elements of the later church's Lord's Supper, in particular bread and wine and the words spoken over them) very possibly preserves a factual tradition—Jesus' significant and memorable act of *washing his disciples' feet*—even though it is missing altogether from the synoptics. (This is my own opinion; the Seminar did not consider the question.)

If some of these details are perhaps unintentionally accurate, the bulk of the events in John, the two blocks that form the substance of Jesus' career in John, are not factual at all: a) In the gospel's first half he is shown voluntarily performing *miracles* as signs of his divine nature, and b) in the second his *death* is portrayed as chiefly his own deed, under his own control, and amounting to victory—in contrast to the starker synoptic portrayals.

From this quick survey of events in John we can see that occasionally an accurate historical datum may be preserved, but often for theological, not factual, reasons. In general, then, the Johannine portrait of Jesus' career is highly distorted historically.

Conclusion

What have we learned? First, that virtually none of the sayings in John can be taken with any confidence as authentic. (Notice the phrase, "with any confidence". As with everything the Jesus Seminar has claimed, there is of course no certainty; but its consensus, arrived at by reducing a usually wide spectrum of voting to a weighted average, is unique and significant—no extended collaborative enterprise of this sort has ever before been attempted.) The one possibly authentic saying ("Prophets have no honor in their own hometown" [4:44]) reflects conventional wisdom, and only in some earlier form are the two questionable ones conceivably authentic:

> I swear to God, unless the kernel of wheat falls to the earth and dies, it remains a single seed; but if it dies, it produces a great harvest. Those who love life lose it, but those who hate live in this world will preserve it for unending, real life. (John 12:24–25)

and,

> I swear to God, if they welcome the person I send, they welcome me; and if they welcome me, they welcome the one who sent me. (John 13:20)

There may of course be other sayings that escaped the Seminar's careful scrutiny – we do not claim that our reconstruction of authentic Jesus material is exhaustive, and probably many of the ambiguous votes need reconsidering—but on the whole, the evidence of John is almost wholly negligible compared to the synoptics.

In the case of deeds and events in the Fourth Gospel, the consensus is slightly more optimistic. But overall, it seems clear that this gospel can hardly be taken as a usable source for the reconstruction of the historical Jesus.

So what value has this gospel? If it is not historically factual, not "true" in that sense, should it not be discarded or at least ignored? Well, no, not at all. None of the gospels as they now stand is historically true in that sense. Yes, the synoptics are the chief sources for reconstructing the Jesus of history, but that reconstruction must be accomplished by the most subtle and intricate methods. The reader of any of the gospels is presented not with an accurate profile, certainly not with a biography, of Jesus, but rather with a highly theological, that is, Christian, interpretation of him and his career. Christianity was not based primarily on the man Jesus, even though the Gospels of Mark, Matthew, and Luke make use of the tradition of the man Jesus to express it. Instead it was based on the resurrection, which in turn forced a radical reinterpretation through the eyes of faith of who Jesus was—or rather who he must have been. So we read John as the most christological gospel, a pure basis for orthodox Christianity. If members of the Jesus Seminar are interested in countering the distortions of a fundamentalist, literal reading of the gospels (see below), they are also concerned to reclaim the Fourth Gospel for a valid reading by Christians and non-Christians alike.

Finally it needs to be said that the result of the Seminar's work is to throw out nothing; we are not in the business of "debunking" the gospels, as many have said. On the contrary, we debunk the kind of simplistic, literal reading of the gospels that leads to fundamentalist and rigid interpretation, and is dangerous in the modern world. (Take, for example, the malevolent and reactionary politics of some fundamentalists, or their savagely homophobic stance.)

Material seen as unhistorical is in a way just as significant as the historical; it shows us with specific clarity what was happening intellectually – that is, theologically – in the otherwise largely obscure first century CE. Such passages are presumably the creation of the early Christians, as they tried to come to terms with Jesus and particularly with his resurrection. They are not factual, but as often as not they form the basis of important Christian belief and interpretation. It is not the Seminar's intent to destroy the Fourth Gospel or its importance in forging early Christianity, but to understand it. It is only for the purely historical understanding of the man Jesus – important of course, fascinating, disarming, but not all-important – that John is of limited import.[5]

Notes

Hoover, *Introduction*

1. The Jesus Seminar voted on whether sayings and deeds attributed to Jesus in the gospel texts probably were or probably were not historical, and represented these judgments by color-coding the gospel texts.

For sayings, the colors signify the following:

    red: Jesus undoubtedly said this or something very like it.

    pink: Jesus probably said something like this.

    gray: Jesus did not say this, but the ideas contained in it are close to his own.

    black: Jesus did not say this; it represents the perspective or content of a later or different tradition.

This is the color-coding used in *The Five Gospels.*

For deeds, the colors signify the following:

    red: The historical reliability of this information is virtually certain. It is supported by a preponderance of the evidence.

    pink: This information is probably reliable. It fits well with other evidence that is verifiable.

    gray: This information is possible but unreliable. It lacks supporting evidence.

    black: This information is improbable. It does not fit verifiable evidence; it is largely or entirely fictive.

This is the color-coding used in *The Acts of Jesus.*

2. Kathleen Corley's essay is concerned with a social issue, Jesus' attitude toward women, rather than with his social location more generally.

3. Bovon, "Review of Crossan's *Birth of Christianity*," 374.

4. These observations are adapted from Becker, *Everyman*, 251.

5. Polybius, *Rise*, 432 [Book 12.12].

6. Berger, *Sacred Canopy*, 51.

Scott, *The Reappearance of Parables*

1. Funk, et al, *The Five Gospels* and *The Acts of Jesus.*

2. For the characteristics of each of the three stages, see my "New Options in an Old Quest."

3. Sanders, *Jesus and Judaism.*

4. Miller, *Historical Method in the Deeds of Jesus*, and Seeley, "Jesus' Temple Act."

5. Meier, *A Marginal Jew*, 2:290. His primary kingdom saying which determines

how he views the kingdom is "Thy Kingdom Come," from the Lord's prayer.

6. Allison, *Jesus of Nazareth: Millenarian Prophet*, 128–29. "Should we not, if at all possible, rather interpret the parables in accord with what we have established about Jesus on other grounds."

7. Crossan, *The Historical Jesus*.

8. Borg, *Meeting Jesus Again for the First Time*.

9. Wright, *Jesus and the Victory of God*, vol. 2, 178.

10. See my *Hear Then the Parable*, 65–68, for a sketch of this distinctive voice.

11. Semeia Supplements, ch. 5.

12. Wheelwright, *Metaphor and Reality*, 78–86. "Here the 'movement' (*phora*) is 'through' (*dia*) certain particulars of experience (actual or imagined) in fresh way, producing new meaning by juxtaposition," 78.

13. Crossan, *Finding Is the First Act*.

14. Taking interest is something clearly forbidden; see Exod 22:25–27; Lev 25:35–38; Deut 23:19–20.

15. Allison, *Jesus of Nazareth*, 70, admits: "it remains true that most of these stories [the miracles stories] have little or nothing to say about the kingdom of God or repentance or anything eschatological," although he then proceeds to assume an apocalyptic reading of them.

16. For example, Paul uses the two sons theme in the traditional way (Gal 4:21–31) and Luke in chapter 15 attempts to situate the parable of the Prodigals so that the younger son is the Gentiles and the elder son the rejected Jews.

17. Sulloway, *Born to Rebel, Birth Order*.

18. Sulloway, *Born to Rebel*, 20.

19. *Born to Rebel*, xiii.

20. Schaberg, *The Illegitimacy of Jesus*.

21. Heaney, *The Redress of Poetry*, 3–4.

22. Sanders, *Jesus and Judaism*, 4.

23. Meier, *A Marginal Jew*, 1:177.

24. Havel, *Disturbing the Peace*, 181.

Hoover, *The Jesus of History*

1. Neusner, *Judaism*, ix.

2. Wilder, *Literary Critic*, 108, 109.

3. A list of the twenty-three parables identified by the Jesus Seminar as probably authentic is published in Funk, et al, *Parables of Jesus*, 74.

4. Kloppenborg Verbin, *Excavating Q*, 112–65; 353–408; and Robinson et al., *Critical Edition of Q*, lix–lxvi.

5. *Literary Critic*, 109.

6. Neusner, *Judaism*, 51.

7. *Judaism*, 52.

8. *Judaism*, 48, 22.

9. *Judaism*, 50.

10. *Judaism*, 71–74.

11. Cited by M. Hengel in *Judaism and Hellenism*, 1, 213.

12. Funk, et al, *Five Gospels*, 144.

13. *Five Gospels*, 152.

14. Robinson et al, *Critical Edition of Q*, lix–lxvi, esp. lxii–lxiii.

15. J. M. Robinson in a prepublication comment cited on the back cover of Kloppenborg Verbin's *Excavating Q*.

16. Kloppenborg Verbin, *Excavating Q*, 391, 392.

17. Reed, *Archaeology and the Galilean Jesus*, 178.

18. *Galilean Jesus*, 213.

19. Niebuhr, *Christian Ethics*, 25.

20. Berger, *Sacred Canopy*, 47–48.

21. Cadbury, *Peril of Modernizing Jesus*, 106.

22. Montefiore, *Old Testament and After*, 248; cited by Cadbury, *Modernizing*, 110–11.

23. Betz, *Sermon on the Mount* (Matt 5:3–7:27 and Luke 6:20–49), 285.

24. Millar, *Roman Near East*, 97.

25. Reed, *Galilean Jesus*, 100.

26. Niebuhr, *Christian Ethics*, 23–24.

Hedrick, *Jesus of Nazareth: A Profile Under Construction*

1. Funk and Hoover, *The Five Gospels*; Funk, *The Acts of Jesus*.

2. See Hedrick, *When History and Faith Collide*.

3. Kee, *Jesus in History. An Approach to the Study of the Gospels*, 48–54.

4. See the readings of the parables in Hedrick, *Parables*, 93–235.

5. Brown, *New Testament Christology*, 89; cf. 71–89. But compare Matt 26:63–64; Luke 22:67–69.

6. Talbert, *What Is a Gospel?* 25–52.

Dewey, *What Do You Make of This?: Jesus as Peasant Artisan*

1. *Tao Te Ching*, LaFargue Translation, 136 (63 [42] 1).

2. Langewiesche, *Inside the Sky*, 240.

3. Scott, *Hear Then the Parable*, 38–40.

Smith, *Israel's Prodigal Son; Reflections on Reimaging Jesus*

1. Crossan, *Historical Jesus*, 426.

2. Funk, "The Issue of Jesus," 12.

3. The Latin verb *fingo, fingere, finxi, fictum*, while often carrying purely aesthetic connotations of decoration or entertainment, was also used to describe the sober tools of education that were "formed by instruction," to teach or train (Lewis and Short, *Latin Dictionary*, 751).

4. "For all the accounts of Jesus contain a constructive element which goes beyond the data contained in the sources. Historical imagination with its hypotheses creates an 'aura of fictionality' around the figure of Jesus, just like the religious imaginations of earlier Christianity. For in both cases a creative power of imagination is at work, sparked off by the same historical figure" (Theissen and Merz, *Historical Jesus*, 13).

5. Johnson, *Real Jesus*, 167, 141.

6. *Real Jesus*, 167

7. *Real Jesus*, 167.

8. Whether or not one accepts the conclusion of most modern gospel scholars that Matthew is a revision of Mark, it is Matthew who explicitly endorses scholarly revision of treasured texts by ascribing this analogy to Jesus: "Every

scholar who is schooled in Heaven's imperial rule is like some proprietor who produces from his storeroom treasures new and old" (Matt 13:52).

9. Theissen and Merz, *Historical Jesus*, 13.

10. *Real Jesus*, 124–25.

11. For example: (a) Matthew sets Jesus' birth under Herod in 4 BCE while Luke locates it during the census under Quirinius in 6 CE; (b) Matthew claims Jesus insisted on observing every detail of the Torah, while the other gospels focus on situations where Jesus or his disciples are criticized for non-observance; (c) the synoptics identify Jesus' last supper as a Passover meal while John insists that Jesus died before the Passover began.

12. *Reimarus*, 64 (italics mine).

13. Funk, *Poetics*, 300.

14. Funk, "Profiles of Jesus: A Protocol," 22.

15. Theissen, *Shadow of the Galilean*, 1.

16. E.g., A. Schweitzer: "The historical Jesus will be to our time a stranger and an enigma" (*Quest*, 397). "We can find no designation which expresses what He is for us. He comes to us as One unknown, without a name, as of old, by the lakeside, He came to those who knew Him not" (*Quest*, 401).

17. *Quest*, 4. W. Wink extended Schweitzer's challenge to the pretense of historical objectivity with this observation: "Biblical scholars have been exceedingly slow to grasp the implications of Quantum Theory: that the observer is always a part of the field being observed, and disturbs the field by the very act of observation" ("Jesus: As Real As," 28–29).

18. The irony of Schweitzer's critique of modern Jesus scholarship is that it concludes with this poetic eulogy: "He was not teacher, not a casuist; *He was an imperious ruler* . . . And to those who obey Him, whether they be wise or simple, He will reveal Himself in the toils, the conflicts, the sufferings which they shall pass through in His fellowship, and as an ineffable mystery, they shall learn *in their own experience* Who He is" (*Quest*, 403, italics mine).

19. *Reimarus*, 64 (italics mine).

20. If the Fellows had been asked to vote on things that Jesus' contemporary opponents said, these slurs would probably have been rated red. The "pal of toll collectors" motif in Q is independently attested in Mark 2:16 as the pretext for a pink Jesus saying (Mark 2:17b // Gospel Fragment 1224 5:2); the Markan Beelzebul charge is echoed in the even pinker Q retort (Luke 11:18–20 // Matt 12:27–28).

21. Johnson, *Real Jesus*, 151–66.

22. Implicit Elijah parallels are integral to both synoptic and Johannine accounts of Jesus' deeds.

23. In the only gospel texts where Jesus explicitly acknowledges being *ho Christos*, the messianic title is introduced by someone else: Peter (Matt 16:16–17), Caiaphas (Mark 14:61–62), and a Samaritan woman (John 4:25–26). The fact that *no* christological confession is credited to Jesus in parallel versions of the first two incidents and there are no independent witnesses in the third supports the conclusion summarized by Borg (*Jesus: A New Vision*, 10): "Regarding Jesus' own sense of identity, the growing historical skepticism produced a consensus. Whether Jesus thought of himself as having a special exalted identity –as 'Messiah' or 'the Son of God'– we cannot know because of the very nature of the documents. When we do find such statements in the gospels . . . the careful

historian (even if he or she is also a Christian) must suspect them as the post-Easter perspective of Jesus' followers projected back into the ministry." Notable dissenters to this scholarly consensus include A. Schweitzer, M. Hengel and N. T. Wright (*Jesus and the Victory of God*, 488).

24. E.g., Bornkamm, *Jesus of Nazareth*, 56–57; Vermes, *Jesus the Jew*, 224–25; Borg, *Meeting Jesus*, 30.

25. Bornkamm noted the dissimilarity between Jesus and these traditional Jewish paradigms even in adopting them: "He is a prophet of the coming kingdom of God . . . Yet he is in no way completely contained in this category, and differs from the customary ways of a prophet. A prophet has to produce his credentials . . . Jesus, on the other hand, never speaks of his calling, and nowhere does he use the ancient, prophetic formula. Even less do we find any trace of that self-justification typical of the apocalyptic visionaries of later Judaism, who claim the authority of ecstatic states of mind and visions, secret revelations of the next world, and miraculous insights into God's decrees" (*Jesus of Nazareth*, 56). "This rabbi differs considerably from the other members of his class. Even external facts reveal this difference . . . There is nothing in contemporary Judaism which corresponds to the immediacy with which he teaches" (*Jesus of Nazareth*, 57).

26. Multiple attestation and the implicit embarrassment gave this pronouncement a pink rating in the Jesus Seminar's voting, just one point below the .75 weighted average required for a red saying.

27. While many details of the *testimonium Flavianum* (*Antiquities* 18.3.3) have obviously been altered by Christian scribes to make Josephus' report confirm orthodox christology, his formula of introduction is probably genuine: "Now about this time came Jesus, a wise man (*sophos aner*). . . ."

28. The Jesus Seminar deemed the Markan form of this critique of scholarly privilege in general (Mark 12:38–39, Luke 20:46) to be closer to Jesus' original pronouncement than the Q version (Luke 11:43, Matt 23:5–7), which singled out the Pharisees for censure, though both versions were weighted pink (.61 versus .53).

29. See Excursus 1.

30. The multiply attested beatitude declaring the divine *basileia* the possession of "the poor" received the third highest weighted average as a genuine Jesus saying in the voting of the Jesus Seminar (.91). Discrepancies in the precise formulation of aphorisms assigning this "kingdom" to children led to a low pink rating (.51) for the canonical version.

31. This aphorism was reviewed three times by the Jesus Seminar and in the final vote fell just short of a red weighted average (.74 pink).

32. Jesus Seminar weighted average: red (.77). See Excursus 2.

33. The Fellows gave the versions of this widely attested Jesus saying that refers to "Father" a pink rating (.60). The versions that use the term "God" (i.e., Mark and Luke) were rated lower.

34. The Markan version of the "Lord of the sabbath" saying – affirming the priority of the generic human being (Adam) over the sabbath in the order of creation – was one of two "son of Man" sayings that the Seminar accepted as genuine Jesus sayings (.55 pink). The synoptic versions that omit reference to the creation account were rated lower.

35. The Fellows rated Matthew's unqualified formulation, "The last will be first

and the first last," pink (.58); qualifications in other versions can be credited to scribal attempts to deradicalize Jesus' principle of inversion.

36. The Jesus Seminar initially voted this saying gray because it has been interpreted as inferring that Jesus' movement is superior to JB's. That interpretation, however, ignores the fact that it obviously precludes exalting even Jesus, who himself had a mother, above John. This saying was reconsidered when the Seminar examined Jesus' relation to JB in detail (Spring '92), and was voted red in substance (weighted average, .85; cf. Tatum, *John the Baptist*, 155).

37. The Matthean version of this Q saying is remarkable not only because it does not fit Matthew's usual theme of the punishment of the wicked, but because it places "the bad" ahead of "the good," an emphasis confirmed by the Lukan paraphrase (Luke 6:35).

38. This saying is clearly out of place in its current setting and thus deserves a separate vote. Recommendation: RED!

39. A conclusion independent of but supported by S. J. Patterson's observation: "Jesus was remembered as a shameless fool. To spend time with expendables is to be a fool – to refuse to recognize the shame of another. Expendables are by definition shamed. To have honor is to have place, to have a recognized role" (*God of Jesus*, 75–76).

40. R. A. Horsley ("Jesus, Itinerant Cynic") in particular has pointed out (a) the differences between Jesus' instructions to itinerants and normal cynic lifestyle and (b) the lack of concrete evidence of cynics – Jewish or otherwise – in the Galilee of Jesus' day (in Charlesworth, *Images of Jesus*, 72–78).

41. Discontinuity between the parable's plot and its gospel context shows that it is was not a free Lukan creation.

42. A notable exception is J. R. Michaels: "The assumption on which this book is based is that what Jesus of Nazareth taught is what he himself first learned by experience . . . Nowhere is this more apparent than in the metaphors and images that dominate Jesus' speech . . . The pictures he draws for disciples and antagonists alike are pictures that he himself has seen . . . The stories he told – his parables – and the stories he acted out – his meals with sinners, his words of forgiveness, his miracles of healing – unfold for us his profound and peculiar vision of what is real" (*Servant and Son*, xi–xii).

43. Scott, "The Reappearance of Parables," 3.

44. R. W. Funk's hermeneutical analysis of "Parable as Metaphor" (*Language*, 133–62) is still the classic study of the genre.

45. Crossan, *In Parables*, 14 (italics author's; boldface mine).

46 "The parables in the special material give many indications that they are not the compositions of the evangelists . . . In the two Lukan parables of the good Samaritan and the prodigal son the narrative shows a Jewish perspective: the Samaritans are aliens; the prodigal son almost comes to grief looking after (unclean) pigs; his family lies in Jewish Palestine. It is improbable that the evangelist composed such parables with a Jewish perspective" (Theissen and Merz, *Historical Jesus*, 338–39).

47. An insight originally independent of but supported by B. B. Scott: "To accept this parable as anything but a fantasy, a hearer must accept the Samaritan as helper-hero instead of expected opponent-villain and oneself as victim in the ditch" ("The Reappearance of Parables," 9).

48. "It is thus possible . . . to affirm that the parable, as metaphor, has not one but many 'points,' as many points as there are situations into which it is spoken. And that applies to the original as well as subsequent audiences" (Funk, *Language*, 151).

49. The Jesus Seminar was almost unanimous in recognizing the principle of turning the cheek in reaction to an opponent's slap as a genuine Jesus saying (.92). The paradoxical injunction to love the opponent was also among the Seminar's top five red sayings (.84), while the non-canonical version of the advice to clear one's own vision before correcting someone else was ranked fiftieth (.60 = pink) among the more than 1500 sayings ascribed to Jesus in antiquity.

50. Most Fellows (.56) accepted the thesis "there is a historical core to the story of Jesus and the Syro-Phoenician woman." That core is the dialectical structure of the repartée between Jesus and the woman. Though a majority considered the dialog historically reliable(.52), it fell shy of a pink rating (.43–.47), because several who doubted that Jesus would insult a woman voted black. Yet, these general statements received an endorsement of almost .60: "A woman turned Jesus' metaphors against him" and "Jesus accepted a woman's witty retort."

51. The Jesus Seminar vote on similar metaphorical advice against throwing valuable things to "dogs" or "pigs" (Matt 7:6 // Thomas 93) was weighted gray, indicating that some of the content, if not the form of the saying could be traced to Jesus.

52. The Seminar accepted the general thesis "Jesus defended his behavior in aphorism (and parable)" as virtually certain (.86 = red).

53. B. B. Scott's reader-response analysis of the impact of this parable is apt: "What is a hearer to make of this?. Was the master being arbitrary in his judgment? Was the accusation of wasting goods true or false? Was the steward's behavior simply harmless fun at the master's expense? The parable offers no answers to these questions, it only provokes them! . . . The hearer has no way to navigate in the world. Its solid moorings have been lost" (*Hear Then*, 265–66).

54. The Jesus Seminar almost unanimously agreed that "Jesus was criticized for eating with 'sinners'" (.92 = red) and that this criticism was based on his actual behavior.

55. Funk, *Language*, 161–62.

56. The Fellows overwhelmingly agreed with the thesis that "some who saw Jesus said he had a demon" (Fall '92, item 21; .90 = red). No vote has yet been taken on the thesis: "some Judeans called Jesus a Samaritan." Recommendation: red.

57. Josephus, *Antiquities* 11.346: "If anyone was charged by authorities in Jerusalem with *eating unclean things* or with *violating the sabbath* or some other sin like this, he fled to the authorities at Shechem, saying that he had been unjustly banished (italics mine)."

58. The Jesus Seminar voted both sayings pink: Mark 7:14–15 (.70) and Mark 2:27–28 (.55).

59. Whether Jesus was responsible for the formulation of the Lord's prayer or not, the wording of the initial petition "Father! . . . Your *basileia* come!" mimics his characteristic emphases. The transactional logic of this demand makes the petitioner the intended recipient of the *basileia*, for it makes absolutely no sense to ask the King to actualize what is his by definition. And there is no third party

in view; so the petition cannot be passed off as selfless mediation. Any child who presumes to ask a parent for *his* car is really demanding the keys for him or herself. After all, this petition is credited to the Jesus who advised others "seek first [your Father's] *basileia*" (Luke 12:31 // Matt 6:33) and assured them: "Ask — and it will be given *to you!*" (Luke 11:9 // Matt 7:7).

60. The Seminar accepted the parable of the rich farmer (.60) and the paradox about saving/losing one's life (.52) as essentially genuine (pink) Jesus sayings. Criticisms for eating openly with "sinners" were almost unanimously accepted (.92) as even more certain (red).

61. The Fellows voted the saying "toll collectors and prostitutes will get into God's *imperium* but you will not" gray primarily because of its questionable Matthean context (as conclusion to the parable of the two sons). Since the statement is not characteristic of Matthew's general ethics and is coherent with genuine aphorisms of Jesus that are socially shocking, it probably would have been voted pink had it been treated separately. See Funk, et al, *Five Gospels*, 232.

62. The Fellows accepted the parable of the dinner party (.69) and the aphorism about wedding guests (.57) as relatively reliable (pink) sayings of Jesus.

63. The Seminar almost unanimously accepted these general theses as historically certain (red): "Jesus had brothers" (.97) and "the family of Jesus played a significant role in the early Jerusalem community" (.91). The majority also agreed that the evidence made it probable (pink) that "Jesus brothers were not in sympathy with him" (.69).

64. The Seminar considered Paul's portrayal of Jesus' brother James (Gal 1–2) as "pre-eminent among the three leaders of 'repute'" among Jerusalem Christians as historically accurate (.95).

65. B. B. Scott notes the lack of congruence between Luke's fictional audience and the elder son and that "in the parable narrative itself there is no rejection" (*Hear Then*, 103).

66. Scott also notes: "The Christian adoption of the [two sons] mytheme . . . is inappropriate to Jesus' context. . . ." (*Hear Then*, 124.)

67. From this angle, the father's words "this brother of yours was dead and has come back to life" (Luke 15:31) reads like a post-crucifixion but pre-Lukan expansion.

68. J. R. Michaels proposed the older son as Jesus' fictive persona because the father identifies that son as his heir who is always with him: "Like most other hearers, Jesus would have found himself drawn into the story of the lost son precisely through the figure of the older brother, and so called upon to share the father's joy and compassion. But for Jesus, unlike other hearers, the self-identification was part of a larger pattern. Here as elsewhere he found his sonship confirmed, while at the same time he learned obedience to his Father's will regarding tax collectors and other prodigals." (*Servant and Son*, 219.) The primary problem with this reading, as Michaels himself notes, is that the parable ends with no indication that the heir is reconciled to the prodigal.

69. Scott, *Hear Then*, 122.

70. Beyond the Lukan parables of the Samaritan, shrewd manager and prodigal, instances of Jesus' rhetorical concession of critics' slander are found in Q (Luke 7:34 // Matt 9:19 and Luke 11:19 // Matt 12:27).

71. Theissen summarizes the consensus of biblical critics since Wrede and Bultmann: "The chronological and geographical outline of Mark is secondary to

the individual traditions; its form is determined by the author's theological premises and therefore [is] historically worthless" (*Historical Jesus*, 27).

72. The Seminar overwhelming endorsed (.85 = red) this unequivocal conclusion: "It is not just the content of the trial but the fact of a trial that lacks historical foundation." (Fall '95; cf. Funk et al, *Acts of Jesus*, 147f.) The thesis on the dating of the crucifixion was less precise – "Jesus was crucified in some conjunction with Passover" – and the vote less conclusive (.48 = gray). But an earlier vote (Spring '94) overwhelmingly rejected the thesis of the synoptic gospels that Jesus' last supper was a Passover meal (.10 = black). Thus, the Seminar decisively rejected the historicity of the synoptic passion narrative without ruling out the Johannine dating of Jesus' execution prior to the paschal seder.

73. Three quarters of the Fellows endorsed this thesis: "The underlying structure of the Passion narrative was taken from the Septuagint texts."

74. The Seminar considered it probable (pink) that the movements focused on John and Jesus were rivals both during (.67) and after (.70) the lifetime of their leaders (Tatum, *John the Baptist*, 163–66). But it deemed the synoptic thesis that "Jesus began his public ministry at the time JB was imprisoned" only possible (.46 = gray). There were no red votes on that chronological marker.

75. The Fellows confirmed the historical basis of the gospel accounts of John's career with the following red votes: "There was a person named John the baptizer" (.96); "JB's exhortations and activities had a widespread appeal" (.86); "JB's time precedes and overlaps that of Jesus" (.81); "JB's activities posed a threat to Herod Antipas' ability to maintain peace and stability" (.89).

76. This saying was weighted gray largely because the second strophe can be interpreted as primitive Christian propaganda. "The Fellows agreed that few in the Christian community would have been willing to say that 'no human is greater than John.'" (Funk et al, *Five Gospels*, 302.) A subsequent vote (Spring '92) affirmed that "Jesus identified JB as a great figure" (.85 = red).

77. The majority of Fellows (.55) deemed this thesis historically probable (pink): "Jesus' disciples considered Jesus to be JB's successor."

78. The Fellows overwhelmingly rejected the thesis that "Mark's temporal statements are historically accurate" (.10 = black; Spring '93).

79. *Pace* Johnson (see above, n. 8).

80. The Fellows agreed that John's baptism was a sign of repentance (.81 = red) but were less certain that it was regarded as a sacrament of forgiveness (.67 = pink). (Tatum, *John the Baptist*, 121–24)

81. Although the Fellows thought the story of the healing of the paralytic (Mark 2:1–12) had a historical core (pink), the Markan parenthesis on the forgiveness of sins (2:6–10) was deemed less probable (Spring '93; *Acts of Jesus*, 63–65). Mark 2:16 was voted pink (.63; Fall '94/5; *Acts of Jesus*, 66). The only time Mark credits Jesus with a call to "repent" is a generalized proclamation of God's *basileia* (Mark 1:15). But there the Greek verb *metanoeite* is is best taken literally ("Change your mind") since Mark gives no clue of the morality of intended auditors. This saying was voted black anyway (.20; Fall '86).

82. The Fellows overwhelmingly agreed John was an ascetic (there was no black and only one gray vote on item 18S; Spring '92). A bare majority opinion (.51) rated the Markan characterization of his rustic diet historically probable. No vote was recorded on his disciples' practices (Tatum, *John the Baptist*, 116–17).

83. The Fellows overwhelming concurred in characterizing Jesus as an exorcist

(.88 = red; Fall '92 item 46; *Acts of Jesus*, 61). An exorcism in the synagogue at Capernaum was weighted possible but historically uncertain (.36 = gray; Fall '92 item 20; *Acts of Jesus*, 57).

84. The Seminar deemed descriptions of Jesus as socially deviant (.79 = red) and opponents' labeling him possessed (.90 = red) historically accurate (Fall '92; items 11 & 15). No vote was recorded on references to his physical contact with people in states of ritual impurity.

85. While questions about the wording of the Q sayings about children in the marketplace (Luke 7:31–35) and the kingdom and violence (Luke 16:16) initially left these passages gray (Spring '89), a subsequent vote (Spring '92) colored the general thesis "Jesus contrasted his behavior with that of JB (Q 7:31–35, 16:16)" bright pink (.71).

86. The Seminar was practically unanimous (.91) in endorsing the historical proposition that John baptized Jesus; there were no black votes (Tatum, *John the Baptist*, 148).

87. The Seminar deemed it virtually certain (red) that John preached repentance (.78) and baptized to signify repentance (.81) (Tatum, *John the Baptist*, 122, 127).

McGaughy, *The Search for the Historical Jesus: Why Start with the Sayings?*
1. Witherington, *Jesus Quest*, ch. 2.
2. Pearson, "Gospel According to the Jesus Seminar," 321.
3. Funk, "The Issue of Jesus."
4. Funk, *Honest to Jesus*, esp. 64.
5. Bornkamm, *Jesus of Nazareth*, 14.
6. Perrin, *Rediscovering*, 33.
7. Perrin, *Rediscovering*, 38–49.
8. Boring, "Criteria."
9. Crossan, "Materials and Methods."
10. See the list of red and pink parables in Funk, *Parables*, 102.
11. Funk, *Five Gospels*, 5, 16–35; see also Funk, *Gospel of Mark: Red Letter Edition*, 29–52.
12. Pearson, "Gospel according to the Jesus Seminar," 321.
13. See Immerwahr, "*Ergon*."
14. The role of Herodotus in creating the conventional pattern of Greek biography is discussed in Homeyer, "Anfangen."
15. Momigliano, *Development of Greek Biography*, 103.
16. Hadas and Smith, *Heroes and Gods*, 3, 58.
17. For the full text, see Hadas and Smith, *Heroes and Gods*, 203.
18. See the classic description in Bultmann, *History*, 209–44.
19. See, e.g., Funk, *Acts*, 61.
20. Vielhauer, "On the 'Paulinism' of Acts."
21. Witherington, *Jesus Quest*, 46; Pearson, "Gospel According to the Jesus Seminar," 321.
22. For a discussion of parable as metaphor, see Funk, *Language*, and *Jesus as Precursor*; Crossan, *In Parables*; Scott, *Jesus, Symbol-Maker* and *Hear then the Parable*. A brief summary of this approach to parables is contained in McGaughy, "Jesus' Parables."

23. Funk, *Jesus as Precursor*, 51–72.
24. See Crossan, *In Fragments*, and Williams, *Those Who Ponder Proverbs*.
25. Schweitzer, *Quest*, 357.
26. Perrin, *Jesus and the Language of the Kingdom*, 15–40. For a discussion of Perrin's work on the kingdom of God as a symbol, see Scott, *Jesus, Symbol-Maker*, chs. 1, 6.
27. For a recent attempt to connect Jesus' parables with his crucifixion, see Herzog, *Parables as Subversive Speech*.

Corley, *Gender and Class in the Teaching of Jesus*
1. Schüssler Fiorenza, *In Memory of Her*, 107.
2. Borg, *Jesus: A New Vision*, 133–35; *Meeting Jesus*, 57–58; Crossan, *Historical Jesus*, 261–64.
3. Slee, "Parables and Women's Experience," 20–31. See also Durber, "Female Reader," 69.
4. Crossan, *In Parables*, 38.
5. Text and Translation by M. Meyer, *The Gospel of Thomas*, 61.
6. Borg, *Jesus: A New Vision*, 133–35; *Meeting Jesus*, 57–58; Crossan, *Historical Jesus*, 261–64; Schüssler Fiorenza, *In Memory of Her*, 118–22; *idem, Miriam's Child*, 93–94.
7. Borg, *Jesus: A New Vision*, 133–35; *Meeting Jesus*, 57–58; Schüssler Fiorenza, *In Memory of Her*, 118–22. In *Miriam's Child* Fiorenza does not mention purity (93–94).
8. Crossan, *Historical Jesus*, 261–64; Schottroff, *Let the Oppressed Go Free*, 93–94; 104.
9. Corley, *Private Women, Public Meals*, 89–95.
10. D. Smith, "Table Fellowship and the Historical Jesus," 160–61.
11. D. Smith, "Table Fellowship and the Historical Jesus," 161.
12. Corley, *Women and the Historical Jesus*, ch. 4.
13. Gibbs and Feldman, "Josephus' Vocabulary for Slavery," 293.
14. Crossan, *In Parables*, 96–120; see also "The Servant Parables," 17–62.
15. Beavis, "Slavery."
16. Jeremias, *Parables*, 97; 213.
17. LSJ, 1289; Josephus, *AJ*, 8.314; 18:192–193; Philo, *Vit. Cont.* 50–51.
18. MM, 474.
19. 1 Clement 55. Text and translation by Kirsopp Lake (LCL)
20. See for example Schüssler Fiorenza, *In Memory of Her*, 145–46.
21. Gen 1:27; 5:2. See 11QTemple 57:17–19; CD 2:14–6:1.
22. Corley, *Women and the Historical Jesus*, ch. 1.
23. See Musonius Rufus 14; Dio Chrysostom 3.122; Lucian, *Demonax*, 9; Seneca, *Ep.* 94.26.
24. Jeremias, *Abba*, 15–67; ET: *The Prayers of Jesus*, 11–65.
25. Hammerton-Kelly, *God the Father*; and "God the Father in the Bible and in the Experience of Jesus: The State of the Question," 95–102.
26. Schüssler Fiorenza, *In Memory of Her*, 145–51.
27. D'Angelo, "Theology in Mark and Q," 149–74; and "*Abba* and 'Father,'" 611–30.
28. The use of God as Father in Jewish prayer is more common than has previ-

ously been supposed. See 4Q372 1; 3 Macc 6:3; Apoc. Ezek. frag. 3; Wis 14:3; Sir 23:1. On the biblical and Jewish precedents to the appelation of God as "father," see D'Angelo, "Theology in Mark and Q," 152–56; "Abba and Father," 618–19; Hammerton-Kelly, *God the Father*, 20–51; Jeremias, *Prayers of Jesus*, 11–29.

29. D'Angelo, "Theology in Mark and Q," 151; and "Abba and Father," 614.

30. D'Angelo, "Theology in Mark and Q," 173–74; and "Abba and Father," 623–30.

31. D'Angelo, "Theology in Mark and Q," 174;

32. So D'Angelo, "Abba and Father," 630.

33. So D'Angelo, "Theology in Mark and Q," 159. Against Jeremias, *Prayers of Jesus*, 55–56.

34. D'Angelo, "Abba and Father," 615.

35. D'Angelo,"Theology in Mark and Q," 174.

36. See Corley, *Women and the Historical Jesus*, ch. 5.

37. See Job 1:20; Isa 22:21; Ezek 7:18; Amos 8:10; Jer 16:6; 41:5; 48:37.

38. 1 Sam 28:39; Deut 26:14; Hos 9:4; Amos 6:10; Jer 16:7; Ezek 24:17; Ps 106:28; 22; see also Cant 2:4; 5:1.

39. Isa 8:19; 19:3; 28:15;18; 29:4; 57:9; 65:4.

40. Jer 16:1–13; Ezek 24:15–18. Priests are directed to go only to funerals of those next of kin. See Lev 21:1–3.

41. Pseudo-Philo, *Bib. Ant.* 33:5. Trans. D. J. Harrington.

42. 2 Bar 85:1; 12.

43. McCane, "Let the Dead," 38–39.

44. See Aristotle, *History of Animals* 7.592b; 11.615a; 30.618b–619b; Prov 30:17.

45. Cumont, *After Life In Roman Paganism*, 65. Unfortunately this citation is made by Cumont without sources.

46. Plato, *Phaedo*, 115C. Trans. H. N. Fowler.

47. See Diog. Laer., 4.52; 4.79; *Cynic Epistles*, 25; Cicero, *Tusc.* 1.104 (quoting Diogenes); Lucian, *Demon.*, 35; 66. I would like to thank David Seeley for these references.

48. Corley, *Women and the Historical Jesus*, ch. 4.

49. Corley, *Women and the Historical Jesus*, ch. 4. I would like to thank John Kloppenborg for his remarks in this regard in a personal correspondence dated June 7, 1996.

50. See Steck, *Israel und das gewaltsame Geschick der Propheten*.

51. This article is an abridged version of a longer article. For the full version of this article with full notes and bibliography, see Corley, *Women and the Historical Jesus*, ch. 3.

Taussig, *Jesus in the Company of Sages*

1. Recent essays exchanged in the *Journal of Biblical Literature* offer in their difference a summary of the current status of the scholarly case for a connection between the historical Jesus and popular cynicism. See Eddy, "Jesus as Diogenes?", 49–69, and Seeley, "Jesus and the Cynics Revisited," 704–12.

2. Hengel and Markschies, *The Hellenization of Judaea*, 44.

3. *Historical Jesus*, 421.

4. Cf. Vaage's Claremont dissertation, "The Community of Q"; F. Downing, *Christ and the Cynics"*; Crossan's *The Historical Jesus;* Borg's *Jesus: A New Vision;* Mack's *A Myth of Innocence and The Lost Gospel.*

5. Objections to the Cynic connection have come from several quarters: H.D. Betz, "Jesus and the Cynics", 462–486; Witherington, *Jesus, the Sage* and *The Jesus Quest;* Robinson, "Building Blocks in the Social History of Q," ; Rhodes, "Jesus as Diogenes," 449–69; and Koester, "Jesus the Victim", 3–15.

6. "Jesus and the Cynics Revisited," 705. The citations from Eddy are from "Jesus as Diogenes", 449–69. The citations from Downing are from "The Social Contexts of Jesus the Teacher", 449; and *Jesus and the Threat of Freedom*, 132. The citations from Mack are from A *Myth of Innocence*, 68, 74.

7. The most extensive and recent documentation of this can be found in the massive new work by Klinghardt, *Gemeinschaftsmahl und Mahlgemeinschaft.* 1–174, 183–92, 251–68. See also the earlier work of Kollmann, *Ursprung und Gestalten,* 190–238; Smith's Harvard disseration "Social Obligation in the Context of Communal Meals" and Smith's and my *Many Tables,* 21–69.

8. *Myth of Innocence,* 53–77, 80–83

9. *The Historical Jesus,* 399–404.

10. Crossan's case for this is the most thoroughly presented. Breech and Borg *New Vision* 130–135, make it into a program. Meals as anti-purity codes are taken to the programmatic level by Bruce Chilton. Cf. also Funk in *Honest to Jesus,* 193, 194.

11. Downing's entire book, *Christ and the Cynics* consists in the listing of such parallels. Vaage's more recent *Galilean Upstarts* is also almost entirely devoted to an updated version of these parallels.

12. See Note 7.

13. Examples of critique of religion in hellenistic Judaism are Josephus, Apion 11, 102–109, and Philo, *De Legatione,* 134; of critique of family Philo, *The Contemplative Life,* 18–41, *In Flaccum,* 84. Josephus, War *II,* 24 1. Examples of Cynic critiques are found ad nauseum, in Vaage and Downing.

14. See Mahlon Smith's profile in this volume.

15. Didache, chapters 11 and 12, Revelation to John chapters 2 and 3.

16. Funk's list of "outsiders" includes "persons with skin disease, the maimed, the halt, the blind, gentiles, Samaritans, as well as petty tax officials, who were Roman collaborators, and women who did not observe the social proprieties." *Honest to Jesus,* 194.

16. Crossan traces this equation in Cynicism in some detail in *The Historical Jesus,* 76–90. Typical of some 35 sayings cited by Downing in *Christ and the Cynics* is this: "You'll not only share table-fellowship with the Gods, you'll share their rule." (Epictetus, *Encheiridion* 15)

17. Crossan lays this out clearly in *The Historical Jesus,* 76–80.

18. Leif Vaage quotes Epictetus, Diss. 2.2.20. as well as the related 3.5; 7; 18.4; 22,12; 4.1.153–154 in *Galilean Upstarts,* 95.

19. *Honest to Jesus,* 155.

20. *Galilean Upstarts,* 102.

21. This notion of the so-called Lord's Prayer consisting of prayer fragments from the historical Jesus subsequently arranged by the Q community into a prayer to be taught is developed on pp. 39, 40 of my "The Lord's Prayer," written for the Atlanta meeting of the Jesus Seminar. The Seminar followed the recommendation of this article, and consequently broke the prayer up into smaller segment, five of which were voted red or pink. For an insightful rendering of the Seminar's discussion of the article and a critique of the notion of prayer frag-

ments within the Lord's Prayer, see Robert Miller, "The Lord's Prayer and Other Items from the Sermon on the Mount " in *Foundations and Facets* 5.2, 177–86.

22. Cf. Meier in *A Marginal Jew* (291–302) and others (Fitzmyer, *The Gospel According to Luke*, 895–904, and Jeremias, *New Testament Theology*, 194–99 for other opinions.

23. See my "The Lord's Prayer" for a summary of these literary unities. See also Jeremias, *The Lord's Prayer, Abba,* and *The Prayers of Jesus;* Lohmeyer, *"Our Father";* Goulder, "The Composition of the Lord's Prayer;" and Carmignac, *Recherches sur le "Notre Pere".*

24. In addition to my "The Lord's Prayer," see also J. Dominic Crossan's discussion of the later character of some of this content in *The Historical Jesus*, 293–95, 39; Taussig, "The Lord's Prayer," 25–30 and 39, 40.

25. Again this proposal is made in the above cited, "The Lord's Prayer."

26. Calling God "Father" in Jesus' day was not a standard way of talking about or praying to God. Although it was not completely unheard of, it was fairly rare. Saying "Father" to God would have produced somewhere between a slight wrinkle on the brow and a bright twinkle in the eye of those who heard it.

27. The use of "Abba/Father" by the historical Jesus may also have had some very personal roots. Cf. Schaberg's thesis in *The Illegitimacy of Jesus.*

28. Jeremias relies somewhat uncritically on the whole range of Kaddish prayers, in a way that is no longer recommended without considering the possibility of their belonging to later second century rabbinic elaboration.

29. Again here the written material on pronouncing YHWH is later, but contains some early first century material.

30. As proposed in "The Lord's Prayer" article (33, 34), I still tend to relegate this prayer fragment to Jesus' followers rather than Jesus.

31. Farmers, who by and large planted small sections of land, were subject to the whims of weather and the market. Merchants often fell behind in their accounts for very similar reasons. Although for the previous twelve hundred years, Palestinian peasants were rarely out of danger of debt, these cycles of indebtedness were acute in the first century.

32. Crossan offers a very articulate example of the impasse presented by this contrast in styles between the aphorisms and the Lord's Prayer.

33. *Cynics and Christian Origins*, 135.

34. That a primary dimension to Jesus' prayer was its social character stands in opposition to the gray saying from Matthew: "When you pray, go into a room by yourself and shut the door behind you." Cf. *Jesus Before God*, 35–49.

35. Perhaps the most dramatic expression of this comes from Wisdom of Solomon 7:15–21 quoted above.

36. *Cynics and Christian Origins*, 133–35.

37. Borg in both *Jesus " A New Vision* (40–51) and *Meeting Jesus Again for the First Time* asserts that Jesus was "a spirit person" or "a holy man" and that he practiced a deep wordless prayer, similar to the practice of many mystics. For this assertion, he relies heavily on a number of passages voted black or gray by the Seminar.

38. The Seminar in one of its extra-textual votes did vote red that "Jesus prayed in seclusion." After this essay was presented to the Seminar, it changed that vote to gray.

39. If one includes the composite "Abba, your name be revered" in the fragments, there are six.

40. In discussing the pink vote for Thom 31:1 (no prophet welcome on his home turf), *The Five Gospels* commentary reads: "In spite of its seemingly proverbial character, a majority of the Fellows were of the opinion that the simple proverb was plausible in the context of Jesus' activity . . ."(49). In discussing the pink vote on Thom 41:1, 2, *The Five Gospels is* most clear about the Seminar bias against Jesus uttering common wisdom: "The opinion of the Fellows was divided between those who thought the saying was a maxim of common wisdom and those who thought Jesus might have uttered it." Such a viewpoint eliminates a priori the possibility that Jesus uttered common wisdom.

41. In *Fragments*, 68–73.

42. On p. 352 of *The History of the Synoptic Tradition* Bultmann cites as examples the accretion of the sentence to some manuscripts of Luke 12:21 and Mark 7:16.

43. In an odd way, the Seminar seems to have sensed that Jesus could have said it, but decided to vote it gray anyway. Hence, *The Five Gospels* explains: "The saying is not particularly distinctive and so could have been said by any sage. Consequently, it does not tell us much about Jesus." This line of thinking seems to miss the obvious possibility that in many ways Jesus was like any sage.

44. *The History of the Synoptic Tradition,* pp. 100–105 contain a series of such observations.

45. See my "The Gospel of Thomas and the Case for Jesus as Teacher of Common Wisdom" in *Foundations and Facets Forum* for a full review of the effect of Thomas on the larger question of common wisdom in Jesus' teachings.

46. Cf. Downing's *Christ and the Cynics: Jesus and other Radical Preachers in First-Century Tradition*

47. *De Abrahamo,* 217–24.

48. *The Five Gospels,* 55.

49. For twentieth century consciousness, Jesus as a not-so-unique sage is a companion piece of discovery to the other growing awareness of the depth of faith, wisdom, and spirit in other non-Christian religions.

50. *Christ and the Cynics,* 35–37.

51. *The Historical Jesus,* 421. In pp. 303–51 Crossan's textual case and cross-cultural study of healing is imposing.

52. I would beg to claim a certain privilege in asserting this limitation of the historical Jesus' significance. I do so on the basis of 20 years as both a New Testament scholar and a pastor of local churches. I believe that I am the only Seminar member who, from the inception of the Seminar until now, has related to the Jesus material as a leader of a congregation as well as a scholar. As noted in an early article of *Forum* ("The Jesus Seminar and Its Public" 2.2), I attempt regularly to use all of my scholarly work in my congregational position. By and large, this has been both successful and rewarding.

It would therefore seem predictable that I would seek to enhance the significance of the historical Jesus, since weekly I must interact with my congregation about the significance of Jesus for our lives. The privilege I claim at this point in the essay and the Seminar's work comes from the fact that I adopt this same position about the limitations of the significance of the historical Jesus, both consciously and pro-actively, within the congregation I serve. In short, the position that the historical Jesus' significance is quite limited belongs to both my ongoing colloquy here in the Seminar and the continuing conversation with my congregations.

Patterson, *Dirt, Shame, and Sin in the Expendable Company of Jesus*
1. *The Point of Christology*, 20–40.
2. Excerpted from the *Res Gestae Divi Augustus*, an account of his accomplishments penned by Caesar Augustus himself near the end of his life (Suetonius, *Augustus*, 101). A translation of this and other documents relevant to understanding the world of Christian origins is to be found in Barrett, *The New Testament Background*, rev. ed. For the *Res Gestae* of Augustus see pp. 2–4.
3. From the *Carmen Seculare* of Horace. The Secular Games were held once a century. Horace was commissioned to write this hymn to commemorate the accomplishments of Augustus on this auspicious occasion. The hymn is to be found in Barrett, *Documents*, 6–7.
4. *Ant* xiv, 272–75; *War* i, 219–20.
5. *Ant* xvii, 288–95; *War* ii, 66–75.
6. *Agricola*, 30.
7. Borg's description is to be found in his essay, "The Palestinian Background for a Life of Jesus," 37–54 (see pp. 48–49) in Patterson, et al, *The Search for Jesus: Modern Scholarship Looks at the Gospels*. Borg is drawing on Lenski's description of agrarian societies in *Power and Privilege*, 189–296.
8. Crossan, *The Historical Jesus*, esp. 3–88.
9. See Moses Hadas' translation in *Three Greek Romances*. The passage of note occurs on p. 77.
10. Douglas, *Purity and Danger*, 35.
11. Harmon trans., *Lucian*, Loeb Classical Library , 1: 69.
12. Jeremias, *Jerusalem in the Time of Jesus* , 303–12.
13. Crossan, *The Historical Jesus*, 225ff.
14. *The Historical Jesus*, 261–62.
15. *The Historical Jesus*, 341.
16. Marxsen, "Jesus Has Many Names," 1–15 (esp. pp. 1–6) in idem, *Jesus and the Church*.

Fortna, *The Gospel of John & the Historical Jesus*
1. Funk, et al, *The Five Gospels*.
2. The title of Albert Nolan's book, *Jesus before Christianity*, says it. By Christianity, Nolan means the belief in Jesus' messiahship, his divinity. But of course many elements of the historical Jesus' teaching also comprise what we call Christianity.
3. In Mark 12:35–37 and parallels, for example, Jesus calls in question the widespread belief in a Davidic messiah, a passage that could hardly have been created by early Christians. Here I differ from the consensus of the Jesus Seminar; see *The Five Gospels*, p. 105.
4. See the second volume of the Seminar's report, Funk, et al, *The Acts of Jesus*.
5. This article was originally written several years ago and for a lay audience. See also my more recent "Jesus Tradition in the Signs Gospel," in Fortna and Thatcher, *Jesus in Johannine Tradition*, 199–208.

Bibliography

Modern Authors

Allison, Dale. *Jesus of Nazareth: Millenarian Prophet*. Minneapolis: Fortress, 1998.

Barrett. C. K. *The New Testament Background: Selected Documents*. Rev. ed. San Francisco: Harper & Row, 1989.

Beavis, Mary Ann. "Ancient Slavery as an Interpretive Context for the New Testament Servant Parables With Special Reference to the Unjust Steward." *Journal of Biblical Literature* 111 (1992), 37–54.

Becker, Carl. *Everyman His Own Historian. Essays on History and Politics*. Chicago: Quadrangle Books, 1935, 1966.

Berger, Peter L. *The Sacred Canopy. Elements of a Sociological Theory of Religion*. Garden City, NY: Doubleday and Co., Anchor Books, 1969.

Betz, H. D. "Jesus and the Cynics: Survey and Analysis of a Hypothesis." *Journal of Religion* 74 (1993), 462–84.

Betz, Hans Dieter. *The Sermon on the Mount, including the Sermon on the Plain (Matthew 5:3–7:27 and Luke 6:20–49)*. Hermeneia–A Critical and Historical Commentary on the Bible. Minneapolis: Fortress Press, 1995.

Borg, Marcus J. *Jesus in Contemporary Scholarship*. Valley Forge, PA: Trinity Press International, 1994.

Borg, Marcus J. *Jesus, A New Vision: Spirit, Culture, and the Life of Discipleship*. San Francisco: HarperSanFrancisco, 1987.

Borg, Marcus J. *Meeting Jesus Again for the First Time: The Historical Jesus and the Heart of Contemporary Faith*. San Francisco: HarperSanFrancisco, 1994.

Borg, Marcus J. "The Palestinian Background for a Life of Jesus" in *The Search for Jesus: Modern Scholarship Looks at the Gospels*. Ed. Hershel Shanks. Washington: Biblical Archeology Society, 1994.

Boring, Eugene. "Criteria of Authenticity." *Forum* 1/4 (1985), 3–38.

Bornkamm, Gunther. *Jesus of Nazareth*. Trans. I. and F. McLuskey and J. M. Robinson. New York: Harper & Row, 1960.

Bovon, François. "A Review of John Dominic Crossan's *The Birth of Christianity*." *Harvard Theological Review* 94.3 (July 2001), 369–74.

Bradley, K.R. *Slaves and Masters in the Roman Empire: A Study in Social Control*. New York: Oxford, 1987.

Breech, James. *The Silence of Jesus: The Authentic Voice of the Historical Man*. Philadelphia: Fortress Press, 1983.

Brown, R. E. *An Introduction to New Testament Christology*. New York/Mahwah: Paulist Press, 1994.

Bultmann, Rudolf. *Form Criticism*. New York: Haper & Brothers, 1962.

Bultmann, Rudolf. *The History of the Synoptic Tradition*. New York: Harper & Row, 1963.

Bultmann, Rudolf. *Jesus and the Word*. New York: Charles Scribner's Sons, 1934, 1958.

Cadbury, Henry J. *The Peril of Modernizing Jesus*. New York: Macmillan, 1937; London: SPCK, 1962.

Charlesworth, James H. and Walter P. Weaver, ed. *Images of Jesus Today*. Faith and Scholarship Colloquies 3, Florida Southern College. Valley Forge, PA: Trinity Press, 1994.

Corley, Kathleen E. *Private Women, Public Meals: Social Conflict in the Synoptic Tradition*. Peabody, MA: Hendrickson, 1993.

Corley, Kathleen E. *Women and the Historical Jesus: Feminist Myths of Christian Origins*. Santa Rosa, CA: Polebridge Press, 2002.

Countryman, L. William. *Dirt, Greed and Sex: Sexual Ethics in the New Testament and Their Implications for Today*. Philadelphia: Fortress Press, 1988.

Crossan, John Dominic. *The Birth of Christianity*. San Francisco: HarperCollins, 1998.

Crossan, John Dominic. *The Cross that Spoke: The Origins of the Passion Narrative*. San Francisco: Harper Collins, 1988.

Crossan, John Dominic. *Finding is the First Act*. Semeia Supplements. Philadelphia: Fortress Press, 1979.

Crossan, John Dominic. *The Historical Jesus: The Life of a Mediterranean Jewish Peasant*. San Francisco: HarperCollins, 1991.

Crossan, John Dominic. *In Fragments: The Aphorisms of Jesus*. San Francisco: Harper & Row, 1983.

Crossan, John Dominic. *In Parables*. Santa Rosa, CA: Polebridge Press, 1992.

Crossan, John Dominic. *Jesus: A Revolutionary Biography*. San Francisco: HarperSanFrancisco, 1994.

Crossan, John Dominic, "Materials and Methods in Historical Jesus Research." *Forum* 4/4 (1988), 3–24.

Crossan, John Dominic. "The Servant Parables of Jesus." *Semeia* 1 (1974) 17–62

Cumont, Franz. *Afterlife in Roman Paganism*. New Haven: Yale University Press, 1922.

D'Angelo, Mary Rose. "'Abba' and 'Father': Imperial Theology and the Jesus Traditions." *Journal of Biblical Literature* 111 (1992) 611–630.

D'Angelo, Mary Rose. "Theology in Mark and Q: 'Abba' and 'Father' in Context." *Harvard Theological Review* 85 (1992) 149–74.

Davies, Stevan. *Jesus, The Healer: Possessions, Trance, and the Origins of Christianity*. New York: Continuum, 1995.

Douglas, Mary. *Purity and Danger, An Analysis of the Concepts of Pollution and Taboo*. London: Routledge & Kegan Paul, 1966.

Downing, F. Gerald. *Christ and the Cynics: Jesus and Other Radical Preachers in First Century Tradition*. Sheffield: JSOT Press, 1988.

Downing, F. Gerald. *Cynics and Christian Origins*. London: SCM Press, 1995.

Dudley, D. F. *A History of Cynicism from Diogenes to the Sixth Century A.D.* London: Methuen, 1937.

Durber, Susan. "The Female Reader of the Parables of the Lost." *Journal for the Study of the New Testament* 45 (1992), 59–78.

Eddy, Paul Rhodes. "Jesus as Diogenes? Reflections on the Cynic Jesus Thesis." *Journal of Biblical Literature* 115 (1996), 449–69.

Finley, Moses. *The Ancient Economy*. Berkeley: University of California Press, 1973.

Fitzmeyer, Joseph A. *The Gospel According to Luke*. Anchor Bible. Garden City: Doubleday, 1981–1985.

Fortna, Robert T. and Tom Thatcher. *Jesus in Johannine Traditions: New Directions*. Louisville: Westminster/John Knox, 2001.

Funk, Robert W. and the Jesus Seminar. *The Acts of Jesus: The Search for the Authentic Deeds of Jesus*. San Francisco: HarperCollins, 1998.

Funk, Robert W. *Jesus as Precursor, Semeia Supplements*. Philadelphia: Fortress Press, 1975. Reprint, Sonoma, CA: Polebridge Press, 1994.

Funk, Robert W. and Roy W. Hoover. *The Five Gospels. The Search for the Authentic Words of Jesus*. New York: Macmillan, 1993.

Funk, Robert W. with Mahlon H. Smith. *The Gospel of Mark: Red Letter Edition*. Sonoma, CA: Polebridge Press, 1991.

Funk, Robert W. *Honest to Jesus: Jesus for a New Millennium*. San Francisco: HarperCollins, 1996.

Funk, Robert W. "The Issue of Jesus." *Forum* 1/1 (1985), 7–12.

Funk, Robert W. *Language, Hermeneutic and Word of God: The Problem of Language in The New Testament and Contemporary Theology*. New York: Harper & Row, 1966.

Funk, Robert W., Bernard Brandon Scott, and James R. Butts. *The Parables of Jesus, Red Letter Edition*. Sonoma, CA: Polebridge Press, 1988.

Funk, Robert W. *The Poetics of Biblical Narrative*. Sonoma, CA: Polebridge Press, 1988.

Funk, Robert W. "Profiles of Jesus: A Protocol." *The Fourth R* 8/5–6 (Sept.–Dec. 1995), 21–22.

Gibbs, John G. and Louis H. Feldman. "Josephus' Vocabulary for Slavery." *Jewish Quarterly Review* 76 (1986), 281–310.

Hadas, Moses and Morton Smith. *Heroes and Gods: Spiritual Biographies in Antiquity*. New York: Harper & Row, 1965.

Hammerton-Kelly, Robert. "God the Father in the Bible and in the Experiences of Jesus: The State of the Question." Pp. 95–102 in *God as Father*. Eds. Johannes-Baptist Metz, and Edward Schillebeeckx. Edinburgh: T and T Clark; New York: Seabury Press, 1981.

Hammerton-Kelly, Robert. *God the Father: Theology and Patriarchy in the Teaching of Jesus*. Philadelphia: Fortress Press, 1979.

Havel, Vaclav. *Disturbing the Peace*. London: Faber and Faber, 1990.

Heaney, Seamus. *The Redress of Poetry*. London: Faber and Faber, 1995.

Hedrick, Charles W. *Parables as Poetic Fictions: The Creative Voice of Jesus*. Peabody, MA: Hendrickson Publishers, 1994.

Hedrick, Charles W. *When History and Faith Collide: Studying Jesus*. Peabody, MA: Hendrickson Publishers, 1999.

Hengel, M. and C. Markschies, *The Hellenization of Judea in the First Century after Christ*. Valley Forge: Trinity Press International, 1990

Hengel, Martin. *Judiasm and Hellenism. Studies in Their Encounter in Palestine during The Early Hellenistic Period*. Philadelphia: Fortress Press, 2 vols., 1974.

Herzog, William R. *Parables as Subversive Speech: Jesus as Pedagogue of the Oppressed.* Louisville: Westminster/John Knox, 1994.

Homeyer, Helene. "Zu den Anfangen der griechischen Biographie." *Philologus* 106 (1962), 75–85.

Horsley, Richard. *Jesus and the Spiral of Violence: Popular Jewish Resistance in Roman Palestine.* San Francisco: Harper & Row, 1987.

Immerwahr, Henry R. "*Ergon:* History as a Monument in Herodotus and Thucydides." *American Journal of Philology* 81 (1960), 261–90.

Jeremias, Joachim. *Abba. Studien zur neutestamentlischen Theologie und Zeitgeschichte.* Göttingen: Vandenhoeck and Ruprecht, 1966.

Jeremias, Joachim. *Jerusalem in the Time of Jesus.* Philadelphia: Fortress, 1969.

Jeremias, Joachim. *New Testament Theology,* vol. 1: *The Proclamation of Jesus.* New York: Scribner's Sons, 1971.

Jeremias, Joachim. *The Parables of Jesus.* New York: Scribner's Sons, 1972.

Jeremias, Joachim. *The Prayers of Jesus.* Trans. John Bowden. Naperville, IL: Alec R. Allenson, 1967.

Johnson, Luke Timothy. *The Real Jesus: The Misguided Quest for the Historical Jesus and the Truth of the Traditional Gospels.* San Francisco: Harper-Collins, 1996.

Kee, Howard C. *Jesus in History.* Second ed. New York: Harcourt Brace Jovanovich, 1970, 1977.

Kloppenborg Verbin, John S. *Excavating Q. The History and Setting of the Sayings Gospel.* Minneapolis: Fortress Press, 2000.

Koester, Helmut. "Jesus the Victim." *Journal of Biblical Literature* 111 (1993), 3–15.

Langewiesche, William. *Inside the Sky.* New York: Pantheon, 1998.

Lenski, Gerhard. *Power and Privilege.* New York: McGraw-Hill, 1966.

Lewis, Charlton T. and Charles Short. *A Latin Dictionary.* Oxford: The Clarendon Press, 1879.

Lewis, Joan. *Ecstatic Religion: An Anthropological Study of Spirit Possession and Shamanism,* Penguin Anthropology Library. Baltimore: Penguin Books, 1971.

Lohmeyer, Ernst. *Our Father: An Introduction to the Lord's Prayer.* New York: Harper and Row, 1966.

Mack, Burton L. *A Myth of Innocence.* Philadelphia: Fortress Press, 1988.

Malina, Bruce. *The New Testament World: Insights from Cultural Anthropology.* Louisville: John Knox Press, 1981.

Marxsen, Willi. *Jesus and the Church.* Trans. and ed. Philip Devenish. Philadelphia: Trinity Press International, 1992.

McCane, Byron R. "Let the Dead Bury Their Own Dead: Secondary Burial and Matt 8:21–22." *Harvard Theological Review* 83 (1990), 31–43.

McGaughy, Lane C. "Jesus' Parables and the Fiction of the Kingdom." *The Fourth R* 3/4 (1990), 8–11.

Meier, John P. *A Marginal Jew: Rethinking the Historical Jesus.* 2 vols. The Anchor Bible Reference Library. Garden City: Doubleday, 1991, 1994.

Meyer, Marvin. *The Gospel of Thomas: The Hidden Sayings of Jesus.* San Francisco: HarperSanFrancisco, 1992.

Michaels, J. Ramsey. *Servant and Son: Jesus in Parable and Gospel.* Atlanta: John Knox Press, 1981.

Millar, Fergus. *The Roman Near East. 31BC–AD 337.* Cambridge, MA: Harvard University Press, 1993.

Miller, Robert J., ed. *The Complete Gospels*. Santa Rosa, CA: Polebridge Press, 1994.

Miller, Robert J. "Historical Method in the Deeds of Jesus: The Test Case of the Temple Demonstration." *Forum* 8/1–2 (1992), 5–30.

Momigliano, Arnoldo. *The Development of Greek Biography*. Cambridge, MA: Harvard University Press, 1971.

Montefiore, C. G. *The Old Testament and After*. Macmillan, 1923.

Niebuhr, Reinhold. *An Interpretation of Christian Ethics*. San Francisco: Harper & Row, 1935, 1963.

Neusner, Jacob. *Judaism: The Evidence of the Mishnah*. Chicago: The University of Chicago Press, 1981.

Nolan, Albert. *Jesus before Christ*. Maryknoll, NY: Orbis, 1976.

Ogden, Shubert. "The Question Christology Answers" in *The Point of Christology*. San Francisco: Harper and Row, 1982.

Patterson, Stephen J. *The God of Jesus: The Historical Jesus and the Search for Meaning*. Harrisburg, PA: Trinity Press International, 1998.

Pearson, Birger A. "The Gospel According to the Jesus Seminar." *Religion* 25 (1995), 317–38.

Perrin, Norman. *Jesus and the Language of the Kingdom*. Philadelphia: Fortress Press, 1976.

Perrin, Norman. *Rediscovering the Teaching of Jesus*. New York: Harper & Row, 1967.

Pitt-Rivers, Julian. *The Fate of Shechem or the Politics of Sex: Essays in the Anthropology of the Mediterranean*. Cambridge: Cambridge University Press, 1977.

Reed, Jonathan L. *Archeology and the Galilean Jesus*. Harrisburg, PA: Trinity Press International, 2000.

Reimarus, Hermann Samuel. *Reimarus Fragments*. Ed. Charles H. Talbott; Trans. Ralph S. Fraser. Philadelphia: Fortress Press, 1970.

Rhodes, P. R. "Jesus as Diogenes: Reflections on the Cynic Jesus Thesis." *Journal of Biblical Literature* 115 (1996), 72–91

Ringe, Sharon. *Luke*. Louisville: Westminster John Knox Press, 1977

Robinson, James M. "Building Blocks in the Social History of Q" in *Reimagining Christian Origins: A Colloquium Honoring Burton L. Mack*. Valley Forge: Trinity Press International, 1966.

Robinson, James M. *A New Quest of the Historical Jesus*. Studies in Biblical Theology. Naperville: Allenson/London: SCM, 1959.

Robinson, James M., Paul Hoffmann, and John S. Kloppenborg. *The Critical Edition of Q*. Minneapolis: Fortress Press, 2000.

Sanders, E. P. *Jesus and Judaism*. Philadelphia: Fortress Press, 1985.

Schaberg, Jane. *The Illegitimacy of Jesus*. San Francisco: Harper and Row, 1987.

Schottroff, Luise. *Let the Oppressed Go Free: Feminist Perspectives on the New Testament*. Louisville, KY: Westminster/John Knox, 1992.

Schüssler Fiorenza, Elisabeth. *In Memory of Her: A Feminist Theological Reconstruction of Christian Origins*. New York: Crossroad, 1983; 1994.

Schüssler Fiorenza, Elisabeth. *Jesus, Miriam's Child, Sophia's Prophet: Critical Issues in Feminist Christology*. New York: Crossroad, 1994.

Schweitzer, Albert. *The Quest of the Historical Jesus*. London: Adam and Charles Black, 1910; New York: The Macmillan Company, 1961.

Scott, Bernard Brandon. "From Reimarus to Crossan: Stages in a Quest" in *Currents in Research: Biblical Studies 2* (1994).

Scott, Bernard Brandon. *Hear Then the Parable: A Commentary on the Parables of Jesus.* Minneapolis: Fortress Press, 1989.

Scott, Bernard Brandon. *Jesus, Symbol-Maker for the Kingdom.* Philadelphia: Fortress Press, 1981.

Scott, Bernard Brandon. "New Options in an Old Quest." Pp. 1–50 in *The Historical Jesus through Catholic and Jewish Eyes.* Ed. Leonard J. Greenspoon, Dennis Hamm and Bryan F. LeBeau. Harrisburg, PA: Trinity Press International, 2000.

Scott, Bernard Brandon. "The Reappearance of Parables." *The Fourth R* 10/1-2 (Jan/Apr 1997).

Seeley, David. "Jesus and the Cynics Revisited." *Journal of Biblical Literature* 116 (1997), 704–12.

Slee, Nicola. "Parables and Women's Experience." *Modern Churchman* 26 (1984), 21–31.

Smith, Dennis E. "Table Fellowship and the Historical Jesus." Pp. 135–62 in In *Religious Propaganda and Missionary Competition in the New Testament World: Essays Honoring Dieter Georgi.* Ed. Lukan Bormann et al. Leiden; New York; Köln: Brill, 1994.

Smith, Dennis E. and Hal Taussig. *Many Tables: The Eucharist in the New Testament and Liturgy Today.* Philadelphia: Trinity Press / London: SCM, 1990.

Sulloway, Frank J. *Born to Rebel: Birth Order, Family Dynamics, and Creative Lives.* New York: Pantheon Books, 1996.

Talbert, Charles H. *What Is a Gospel? The Genre of the Canonical Gospels.* Philadelphia: Fortress Press, 1977.

Tatum, W. Barnes. *John the Baptist and Jesus: A Report of the Jesus Seminar.* Sonoma, CA: Polebridge Press, 1994.

Taussig, Hal. "The Gospel of Thomas and the Case for Jesus as Teacher of Common Wisdom." *Forum* 10,1-2 (1994) 31-46.

Taussig, Hal. "The Lord's Prayer." *Forum* 4/2 (1990), 25–41.

Taussig, Hal and Castelli, Elizabeth; eds. *Re-imaging Christian Origins: A Colloquium Honoring Burton L. Mack.* Valley Forge: Trinity Press International, 1966.

Taussig, Hal. *Jesus before God: The Prayer Life of the Historical Jesus.* Santa Rosa: Polebridge Press, 1999.

Theissen, Gerd and Annette Merz. *The Historical Jesus: A Comprehensive Guide.* Trans. by John Bowden. Philadelphia: Fortress Press, 1998.

Theissen, Gerd. *The Shadow of the Galilean. The Quest of the Historical Jesus in Narrative Form.* Trans. by John Bowden. Philadelphia: Fortress Press, 1987.

Vaage, Leif. *Galilean Upstarts.* Valley Forge: Trinity Press International, 1995.

Vermes, Geza. *Jesus the Jew: A Historian's Reading of the Gospels.* Philadelphia: Fortress Press, 1973.

Vielhauer, Philipp. "On the 'Paulinism' of Acts" in *Studies in Luke-Acts.* Ed. L. E. Keck, and J. L. Martyn. Nashville: Abingdon Press, 1966.

Wheelwright, Philip. *Metaphor and Reality.* Bloomington, IN: Indiana University Press, 1962.

Wilder, Amos N. *The Bible and the Literary Critic.* Minneapolis: Fortress Press, 1991.

Wilder, Amos N. *Jesus' Parables and the War of Myths.* Ed. James Breech. Philadelphia: Fortress Press, 1982.

William, James G. *Those Who Ponder Proverbs: Aphoristic Thinking and Biblical Literature.* Sheffield, England: Almond Press, 1981.

Wink, Walter. "Jesus as Real as We Can Get Him." *Jesus Seminar Papers* (March 1997).

Witherington, Ben, III. *The Jesus Quest: The Third Search for the Jew of Nazareth.* Downers Grove, IL: InterVarsity Press, 1995.

Wright, N. T. *Jesus and the Victory of God. Christian Origins and the Question of God.* Vol. 2. Minneapolis: Fortress Press, 1996.

Ancient Authors

Cicero. *Tusculan Disputations.* Loeb Classical Library, 1945.

Epictetus. *Encheiridion.* Ed. H. Schenkl. Leipzig, 1894.

First Letter of Clement. Vol 1 of *The Apostolic Fathers.* Loeb Classical Library, 1962.

Horace, *Carmen Seculare* in Barrett, C. K. *The New Testament Background: Selected Documents.* Rev. ed. San Francisco: Harper & Row, 1989.

Josephus. *Antiquities.* Loeb Classical Library, 1930 –1965.

Lucian. *De Fugitivi.* Loeb Classical Library, 1979.

Philo. *De Abrahamo.* Loeb Classical Library, 1967.

Philo. *De Legatione.* Loeb Classical Library, 1967.

Philo. *The Contemplative Life.* Loeb Classical Library, 1967.

Philostratus. *Life of Apollonius of Tyana.* Loeb Classical Library, 1960.

Plato. *Phaedo.* Loeb Classical Library, 1971.

Pseudo-Philo. *Biblical Antiquities.* Pp. 297–377 in *Old Testament Pseudepigrapha.* Vol. 2. Text and trans. Daniel J. Harrington. Ed. James H. Charlesworth. Garden City, New York: Doubleday, 1985.

Polybius. *The Rise of the Roman Empire.* New York: Penguin Books, 1979.

Suetonius. "Res Gestai Divi Augustus" in Barrett, C. K. *The New Testament Background: Selected Documents.* Rev. ed. San Francisco: Harper & Row, 1989.

Tacitus. *Agricola and Germania.* Loeb Classical Library, 1970.

The Tao Te Ching of Lao Tzu: A Translation and Commentary. LaFargue, Michael. Albany: State University of New York Press, 1992.

Xenophon. *An Ephesian Tale.* In *Three Greek Romances.* Trans. and presented Moses Hadas. Indianapolis: Bobbs-Merrill, 1964.

Contributors

Marcus J. Borg is Hundere Distinguished Professor of Religion and Culture at Oregon State University. He has written eleven books, including *Meeting Jesus Again for the First Time*, *The God We Never Knew*, *The Meaning of Jesus* (with N. T. Wright); and *Reading the Bible Again for the First Time*. He has been chair of the Historical Jesus Section of the Society of Biblical Literature and president of the Anglican Association of Biblical Scholars.

Kathleen E. Corley is the Thrivent Financial for Lutherans Professor of the University of Wisconsin-Oshkosh. She has also served as a member of the Steering Committee of the Historical Jesus Section of the Society of Biblical Literature and of the Committee on the Status of Women in the Profession of the Society of Biblical Literature. Her books include *Private Women, Public Meals* and *Women and the Historical Jesus: Feminist Myths of Christian Origins*.

John Dominic Crossan is Professor Emeritus of Religious Studies, DePaul University, Chicago. He has written twenty books on the historical Jesus in the last thirty years, including *The Historical Jesus* (1991), *Jesus: A Revolutionary Biography* (1994), *Who Killed Jesus* (1995), and *The Birth of Christianity* (1998). He is a former co-chair of the Jesus Seminar, and a former chair of the Historical Jesus Section of the Society of Biblical Literature.

Arthur J. Dewey is Professor of Theology, Xavier University, Cincinnati, Ohio. He is co-founder of the Healing Deadly Memories Program and co-chair of the Bible in Ancient and Modern Media Group of the Society of Biblical

Literature. His books include *The Word in Time* (1990) and *Spirit and Letter in Paul* (1996). His poetic perspective, the bi-weekly Friday Morning Commentary, can be heard on the Public Radio Station WVXU (91.7) in Cincinnati.

Robert T. Fortna is Weyerhaeuser Professor Emeritus of Biblical Studies, Vassar College, Poughkeepsie, New York.. He has been Annual Professor at the W. F. Albright Archaeological Institute and a Visiting Scholar at the Ecumenical Institute for Advanced Theological Studies (Tantur), both in Jerusalem. His books include *The Gospel of Signs* (1970), *The Fourth Gospel and its Predecessor* (1988), and *Jesus in Johannine Tradition* (2001, co-edited with Tom Thatcher).

Robert W. Funk is Director of the Westar Institute and founder of the Jesus Seminar. A Guggenheim Fellow and Senior Fulbright Scholar, he has served as Annual Professor of the American School of Oriental Research in Jerusalem and as chair of the Graduate Department of Religion at Vanderbilt University. His many books include *A Credible Jesus* (2002), *The Five Gospels* (1993) and *The Acts of Jesus* (1998) (both with the Jesus Seminar), and *Honest to Jesus* (1996).

Charles W. Hedrick is Distinguished Professor of Religious Studies, Southwest Missouri State University. A retired U.S. Army Reserve Chaplain (Colonel) and Juvenile Probation Officer, Los Angeles County Probation Department; he has served as pastor of churches in Mississippi, California, and New York City. He is the author of *The Gospel of the Savior. A New Ancient Gospel* (with Paul Mirecki, 1999), *When History and Faith Collide* (1999), *and Parables as Poetic Fictions* (1994).

Roy W. Hoover is Weyerhaeuser Professor of Biblical Literature and Professor of Religion Emeritus, Whitman College, Walla Walla, Washington. He is the author of articles that have appeared in *Forum, The Fourth R, Bible Review,* and *Harvard Theological Review* and co-author (with Robert W. Funk) of *The Five Gospels. The Search for the Authentic Words of Jesus,* 1993. In 1992, he received the Whitman College Award for Faculty Achievement.

Lane C. McGaughy is the Geo. H. Atkinson Professor of Religious and Ethical Studies and chairs both the Religious Studies Department and Classical Studies program at Willamette University in Salem, Oregon. The former president and executive secretary of the Pacific Northwest Region of the American Academy of Religion and Society of Biblical Literature, he serves on the Board of Directors of the Alton L. Collins Retreat Center and directs its annual Summer Institute of Biblical Studies.

Stephen J. Patterson is Professor of New Testament at Eden Theological Seminary in St. Louis, Missouri. A Fulbright Fellow at the University of Heidelberg in Germany in 1986, his books include *The God of Jesus* (1998) and *The Gospel of Thomas and Jesus* (1993) and *The Q-Thomas Reader* (1990, with M. Meyer, M. Steinhauser, and J. Kloppenborg).

James M. Robinson is the former director of the Institute for Antiquity and Christianity and Professor Emeritus at The Claremont Graduate School. A Fulbright Scholar, American Council of Learned Societies Fellow, and American Association of Theological Schools Fellow, his books include *The Critical Edition of Q* (editor, 2000) and *A New Quest of the Historical Jesus* (1959. He is best know as the General Editor of *The Nag Hammadi Library in English* (1977).

Bernard Brandon Scott is Darbeth Distinguished Professor of New Testament at the Phillips Theological Seminary, University of Tulsa, Oklahoma and the author of several books, including *Re-Imagine the World: An Introduction to the Parables of Jesus* (2002), *Hear Then the Parable* (1989), *Hollywood Dreams and Biblical Stories* (1994), and the editor of several more. He has been a consultant to the American Bible Society experimental film translations.

Mahlon H. Smith is Associate Professor and Vice Chair, Department of Religion, Rutgers University, and founder of the program in religious studies at Rutgers College where he served as the first chair of the Department of Religion. His draft report on the Q sayings provided the basis for the commentary in *The Five Gospels*. He has pioneered electronic publication in the field of religion and is author of several award-winning academic websites.

Hal Taussig is Visiting Professor of New Testament at Union Theological Seminary in New York. He also teaches biblical studies at Chestnut Hill College and the Reconstructionist Rabbinical College and is the pastor of the Chestnut Hill United Methodist Church in Philadelphia. His books include *Re-imagining Life Together in America* (2002, with Catherine T. Nerney), *Jesus Before God* (1999), and *Many Tables* (1999, with Dennis E. Smith).